Future of Business and Finance

The Future of Business and Finance book series features professional works aimed at defining, describing and charting the future trends in these fields. The focus is mainly on strategic directions, technological advances, challenges and solutions which may affect the way we do business tomorrow, including the future of sustainability and governance practices. Mainly written by practitioners, consultants and academic thinkers, the books are intended to spark and inform further discussions and developments.

More information about this series at http://www.springer.com/series/16360

Kai-Ingo Voigt • Julian M. Müller
Editors

Digital Business Models in Industrial Ecosystems

Lessons Learned from Industry 4.0 Across Europe

Springer

Editors
Kai-Ingo Voigt
Chair of Industrial Management
University of Erlangen-Nuremberg
Nuremberg, Germany

Julian M. Müller
University of Applied Sciences Kufstein
Kufstein, Austria

ISSN 2662-2467 ISSN 2662-2475 (electronic)
Future of Business and Finance
ISBN 978-3-030-82002-2 ISBN 978-3-030-82003-9 (eBook)
https://doi.org/10.1007/978-3-030-82003-9

This Springer imprint is published by the registered company Springer Nature Switzerland AG
The registered company address is: Gewerbestrasse 11, 6330 Cham, Switzerland

Introduction: From Industry 4.0 to Digital Industrial Business Models

Abstract

Ten years after the concept of "Industrie 4.0" was announced at the Hanover Fair as part of the German High-Tech Strategy, nowadays often referred to in its English spelling "Industry 4.0," research and practice has increasingly recognized the concept and it has become a focus of investigation from various perspectives. This book subsumes insights from research and practice on Industry 4.0 with special regard to digital business models and industrial ecosystems. Thus, it aims to contribute to understanding the socioeconomic implications of Industry 4.0 that go beyond technological enablers or use cases. The book thereby aims to contribute to unfolding the concept across entire industrial supply chains or even ecosystems, as referred to as a central characteristic of horizontal and vertical integration in the initial concept of Industry 4.0. Likewise, the potential for digital or data-driven business models is regarded in detail, especially in conjunction with the aforehand mentioned supply chain or even ecosystem spanning nature of Industry 4.0. The following chapter aims to conceptualize the main themes of this book, Industry 4.0, digital business models, and industrial ecosystems and put them into context. Further, the 15 contributions grouped into six parts are introduced briefly to the reader, highlighting different perspectives on Industry 4.0 research, managerial insights, and lessons learned from across Europe.

At the Hanover Fair in 2011, the German government announced the concept of "Industrie 4.0" as part of its High-Tech Strategy to secure the future competitiveness of the German manufacturing industry. The abbreviation "4.0" points towards a potential fourth industrial revolution that shall, in contrast to the three previous industrial revolutions, be introduced proactively and a priory. The concept of Industry 4.0 is based on several technological enablers that have gained maturity in the last decade, most notably Cyber-Physical Systems (CPS) and the Internet of Things (IoT). CPS aim to resemble and extend the physical world through a virtual one, using technologies such as advanced sensors or digital twins. This allows to better simulate and thus better analyze and understand the physical world due to data generated. Thereupon, this data generated is shared using the IoT, allowing to interconnect humans, production facilities, and products across the entire industrial value chain. Therefore, several authors also refer to the Industrial IoT. CPS and the

IoT foundations enable horizontal and vertical integration, i.e., across entire industrial value chains, across the entire lifecycle of products, and across several functional departments. Horizontal and vertical integration then allow multiple potentials on an operational and strategic levels (Kagermann et al., 2013; Lasi et al., 2014).

Ten years afterwards, the concept has gained broad international recognition in research and practice, increasingly using its English spelling "Industry 4.0." The majority of research in the field of Industry 4.0 considers the technological enablers of Industry 4.0 that, in addition to CPS and the IoT, often include artificial intelligence, cloud computing and technologies for secure data transmission, technologies to interconnect humans and machines, or advanced manufacturing technologies. The latter include, e.g., additive manufacturing technologies or advanced robotics technologies such as collaborative robots. This resembles that Industry 4.0 is often understood from the perspective of digital production, but less from the perspective of digital, integrated supply chains, as intended by the original concept of Kagermann et al. (2013). In response, this book aims to further investigate Industry 4.0 from the perspective of digital supply chains (Hofmann et al., 2019), or extending this perspective, industrial ecosystems. These comprise, in addition to supply chains, further stakeholders such as research institutions, or political and social institutions (Benitez et al., 2020; Schmidt et al., 2020).

Also considerably less regarded in comparison to technological perspectives on Industry 4.0, but growing rapidly, a research stream on the socioeconomic effects of Industry 4.0 has emerged. Alongside analyzing performance effects on industrial value creation or effects for ecology and society, new or changed business models through Industry 4.0 receive increasing attention in Industry 4.0 research. Business models comprise the logic on value proposition, value creation, and value capture, i.e., the monetization of the value proposition. The potentials of innovative business models go hand in hand with its technological enablers and even enhance them (Müller et al., 2018; Voigt et al., 2017). In the context of Industry 4.0, digital and data-driven business models enable several potentials (Paiola & Gebauer, 2020; Sorescu, 2017). These become increasingly powerful if unfolded across the entire supply chain, or even ecosystem (Frank et al., 2019; Müller et al., 2020).

In sum, this book aims to investigate the potentials of digital business models when regarded from a supply chain, or even ecosystem perspective. Therefore, 15 contributions by practitioners and researchers across Europe share their insights and lessons learned. The 15 contributions are again subdivided into six parts: (I) Digital Supply Chain Management and Business Models, (II) Digital Business Models in Manufacturing, (III) Digital Industrial Platforms, (IV) Industrial Data-driven Business Models, (V) AI and Blockchain in Production and Supply Chain Management, and (VI) Lessons learned from European Ecosystems. Each of the six parts include contributions from research and practice and will be introduced briefly in the following.

The *first part, Digital Supply Chain Management and Business Models*, comprises insights into how Industry 4.0 affects supply chain management and what potentials arise for digital business models. As mentioned above, the potentials of

Industry 4.0 can be found especially when horizontal and vertical integration, i.e., across the entire value chain, is established. Likewise, data-driven business models become especially powerful when data is shared, analyzed, and put to use across entire supply chains.

The *second part, Digital Business Models in Manufacturing*, focuses on digital or data-driven business models in manufacturing, but with a strong interconnection to customers, suppliers, or partners in the supply chain. The examples described refer to the potentials data has to generate new, digital or data-driven business models, and provides both an overview as well as cases from industrial application on the topic.

In the *third part, Digital Industrial Platforms,* the perspective of ecosystems is extended towards digital platforms. Aiming to bring together many different actors on a platform, both concepts of ecosystem and platform are partially interconnected, as shown in these contributions.

In *part four, Industrial Data-Driven Business Models* are investigated in an industrial context, highlighting potentials in industrial application and industrial supply chains. A classification of data-driven business models is developed, highlighting several types and forms in an industrial context. It is followed by an application case for data-driven business models in an industrial supply chain.

Part five, AI and Blockchain in Production and Supply Chain Management, gives detailed insights into how both technologies can be applied in production and supply chain environments. AI and Blockchain both represent a set of technologies with far-reaching implications by themselves. They can unfold further potentials in the context of Industry 4.0 if used for horizontal and vertical integration, such as in digital or data-driven business models.

In the *sixth part, Lessons Learned from European Ecosystems,* insights from three European ecosystems are presented. The three contributions include the Basque Country in Spain, Central Eastern Europe, illustrated by data from Slovakia, Hungary, Romania, and Serbia, as well as from Krakow in Poland. These three contributions present a broader perspective on relevant factors for Industry 4.0 implementation while focusing on respective manufacturing ecosystems.

We want to thank all authors once again for their valuable contributions to this book. Further, we thank Springer for their support in publishing this book.

We wish all readers an insightful and pleasant reading!

Kai-Ingo Voigt
kai-ingo.voigt@fau.de

Julian M. Müller
julian.mueller@fh-kufstein.ac.at

References

Benitez, G. B., Ayala, N. F., & Frank, A. G. (2020). Industry 4.0 innovation ecosystems: An evolutionary perspective on value cocreation. *International Journal of Production Economics*, *228*, 107735.

Frank, A. G., Mendes, G. H., Ayala, N. F., & Ghezzi, A. (2019). Servitization and Industry 4.0 convergence in the digital transformation of product firms: A business model innovation perspective. *Technological Forecasting and Social Change*, *141*, 341–351.

Hofmann, E., Sternberg, H., Chen, H., Pflaum, A., & Prockl, G. (2019). Supply chain management and Industry 4.0: conducting research in the digital age. *International Journal of Physical Distribution & Logistics Management*, 49(10), 945–955.

Kagermann, H., Wahlster, W. & Helbig, J. (2013). *Recommendations for implementing the strategic initiative INDUSTRIE 4.0*, in: Final report of the Industrie 4.0 Working Group, Acatech, Frankfurt am Main, Germany.

Lasi, H., Fettke, P., Kemper, H. G., Feld, T. & Hoffmann, M. (2014). Industrie 4.0. *Business & Information Systems Engineering*, *56*(4), 261–264.

Müller, J. M., Buliga, O., & Voigt, K. I. (2018). Fortune favors the prepared: How SMEs approach business model innovations in Industry 4.0. *Technological Forecasting and Social Change*, *132*, 2–17.

Müller, J. M., Veile, J. W., & Voigt, K. I. (2020). Prerequisites and incentives for digital information sharing in Industry 4.0—An international comparison across data types. *Computers & Industrial Engineering*, *148*, 106733.

Paiola, M., & Gebauer, H. (2020). Internet of things technologies, digital servitization and business model innovation in BtoB manufacturing firms. *Industrial Marketing Management*, 89, 245–264.

Rachinger, M., Rauter, R., Müller, C., Vorraber, W., & Schirgi, E. (2019). Digitalization and its influence on business model innovation. *Journal of Manufacturing Technology Management*, 30(8), 1143–1160.

Schmidt, M. C., Veile, J. W., Müller, J. M., & Voigt, K. I. (2020). Ecosystems 4.0: redesigning global value chains. *International Journal of Logistics Management*, in press.

Sorescu, A. (2017). Data-driven business model innovation. *Journal of Product Innovation Management*, *34*(5), 691–696.

Voigt, K. I., Buliga, O., & Michl, K. (2017). *Business model pioneers. How Innovators Successfully Implement New Business Models*. Springer.

Contents

Digital Supply Chain Management and Business Models

Digital Transformation of Logistics and SCM: The Long Way from Digitization to Digital Business Models 3
Birgit von See, Beverly Grafe, Sebastian Lodemann, and Wolfgang Kersten

Development of a Trend Management Process for Supply Chain Management in the Context of Industry 4.0 23
Hendrik Birkel and Evi Hartmann

Unlocking the Hidden, Data-Driven Potential of the Supply Chain 35
Stefan Asenkerschbaumer

Digital Business Models in Manufacturing

Digitalization as an Enabler of Subscription Business Models in the Manufacturing Industry 49
Günther Schuh, Jana Frank, Lennard Holst, Daniela Müller, Tobias Leiting, and Lukas Bruhns

Digital Business Models for Industrial Suppliers—The Case of Schaeffler OPTIME 71
Philipp Jussen, Martin Meinel, and Tim Hosenfeldt

Digital Industrial Platforms

German B2B Platforms' Contribution Towards a Resilient Economy 89
Dieter Kempf and Steven Heckler

Digital Logistics Platforms—Initial Approaches to Market Segmentation in Light of Traditional and New Providers 105
Wolfgang Stölzle and Ludwig Häberle

Industry 4.0 Digital Platforms: Collaborative Business Models for SMEs 125
Nikolai Kazantsev and Ingo Martens

Industrial Data-Driven Business Models

Industrial Data-Driven Business Models: Towards a Goods-Service-Data Continuum . . . 137
Kai-Ingo Voigt, Fabian Brechtel, Marie-Christin Schmidt, and Johannes Veile

Realizing New Data-Driven Business Models by Launching Containers into the Cloud . . . 155
Mathias Zink, Victor Naumann, Andreas Harth, and Alexander Pflaum

AI and Blockchain in Production and Supply Chain Management

If You Go for AI, Be Aware of the Psychological Hurdles Around It—Practical and Theoretical Insights on the Industrial Application of Artificial Intelligence . . . 173
Quirin Demlehner, Daniel Schoemer, and Sven Laumer

Blockchain for Supply Chain Traceability: Case Examples for Luxury Goods . . . 187
Christoph G. Schmidt, Maximilian Klöckner, and Stephan M. Wagner

Lessons Learned from European Ecosystems

The Interrelationship Between Industry 4.0 and Servitization in Manufacturing SMEs: The Case of the Basque Country . . . 201
Eduardo Sisti, Miren Estensoro, and Miren Larrea

Beyond Excellence in the Automotive Industry in Industry 4.0? Lessons Learned from the creative Business Sector . . . 217
Jerzy Rosiński

Geographical Factors for the Implementation of Industry 4.0 in Central Eastern Europe . . . 235
Roland Z. Szabó and Lilla Hortoványi

About the Editors

Kai-Ingo Voigt is a Full Professor for Industrial Management at Friedrich–Alexander-University Erlangen-Nuremberg, Germany. His research areas are Digital Transformation of Industry and Technology and Innovation Management.

Julian M. Müller is Professor at Kufstein University of Applied Sciences, Austria. His research areas include Industry 4.0 and Digital Transformation, Technology and Innovation Management, and Supply Chain Management.

Digital Supply Chain Management and Business Models

Digital Transformation of Logistics and SCM: The Long Way from Digitization to Digital Business Models

Birgit von See, Beverly Grafe, Sebastian Lodemann, and Wolfgang Kersten

Abstract

The need to digitally transform is omnipresent in almost every company. Nevertheless, many companies are currently still failing to holistically apply the implications of increasing digitalization to their business model. Thus, this paper aims to analyze drivers, technological elements as well as the success of companies on their way from digitization efforts to a digital business model. This study utilizes a representative longitudinal online survey that covers key stakeholders in logistics and SCM. Our findings show that on the way from digitization (simply transferring analog processes to digital ones) to a digital business model, companies perceive increased opportunities and reduced risks. They expand their focus on cost reductions to new ways of increasing revenues. Technological concepts that contribute to generate a digital twin of the material flow, as well as the usage of platforms/IT services and forecasting methods, are of essential and increasing importance. Companies in the early stages of their way to a digital business model seem to misjudge the potential of concepts like predictive analytics. We finally can show that it is worth taking the long way. The further companies are on their path, the higher is their adaptability to key trends. Our results contribute to the research on digital business models and provide insights for practitioners on how to effectively tread the path to a digital business model.

B. von See (✉) · B. Grafe · S. Lodemann · W. Kersten
Hamburg University of Technology, Institute of Business Logistics and General Management, Am Schwarzenberg-Campus 4, 21073 Hamburg, Germany
e-mail: logu@tuhh.de

K.-I. Voigt and J. M. Müller (eds.), *Digital Business Models in Industrial Ecosystems*, Future of Business and Finance, https://doi.org/10.1007/978-3-030-82003-9_1

1 Introduction

Owing to their multifunctional as well as inter-organizational character, digital transformation is of particular relevance for the areas of logistics and supply chain management (ten Hompel & Henke, 2017, p. 247). There is a big variety of potential value-adding initiatives for digital supply chain management (SCM), such as digital transport marketplaces, optimization and visibility data services, as well as digitally supported fulfillment and warehouse service providers (Möller et al., 2019, p. 12). In this context, digital transformation may improve efficiency in operations, increase customer value as well as offer new ways of creating data-based services and platform business models in logistics and SCM (Cichosz et al., 2020, pp. 218-219). New technological concepts like blockchain, artificial intelligence, big data analytics, cloud computing platforms, or IoT-sensor-driven applications, which are currently often in trial phases, may pave the way for the transparency in supply chains that has always been required and asked for, especially from a sustainability perspective (Ebinger & Omondi, 2020, p. 11).

Digitalization in logistics and SCM is not a new phenomenon but has experienced a surge in awareness since the proclamation of Industry 4.0 in 2011 (von See, 2019, p. 20). The innovation shift is reflected in the growing number of startups in SCM and logistics. Within the logistics sector, their growth in 2017 was over 30% (Borreck et al., 2018, p. 13). The start-ups are mainly focusing on business models such as online platforms, last-mile delivery concepts, transparency, and control of supply chains (Borreck et al., 2018, p. 13; Göpfert & Seeßle, 2019, p. 263).

Since the Covid-19 pandemic at the latest, the need to further digitalize is ubiquitous in almost every company. The crisis has given a boost to the digital transformation in companies (Carroll & Conboy, 2020, p. 1; Dell Technologies, 2020, pp. 7–12; Falk et al., 2020, p. 2; Schroeder et al., 2021, p. 14). Concerning established companies, the scope ranges from incremental process optimizations to radical innovations of the entire business model (Leyh & Gäbel, 2017, pp. 36–37). As already indicated in the title of this paper, it is a long way from individual digitization to digital business models. Intending to provide companies with guidelines on the long way from digitization to digital business models, we analyze in the following paper how different actors in logistics and SCM (in the following L&SCM) proceed and how successful they are in doing so. Our research questions (RQs) are:

RQ 1 What drives companies in L&SCM on the path to a digital business model?
RQ 2 Which role do technological elements play in L&SCM for the path to a digital business model?
RQ 3 How successful are the players along the path to a digital business model?

Before answering those research questions based on an online survey, we give a brief introduction to the theoretical background.

2 Theoretical Background

In this paper, we discuss the path from digitization to digital business models in L&SCM. For this reason, we will briefly present the theoretical foundations of digital transformation and the central concepts of digital business models in the following.

2.1 Digital Transformation in L&SCM

As already mentioned above, a digital transformation is of particular relevance for logistics and SCM (ten Hompel & Henke, 2017, p. 247). From a unionist perspective (Larson, Poist & Halldórsson, 2007, pp. 3–5; Mentzer et al., 2001), SCM can be seen as "the logical progression of developments in logistics management" (Metz, 1998, p. 48). According to Mentzer et al. (2001), we define SCM as "the systemic, strategic coordination of the traditional business functions and the tactics across these business functions within a particular company and across businesses within the supply chain, for the purposes of improving the long-term performance of the individual companies and the supply chain as a whole" (Mentzer et al., 2001, p. 18). In addition to the primarily unidirectional flow of materials in logistics, the bidirectional flow of information is thus of central importance.

There are various terms, some of which are used inconsistently and misleadingly: 'digitization', 'digitalization', 'digital (business) transformation', 'digital business model', and 'Industry 4.0' are just a few of them. Based on a comparison of different definitions by von See (2019, pp. 21–22), however, a clear distinction can be made, which will serve as a basis for this paper and is summarized in Fig. 1.

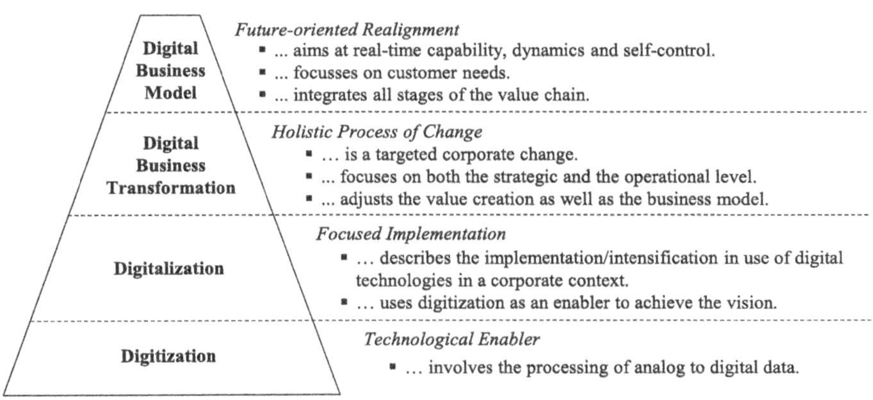

Fig. 1 Systematization of central terms of the digital Transformation (extended representation based on Kersten, von See & Indorf, 2018, p. 104 and von See, 2019, p. 24)

According to Brennen and Kreiss (2016), digitization can be defined "as the material process of converting analog streams of information into digital bits" (Brennen & Kreiss, 2016, p. 556). Digitalization, in contrast, is the "adoption or increase in use of digital or computer technology by an organization, industry, country, etc." (Brennen & Kreiss, 2016, p. 556, based on Oxford English Dictionary). When solely focusing on individual digitization actions, many companies fail to fundamentally question those processes. Digitalization considers the aggregate of multiple digitization efforts (Gobble, 2018, p. 56), leading to meta-structures such as organizations being perceived 'digital' (which previously was a characterization only assigned to products or processes). From the perspective of a corporate context, digitalization thus involves the consideration of individual framework conditions when implementing new digital technologies. Enabling digital technologies discussed within this context are, for example, cloud computing, big data analytics, and Internet of Things (Agrawal & Narain, 2018, p. 3; Büyüközkan & Göçer, 2018, p. 166; Garay-Rondero et al., 2020, pp. 895–897).

Taking a holistic supply chain perspective, digital business transformation highlights the process of change (Bowersox et al., 2005, p. 22). Within this digital transformation process, several authors point out the need to take a socio-technical perspective (Brödner, 2018, p. 247; Dregger et al., 2016, p. 3; Kagermann, Wahlster, & Helbig, 2013, p. 28) – a theory that originally emerged over 60 years ago and further evolved interdisciplinarily (Davis et al., 2014, pp. 171–172). A digital business model builds the top of the 'digitization pyramid'. It is the culmination of this process and entails fundamental changes to businesses leading to digital business models which cover a holistic perspective. It focuses on customer needs and digital value creation (Berman, 2012 p. 18) and incorporates customers as well as partners digitally (Galimova et al., 2019, pp. 2–3). A detailed description follows in the next section.

2.2 Digital Business Models in Logistics and SCM

Even though the term 'business model' has been discussed for many years (Kersten, 2018, p. 1289), a commonly accepted and widespread definition of the phrase is still missing (Weking et al., 2020, p. 3). Nevertheless, there is a converging understanding regarding the core elements that characterize business models (Foss & Saebi, 2017, p. 201); Kersten, 2018, p. 1290: The design of the value creation process, the value proposition as well as the mechanisms to capture value mark central components of business models (Foss & Saebi, 2017, p. 202; Johnson et al., 2008, pp. 52–53; Kersten, 2018, p. 1290; Teece, 2018, p. 40). In this paper, business models are defined as "the architecture of the value creation process that aims at generating benefits for customers and value-added partners and based on that the model to achieve revenue" (Kersten, 2018, p. 1290). Business models can therefore be understood as the interface between the corporate strategy and the business processes (Guggenberger et al., 2020, p. 3; Kersten, 2018, p. 1291).

As business models consist of various components and elements, several tools for describing and operationalizing business models have been developed so far (Möller et al., 2019, p. 3). The most common concepts are represented by the Business Model Canvas (Osterwalder & Pigneur, 2010) and the St. Gallen Business Model Navigator (Gassmann, Frankenberger & Csik, 2014). According to Osterwalder and Pigneur (2010), business models can be described with the help of nine building blocks that touch upon customers, infrastructure, offer, and financial viability as the four central elements of a business (Osterwalder & Pigneur, 2010, p. 15). Inspired by a painter's canvas, the nine blocks – customer segments, value propositions, channels, customer relationships, revenue streams, key resources, key activities, key partnerships, and cost structure – form the Business Model Canvas (Osterwalder & Pigneur, 2010, pp. 43–44). As the sections on the canvas are addressed and filled in several iterative steps, the Business Model Canvas allows developing as well as frequently questioning business models (Kersten, 2018, p. 1293).

Compared to the Business Model Canvas, the St. Gallen Business Model Navigator by Gassmann et al. (2014) appears to be less complex but offers a more focused and holistic reflection of business models at the same time (Kersten, 2018, p. 1293). To describe business models, Gassmann et al. (2014) propose four dimensions that are presented in a 'magic triangle'. The first dimension concentrates on the customer and is related to the question "Who are our target customers?" (Gassmann et al., 2014, p. 6). Second, the value proposition, which deals with the products and services that are valuable for customers and the question of "What do we offer to customers?" (Gassmann et al., 2014, p. 6) needs to be addressed. The question "How do we produce our offerings?" (Gassmann et al., 2014, p. 6) is raised in the third dimension and focuses on the value chain. Lastly, the fourth dimension describes the profit mechanisms and "Why does the business model generate profit?" (Gassmann et al., 2014, p. 7). As soon as a minimum of two of the four dimensions is subject to a change, one can call it a business model innovation (Gassmann et al., 2014, pp. 6–8).

The innovation of business models does not only comprise the development of completely new business models but also includes the incremental refinement of existing business models (Schallmo, 2013, p. 29). In light of the digital transformation during the past years, business model innovation has primarily been driven by advances in IT (Fichman et al., 2014, p. 335). Against this background, the innovation of digital business models presents "a significantly new way of creating and capturing business value that is embodied in or enabled by IT" (Fichman et al., 2014, p. 335), meaning that if new digital technologies cause fundamental changes of the business, a business model can be called digital (Veit et al., 2014, p. 48). Especially the logistics sector will be shaped by technological developments triggering the digital transformation of business models (Möller et al., 2019, p. 1; Remane et al., 2017, p. 41). "Effects on the corresponding supply chains are inevitable" (Pflaum et al., 2020, p. 4504), which stresses the importance of adapting accompanying business models.

The concept of Osterwalder and Pigneur as well as the operationalization by Gassmann et al. as global approaches (Kersten, 2018, p. 1298) form an essential prerequisite that helps to innovate business models systematically (Kersten, 2018, p. 1294). Based on this, several researchers have developed operationalizations to describe business models in the framework of digitalization and to map accompanying changes. A selection of exemplary operationalizations is listed in Table 1.

Table 1 Overview of exemplary operationalizations for digital business models

References	Type of Operationalization	Specification of Operationalization	Data Basis/Data Source
Staub et al. (2021)	Taxonomy based on the St. Gallen Business Model Navigator	Digital business models in general	Ten digital platform cases from the real estate industry and literature on digital platforms and business ecosystems
Kifokeris and Koch (2020)	Business model canvas	Logistics	Observations, interviews, participant mapping, and photo-elicitation
Schlimbach and Asghari (2020)	Business model canvas	Digital business models in general	Online survey and 16 semi-structured expert interviews
Weking et al. (2020)	Taxonomy	Industry 4.0	32 Industry 4.0 business model innovation cases
Möller et al. (2019)	Taxonomy	Logistics	Randomized samples from the startup database AngelList
Bock and Wiener (2017)	Taxonomy	Digital business models in general	56 empirical and key conceptual business model studies that are digitally related
VDI/VDE (2016)	Business model canvas	Industry 4.0	Not specified
Alias et al. (2015)	Business model canvas	Logistics	Expert interviews

To give an example, Weking et al. (2020) derive a taxonomy that enables to describe, classify, and analyze Industry 4.0 business models (Weking et al., 2020). The developed taxonomy comprises five meta-dimensions that address and complement the dimensions of the St. Gallen Business Model Navigator (Weking et al., 2020, p. 8). Moreover, the taxonomy facilitates the evaluation of the Industry 4.0 status of companies' business models and shows opportunities for leveraging Industry 4.0 (Weking et al., 2020, p. 1).

To face the challenges of digital transformation, business models must be continuously benchmarked, put into question, and adapted to changes that emerge from new technologies (Becker et al., 2020, p. 53). Operationalizations of business models do not only pave the way for the digital transformation of business models but also constitute a guideline for firms, which helps to innovate business models toward digitalization. The current status of the digital transformation of business models in companies, more specifically the extent to which questioned companies have transformed their business models digitally, will be discussed in the following analysis.

3 Research Methodology

The data was collected as part of a large-scale study on trends and strategies in L&SCM in cooperation with the German Logistics Association (BVL). BVL is an interest group for L&SCM with more than 10,000 members. Owing to its membership structure, BVL reflects a broad view of the considered core roles in supply chains: manufacturing industry, logistics services, and retail. An online questionnaire was designed in 2016 based on an extensive mixed-methods approach in which expert interviews served as the starting point (Kersten et al., 2017). To be able to make statements that are as representative as possible, the questionnaire was distributed via the network. Data were collected in two periods from mid-July to mid-October 2016 and from the beginning of February to the beginning of March 2020. The first phase of the survey in 2016 was characterized by a period in which many digitalization efforts were being pursued. The second survey period in 2020 extended immediately before or during the Covid-19 pandemic outbreak. This circumstance must therefore be taken into account when discussing and reflecting on the results.

In 2016, 331 responses were generated from German company representatives compared to 276 in 2020. The respective breakdown of the samples can be seen in Fig. 2. A large proportion of the respondents come from the manufacturing industry (approx. 43% in both years) or logistics services (approx. 41% and 40%) and a smaller proportion from the retail sector (approx. 15 and 17%). This distribution corresponds to the membership structure of the BVL with a deviation of max. 5.3% in each case (BVL, 2017, pp. 4–58, 2020, pp. 3–57) and can be regarded as representative. Our breakdown into three different size classes is based on Grüninger et al. (2013). Almost half of the respondents come from large companies and approx. 30% and 20% from medium-sized to small companies, respectively.

To answer the research questions raised in Sect. 1, we use the following survey questions: First, we classify the respondents into groups based on their assessment of the progress of digital transformation in their business model. Second, we discuss

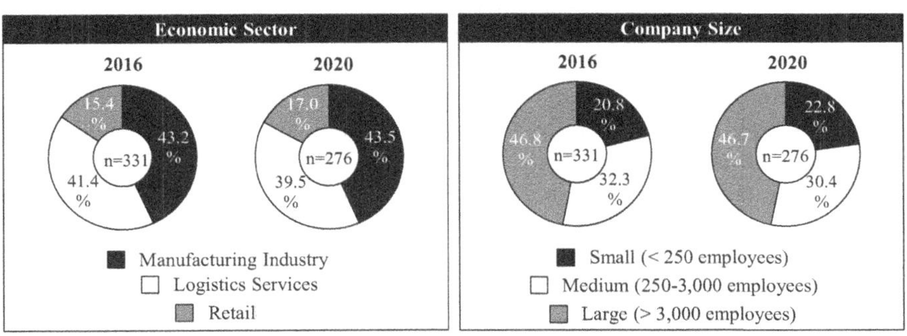

Fig. 2 Demographics of the sample

why the respondents transform their business model based on their opportunity and risk as well as cost and revenue assessment. Third, a look into the assessment of central technological concepts which are relevant for L&SCM gives us the opportunity to discuss how respondents digitalize. Finally, we assess the respondents' success based on their ability to adapt to key trends. Descriptive evaluation is carried out with the software IBM® SPSS® Statistics Version 23 and will be presented in the following section.

4 Findings

For evaluation purposes, we divide our sample into four groups. These groups represent different strategy types for digitally transforming companies' business models. Table 2 shows a description of the strategy types identified. Allocation of participants to groups is based on respondents' answers on the extent of their company's business model transformation.[1]

Figure 3 shows a breakdown of the groups. Comparing those groups, we can first observe that from 2016 to 2020 the share of followers pursuing strategy type A has decreased in favor of the other strategy types B, C, and D. This means that there has been a shift toward an increasing digital business model transformation. Some of the digital observers seem to have put forward first implementation actions, digital adapters, and transformers have focused and expanded their previous activities. Many companies seem to have successfully completed the first steps and have been able to reap the first fruits of their digital business model transformation.

Nevertheless, the proportion of each strategy type is still nearly equally distributed – thus allowing a statistical comparative analysis. In the following, we first analyze why companies in L&SCM digitally transform their business model. We second focus on how (on a technological basis) they actually digitalize, and finally third elaborate their success in doing so.

4.1 What Drives Companies in L&SCM on the Path to a Digital Business Model?

The above observation of a shift toward the digital transformation of the entire business model can be justified by the potential that companies increasingly see in digital transformation. Figure 4 shows that regardless of the type of strategy pursued, opportunities seen in digital transformation by the companies increased in

[1]Related questions were asked as follows: To what extent will the business model of your company be digitally transformed? (I) We extend our offer by digital services in addition to our current offerings. (II) We are extending our business model by a business division for digital services and goods. (III) We are transforming our existing business model to a digital one. The answers are based on a Likert-type scale: not planned, planned > 5 years, planned < 5 years, already today to a minor extent, already today partially, already today to a broad extent.

Table 2 Strategy types identified for digitally transforming companies' business models

#	Strategy Type	Companies that...
A	Digital Observers	... do not digitally transform their business model at all
B	Digital Adapters	... extend their offer by digital services and/or extend their business model by a business division for digital services and products
C	Digital Transformers	... transform their existing business model to a digital one
D	Digital Pioneers	... have already completed a digital transformation of their business model to a digital one

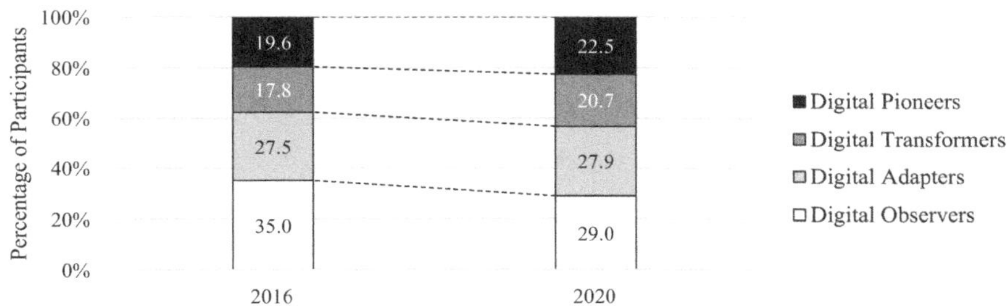

Fig. 3 Longitudinal breakdown of the distribution of strategy types

importance and risks decreased in importance from 2016 to 2020. While the opportunities are rated as high to very high on average, the risks associated with digital transformation are rated as medium on average. What is striking here is that digital pioneers in particular rate the opportunities higher and the risks lower than the other groups. This is certainly a potential explanation for the pioneer strategy they are pursuing.

Digital transformation in L&SCM is often seen as a measure to cut costs and make complexity manageable (Agrawal & Narain, 2018, p. 3; Kersten et al., 2017, p. 19). In that vein, Osterwalder and Pigneur's Business Model Canvas contrasts the cost structure with the revenue sources. In the following, we focus on the respondents' assessment of the impact of digital transformation on their cost and revenue situation.[2] In general, the companies agree with the statement that digital transformation enables a reduction in costs and an increase in revenue, irrespective of the strategy pursued. While in 2016, the average level of agreement regarding the revenue increase option was still higher (mean = 0.60) than the average level of agreement regarding the cost reduction option (mean = 0.53), both have increased

[2]Questions: (i) The digital transformation allows our company to generate additional revenues. (ii) The digital transformation allows our company additional cost reduction. Rated on a bipolar likert-scale: strongly disagree, disagree, neither agree nor disagree, agree, strongly agree.

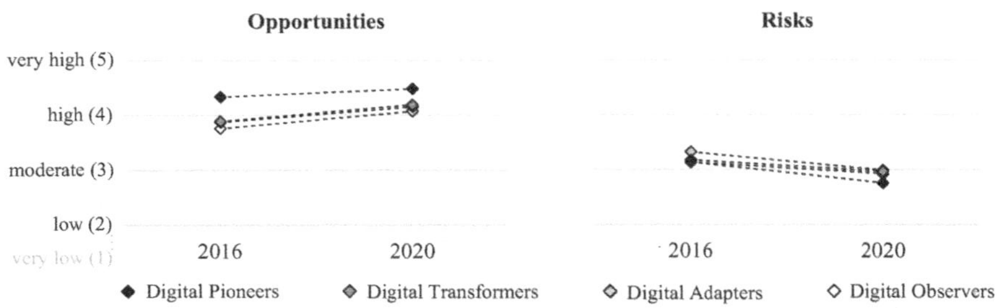

Fig. 4 Longitudinal assessment of the opportunities and risks of digital transformation

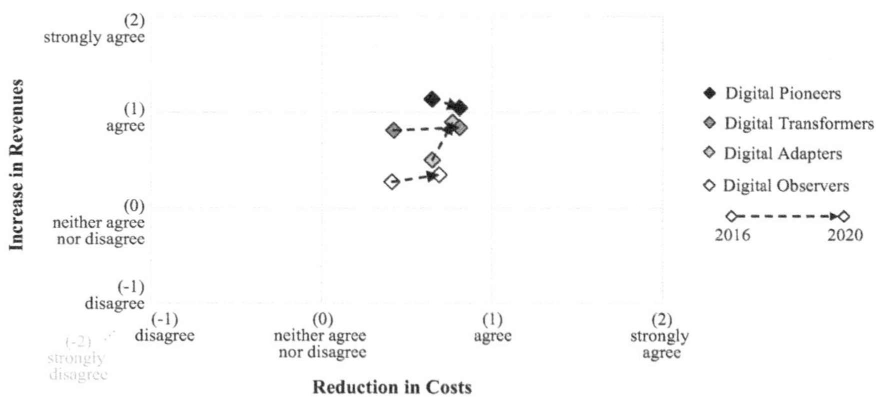

Fig. 5 Evaluation of the opportunity to reduce costs and increase revenues in the longitudinal section of the strategy types

in 2020 and have settled at an even level (mean = 0.76 both). This signals a focus of our respondents on cost-cutting measures during the past 5 years. Figure 5 shows a detailed breakdown of the group responses.

A comparison of the different strategy types revealed the following patterns in 2016: Digital pioneers saw a high degree of opportunities to reduce costs and increase revenues. While digital transformers rather focused on revenue increases, digital adapters prioritized the ability to reduce costs. Compared to the others, digital observers agreed with the possibility of revenue increases or cost reductions to an only proportionally smaller degree. Five years later, in 2020 we see a coalescence of the groups in terms of their prioritization. Digital pioneers, transformers as well as adapters rate the opportunities to achieve cost reductions and revenue increases through digital transformation equally highly. Only the digital observers rate the opportunities for revenue growth much lower. Thus, all three different strategy types for digitally transforming companies' business models (pioneers, transformers as well as adapters) have recognized the opportunity to not only reduce their internal costs through a digital transformation but more importantly to achieve potential revenue increases and new revenue streams.

4.2 Which Role do Technological Elements Play in L&SCM for the Path to a Digital Business Model?

Digital technologies are decisively shaping the digital transformation of the business model. In a previous analysis, von See (2019, p. 107) clustered relevant technological concepts to SCM technology groups, namely assistance systems, automation, digital twin, forecasting tools, business management systems, platforms, IT services, and customer interfaces, which will be used as a basis for our further analysis. The following section analyzes the relevance of individual technologies for the respondents and the extent to which they have been implemented. For the sake of clarity, the comparative analysis is based on two strategy types, namely digital pioneers and digital observers.

Figure 6 provides an overview of the relevance and implementation status of the technologies that enable digitization along with the material flow. When comparing digital pioneers with observers, a clear difference emerges: Digital pioneers rate all technologies as more relevant than digital observers. Thus, technologies are also more common among the pioneers. In SCM, technologies that enable a digital twin

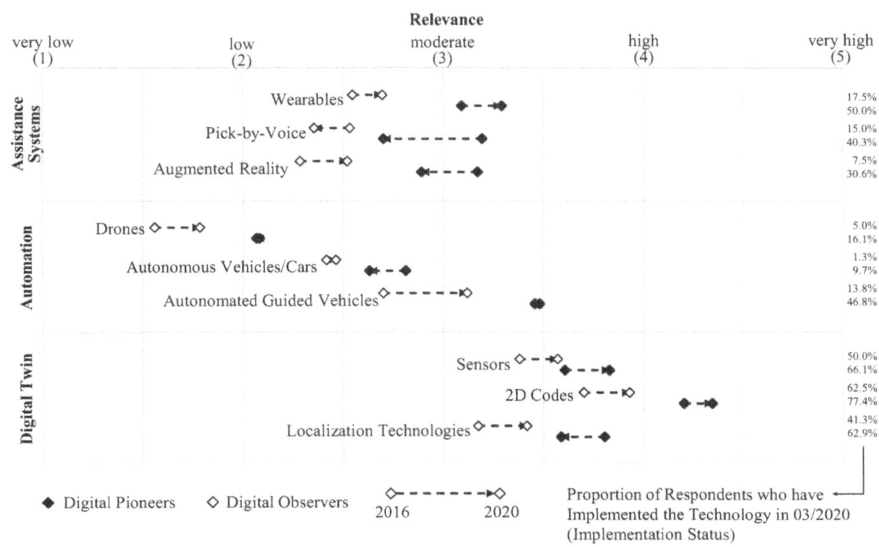

Fig. 6 Importance and implementation of technologies for digitalization along with the material flow in L&SCM

of the material flow are considered particularly relevant: sensor technology, 2D codes, and localization technologies. Automated guided vehicles that serve to automate the flow of materials also occupy an accentuated position. Digital observers, in particular, rate its relevance in 2020 much higher than in 2016. They seem to have recognized their importance for a digital transformation of the companies' business model, even if they have not yet introduced them to the same extent. Among the digital assistance systems, wearables are particularly noteworthy. Based on the relevance rating, augmented reality on the other hand does not seem to have achieved the desired success among the pioneers.

Technologies that support the flow of information are considered to be even more important than the technology-based digitization of the material flow. Figure 7 shows the relevance and implementation status of related technologies. Again, digital pioneers rate those technologies as more relevant than the observers and, accordingly, show a more advanced stage of implementation. Of utmost importance and thus the highest degree of implementation are established business management systems like warehouse management and enterprise resource planning systems. Newer concepts such as platform as a service and digital marketplaces have gained importance in recent years.

Against the background that the value proposition and customer relationship are central building blocks of the business model, it is particularly striking that the

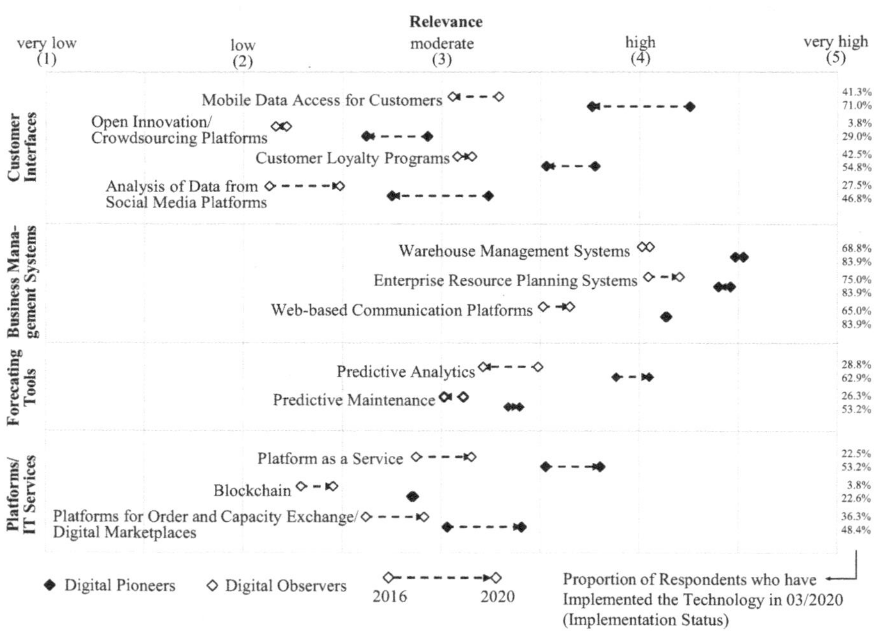

Fig. 7 Importance and implementation of technologies that support the flow of information in L&SCM

technologies that map the customer interfaces are rated as declining in relevance from 2016 to 2020. Especially digital pioneers seem to rather rely on, for example, predictive analytics to create concepts of higher customer value. Surprisingly, digital observers on the other hand estimate this technology to be of decreasing importance in the last 5 years and seem to be in danger of misjudging its potential.

4.3 How Successful Are the Players Along the Path to a Digital Business Model?

To evaluate the success of different strategies, we use the respondents' perceived ability to adapt to key trends from the field of SCM. Figure 8 provides a strategy type-specific evaluation of six central trends from which several key insights can be drawn:

First, the perceived relevance of trends has mostly increased or remained constantly high from 2016 to 2020 in all groups analyzed, except for e-commerce among the digital pioneers, demand fluctuations among digital adapters as well as business analytics among digital transformers and digital observers.

Second, from 2016 to 2020, across all groups and trends – except for digital observers' adaptability to e-commerce – respondents' perceived adaptability decreased. This means that, from today's perspective, respondents are less able to deal with the trends despite their increasing relevance. This effect can possibly be attributed to the fact that, when looking back, respondents have found that their adaptability in the past was lower than originally assessed. But third, with the trends of e-commerce, demand fluctuations, complexity, and transparency primarily impacting the company from the outside, an ascending adaptability can be seen from strategy type A to D. This leads to the conclusion that with an increasing degree of digital transformation of the business model, an increasing adaptability to key trends can be expected.

5 Conclusions

This paper aimed to analyze the long way from digitization to digital business models, providing companies with guidelines on how to proceed in the future. Based on a longitudinal online survey in 2016 and 2020 with 331 and 276 participants, respectively, the following core findings related to the research questions were obtained:

In general, we observed a shift toward an increasing digital business model transformation during 2016 and 2020. Many companies seem to be on a good path of this long way. Regardless of the type of strategy pursued, increasing opportunities and decreasing risks seem to drive companies in L&SCM on the path to a digital business model (RQ 1). Hereby the particularly high assessment of opportunities and low assessment of risks puts digital pioneers one step ahead in

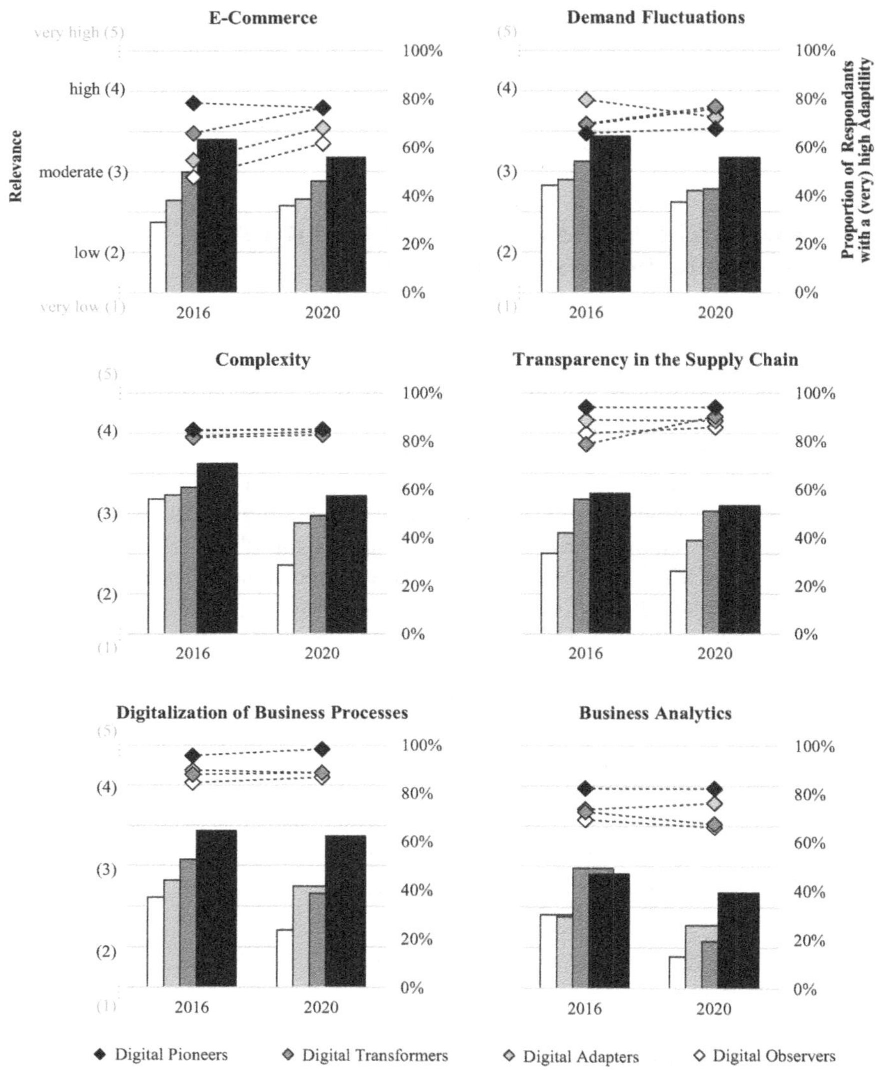

Fig. 8 Relevance and adaptability of respondents to key trends in logistics and SCM

implementation. Furthermore, while digital observers tend to see only minor potential in cost reductions through a digital transformation, companies that are already on their path to a digital business model tend to be driven by both, cost reductions as well as revenue increases. This indicates a holistic consideration of all components of the business model (see Sect. 2.2).

In addition to the customer perspective and thus the revenue sources, the core resources of the digital business model should also be addressed. A variety of technologies exist that come into play along the path toward a digital business model in L&SCM (RQ 2). In terms of material flow, there is a particular focus on technologies that create a digital twin of the physical flow of materials. Additionally, automated guided vehicles and wearables are increasingly supporting employees. Our comparison of different strategy types shows that digital pioneers are clearly ahead of digital observers in the implementation of these technologies. This is also true for technologies that support the flow of information in L&SCM. Here, platform technologies/IT services, as well as forecasting tools, have recently been in the focus of digital pioneers. Concerning companies that are taking their first steps on the way to a digital business model, we observed the danger of misjudging the potential of technologies, for example, predictive analytics. Especially in the early stages, companies, therefore, need to question the digitization of their core resources and closely link it to potential revenue streams in their business model. Our results finally clearly show that the further companies are on their way from digitization to a digital business model, the better they are positioned to deal with future requirements (RQ 3).

Despite it being a long way from individual digitization to digital business models, it is a path certainly worth exploring. Hereby, companies have to bear different things in mind: First, there is no one-size-fits-all approach. Diversity of company backgrounds implies a variety of potential business model adaptations. Second, there are different maturities and connected development processes. Thus, it is initially worth exploring 'digital add-ons' before jumping into entirely digital business models (Bouwman, Nikou & Reuver, 2019, p. 3). Third, of course, the core business of the company must not be neglected despite the hype and potential lure around 'digital-first' companies. Core competence remains a central element of the business model which must not be sacrificed for the sake of digitalization. A clear focus should lie on value addition.

It is one of the success factors of value-adding digital transformation initiatives to find, through intellectual openness and conscious reflection, the right balance between the limitations on the one hand and the potentials of digital innovations on the other (Pearce & Pearce, 2020, p. 23). This is embodied by the 'fast failure' mentality which accepts failure in the knowledge of the big potential upsides of fast progress regarding a company's digital transformation (Neus et al., 2017, p. 35). Trying out digital products or processes in this exploratory way is a sign of digital maturity (Gudergan et al., 2019, p. 8). Following this approach, even though one may not be sure of the eventual value-adding potential of an individual initiative, still retaining a firm grasp of the underlying factors in the organization enable competitiveness – that is the pinnacle of digitalization competence. Doing so will take companies one step further on the way to the digital business model either way.

Our results must be considered in light of their limitations. In determining the sample, a regional restriction was made to Germany. Consequently, it is not possible to transfer the findings to other regions without restrictions. For future research, therefore, it makes sense to extend our investigation toward various other countries as well and to reveal commonalities and differences through comparative analyses. The results are based on self-assessments by the companies on the basis of selected Likert scales. Although the questions were formulated to the best of our knowledge and belief, a bias in the answers cannot be ruled out because of this design. Making digital transformation objectively and better measurable should be the focus of further research. Our findings are based on descriptive evaluations. Further statistical comparative analyses will help to better substantiate them. Besides, we were only able to highlight technological aspects as support for the path to the digital business model. As mentioned in Sect. 2.1 and 2.2, following a socio-technical perspective as well as addressing all parts of a business model is essential. Future research should therefore expand our analyses to include investigations considering employee, organizational as well as customer perspectives.

Despite the continued need for research, this paper made an important contribution to research on digital business models. With the recommendations derived, we were also able to give, in particular, those companies which are already on their path to a digital business model implications for their further course of action.

References

Agrawal, P. & Narain, R. (2018). Digital Supply Chain Management: An Overview. *IOP Conference Series: Materials Science and Engineering*, 455, 012074. https://doi.org/10.1088/1757-899X/455/1/012074.

Alias, C., Goudz, A., Jawale, M. & Noche, B. (2015). Generating a Business Model Canvas for Future-Internet-Based Logistics Control Towers. *Proceedings of the 4th International Conference on Advanced Logistics and Transport (ICALT)*, Valenciennes, France.

Becker, J., Schnaider, M., Cordes, A.-K., Barann, B., Hermann, A. & Gollhardt, T. (2020). Vorgehensmodell zur Umsetzung datengetriebener Geschäftsmodelle. In: Begleitforschung Mittelstand-Digital (Ed.), *Mittelstand-Digital Magazin. Wissenschaft trifft Praxis: Digitale Daten – Treibstoff für Prozess- und Geschäftsmodellinnovationen* (No. 13, 52–58).

Berman, S. J. (2012). Digital transformation: Opportunities to create new business models. *Strategy & Leadership, 40*(2), 16–24. https://doi.org/10.1108/10878571211209314.

Bock, M. & Wiener, M. (2017). Towards a Taxonomy of Digital Business Models - Conceptual Dimensions and Empirical Illustrations. *Proceedings of the 38th International Conference on Information Systems*, South Korea.

Borreck, M.-A., D'Incà, J., Maul, B., Wiehmeier, M., Schambach, S. & Bender, K. (2018). *How Start-ups Digitalize Logistics – 2018: The Acceleration of Disruption*. Retrieved from https://www.presseportal.de/pm/66435/3855682.

Bouwman, H., Nikou, S. & de Reuver, M. (2019). Digitalization, business models, and SMEs: How do business model innovation practices improve performance of digitalizing SMEs? *Telecommunications Policy, 43*(9), 101828.

Bowersox, D. J., Closs, D. J., & Drayer, R. W. (2005). The digital transformation: Technology and beyond. *Supply Chain Management Review, 9*(1), 22–29.

Brennen, J. S. & Kreiss, D. (2016). Digitalization. In: K. Jensen, R. T. Craig, J. Pooley & E. W. Rothenbuhler (Eds.), *The Wiley Blackwell-ICA international encyclopedias of communication. The International Encyclopedia of Communication Theory and Philosophy* (pp. 556–566). Hoboken, John Wiley & Sons.

Brödner, P. (2018). Industrie 4.0 und Big Data – wirklich ein neuer Technologieschub? In: H. Hirsch-Kreinsen, P. Ittermann & J. Niehaus (Eds.), *Digitalisierung industrieller Arbeit* (pp. 323–346). Baden-Baden, Nomos. https://doi.org/10.5771/9783845283340-322.

Büyüközkan, G., & Göçer, F. (2018). Digital supply chain: Literature review and a proposed framework for future research. *Computers in Industry, 97*(4), 157–177. https://doi.org/10.1016/j.compind.2018.02.010.

BVL (2017). *Jahresbericht der Regionalgruppen 2016*. Bremen.

BVL (2020). *Jahresbericht der Regionalgruppen 2020*. Bremen.

Carroll, N. & Conboy, K. (2020). Normalising the „New Normal": Changing Tech-driven Work Practices under Pandemic Time Pressure. *International Journal of Information Management, 55*, 102186. https://doi.org/10.1016/j.ijinfomgt.2020.102186.

Cichosz, M., Wallenburg, C. M., & Knemeyer, A. M. (2020). Digital transformation at logistics service providers: barriers, success factors and leading practices. *The International Journal of Logistics Management, 31*(2), 209–238. https://doi.org/10.1108/IJLM-08-2019-0229.

Davis, M. C., Challenger, R., Jayewardene, D. N. W., & Clegg, C. W. (2014). Advancing socio-technical systems thinking: a call for bravery. *Applied Ergonomics, 45*(2), 171–180. https://doi.org/10.1016/j.apergo.2013.02.009.

Dell Technologies (2020). *Digital Transformation Index 2020*. Retrieved from https://www.delltechnologies.com/en-vn/collaterals/unauth/briefs-handouts/solutions/dt-index-2020-executive-summary.pdf.

Dregger, J., Niehaus, J., Ittermann, P., Hirsch-Kreinsen, H. & ten Hompel, M. (2016). The Digitization of Manufacturing and its Societal Challenges: A Framework for the Future of Industrial Labor. *IEEE International Symposium on Ethics in Engineering, Science and Technology (ETHICS)*, Vancouver, Canada, (pp. 1–3). https://doi.org/10.1109/ETHICS.2016.7560045.

Ebinger, F., & Omondi, B. (2020). Leveraging Digital approaches for transparency in sustainable supply chains: a conceptual paper. *Sustainability, 12*(15), 6129. https://doi.org/10.3390/su12156129.

Falk, S., Lehmann-Brauns, S., Schmidt, F., Piller, F., Matischok, L., Brachmann, D. & Madeja, N. (2020). *Position Paper. Corona and the Consequences: Ten Propositions on the Future of Digital Business Models for Industrie 4.0 in the Post-Corona Economy*. Retrieved from https://www.plattform-i40.de/PI40/Redaktion/EN/Downloads/Publikation/Corona_Thesen.pdf?__blob=publicationFile&v=6.

Fichman, R. G., Dos Santos, B. L., & Zheng, Z. (2014). Digital innovation as a fundamental and powerful concept in the information systems curriculum. *MIS Quarterly, 38*(2), 329–343. https://doi.org/10.25300/MISQ/2014/38.2.01.

Foss, N. J., & Saebi, T. (2017). Fifteen years of research on business model innovation. *Journal of Management, 43*(1), 200–227. https://doi.org/10.1177/0149206316675927.

Galimova, M., Gileva, T., Mukhanova, N., & Krasnuk, L. (2019). Selecting the path of the digital transformation of business-models for industrial enterprises. In *IOP Conference Series: Materials Science and Engineering*, 497, 12071. https://doi.org/10.1088/1757-899X/497/1/012071.

Garay-Rondero, C. L., Martinez-Flores, J. L., Smith, N. R., Caballero Morales, S. O., & Aldrette-Malacara, A. (2020). Digital supply chain model in industry 4.0. *Journal of Manufacturing Technology Management, 31*(5), 887–933. https://doi.org/10.1108/JMTM-08-2018-0280.

Gassmann, O., Frankenberger, K., & Csik, M. (2014). *The business model navigator: 55 models that will revolutionise your business*. Harlow, England, New York: Pearson.

Gobble, M. M. (2018). Digitalization, digitization, and innovation. *Research-Technology Management, 61*(4), 56–59.

Göpfert, I., & Seeßle, P. (2019). Innovative Startups in der Logistikbranche – Eine Betrachtung der neuen Marktteilnehmer und empirische Erkenntnisse einer Fragebogenstudie. In: I. Göpfert

(Ed.), *Logistik der Zukunft – Logistics for the future* (8th ed., pp. 253–280). Wiesbaden, Springer Gabler. https://doi.org/10.1007/978-3-658-23805-6_10.

Grüninger, S., Jantz, M., & Schweikert, C. (2013). *Begründung für die Festlegung der Größengrenzen zur Einteilung von Unternehmen in die verschiedenen Leitfäden. KICG-Forschungspapiere: 6, 2013.* Konstanz: Konstanz Institut für Corporate Governance.

Gudergan, G., Mugge, P., Kwiatkowski, A., Abbu, H., Michaelis, T. L., & Krechting, D. (2019). Patterns of digitization – What differentiates digitally mature organizations? In *IEEE International Conference on Engineering, Technology and Innovation (ICE/ITMC)*, Valbonne Sophia-Antipolis, France, (pp. 1–8).

Guggenberger, T. M., Möller, F., Boualouch, K., & Otto, B. (2020). Towards a unifying understanding of digital business models. In *Proceedings of the Pacific Asia Conference on Information Systems (PACIS) 2020,* Dubai.

Johnson, M., Christensen, C., & Kagermann, H. (2008). Reinventing your business model. *Harvard Business Review, 86*(12), 50–59.

Kagermann, H., Wahlster, W., & Helbig, J. (2013). *Recommendations for implementing the strategic initiative Industrie 4.0. Securing the future of German manufacturing industry.* Final report of the Industrie 4.0 Working Group, Munich: Acatech-National Academy of Science and Engineering and Forschungsunion.

Kersten, W. (2018). Geschäftsmodelle in der Industrie 4.0. In: H. Corsten, R. Gössinger & T. S. Spengler (Eds.), *Handbuch Produktions- und Logistikmanagement in Wertschöpfungsnetzwerken* (pp. 1286–1303). Berlin, Boston: de Gruyter. https://doi.org/10.1515/9783110473803-063.

Kersten, W., Seiter, M., von See, B., Hackius, N., & Maurer, T. (2017). *Trends and strategies in logistics and supply chain management: Digital transformation opportunities.* Hamburg, DVV Media Group.

Kersten, W., von See, B., & Indorf, M. (2018). Digitalisierung als Wegbereiter für effizientere Wertschöpfungsnetzwerke. In A. Khare, D. Kessler, & J. Wirsam (Eds.), *Marktorientiertes Produkt- und Produktionsmanagement in digitalen Umwelten* (pp. 101–117). Wiesbaden: Springer. https://doi.org/10.1007/978-3-658-21637-5_8.

Kifokeris, D., & Koch, C. (2020). A conceptual digital business model for construction logistics consultants, featuring a sociomaterial blockchain solution for integrated economic, material and information flows. *Journal of Information Technology in Construction, 25*, 500–521. https://doi.org/10.36680/j.itcon.2020.029.

Larson, P. D., Poist, R. F., & Halldórsson, Á. (2007). Perspectives on logistics vs. SCM: A survey of SCM professionals. *Journal of Business Logistics*, *28*(1), 1–24. https://doi.org/10.1002/j.2158-1592.2007.tb00230.x.

Leyh, C., & Gäbel, D. (2017). Industrie 4.0: Disruptive Geschäftsmodellonnovationen oder „nur" Geschäftsprozessoptimierung? *Industrie 4.0 Management, 33*(5), 33–38.

Mentzer, J. T., DeWitt, W., Keebler, J. S., Min, S., Nix, N. W., Smith, C. D., & Zacharia, Z. G. (2001). Defining supply chain management. *Journal of Business Logistics, 22*(2), 1–25. https://doi.org/10.1002/j.2158-1592.2001.tb00001.x.

Metz, P. (1998). Demystifying supply chain management. *Supply Chain Management Review, 1* (4), 46–55.

Möller, F., Bauhaus, H., Hoffmann, C., Niess, C., & Otto, B. (2019). Archetypes of digital business models in logistics start-ups. *Research Papers*. Retrieved from https://aisel.aisnet.org/ecis2019_rp/17.

Neus, A., Buder, F., & Galdino, F. (2017). Are you too successful to digitalize? How to fight innovation blindness. *NIM Marketing Intelligence Review, 9*(1), 30–35.

Osterwalder, A., & Pigneur, Y. (2010). *Business model generation: A handbook for visionaries, game changers, and challengers*. Hoboken: John Wiley & Sons.

Pearce, D. D., & Pearce, J. A. (2020). Distinguishing attributes of high-growth ventures. *Business Horizons, 63*(1), 23–36.

Pflaum, A., Bodendorf, F., Prockl, G., & Chen, H. (2020). The digital supply chain of the future: from drivers to technologies and applications. In *Proceedings of the Hawaii International Conference on System Sciences 2020,* Honolulu, Hawaii.

Remane, G., Hanelt, A., Nickerson, R. C., & Kolbe, L. M. (2017). Discovering digital business models in traditional industries. *Journal of Business Strategy, 38*(2), 41–51. https://doi.org/10.1108/JBS-10-2016-0127.

Schallmo, D. (2013). *Geschäftsmodell-Innovation.* Springer Fachmedien. https://doi.org/10.1007/978-3-658-00245-9.

Schlimbach, R., & Asghari, R. (2020). Das Digital Canvas: Ein Instrument zur Konzeption digitaler Geschäftsmodelle. *HMD Praxis Der Wirtschaftsinformatik, 57*(4), 866–878. https://doi.org/10.1365/s40702-020-00624-9.

Schroeder, M., von See, B., Schnelle, J., & Kersten, W. (2021). Impact of the Covid-19 pandemic on supply chain management. In: R. Fritzsche, S. Winter & J. Lohmer (Eds.), *Logistik in Wissenschaft und Praxis: Von der Datenanalyse zur Gestaltung komplexer Logistikprozesse.* (pp. 3-24). Wiesbaden: Springer Gabler. https://doi.org/10.1007/978-3-658-33480-2_1

Staub, N., Haki, K., Aier, S., & Winter, R. (2021). Taxonomy of digital platforms: A business model perspective. In *Proceedings of the 54th Hawaii International Conference on System Sciences,* Honolulu, Hawaii.

Teece, D. J. (2018). Business models and dynamic capabilities. *Long Range Planning, 51*(1), 40–49. https://doi.org/10.1016/j.lrp.2017.06.007.

Ten Hompel, M., & Henke, M. (2017). Logistik 4.0 – Ein Ausblick auf die Planung und das Management der zukünftigen Logistik vor dem Hintergrund der vierten industriellen Revolution. In: B. Vogel-Heuser, T. Bauernhansl & M. ten Hompel (Eds.), *Handbuch Industrie 4.0 Bd.4* (pp. 249–259). Berlin, Heidelberg: Springer. https://doi.org/10.1007/978-3-662-53254-6_13.

VDI/VDE (2016). *Statusreport Digitale Chancen und Bedrohungen – Geschäftsmodelle für Industrie 4.0.* Retrieved from https://www.vdi.de/ueber-uns/presse/publikationen/details/geschaeftsmodelle-fuer-industrie-40-digitale-chancen-und-bedrohungen.

Veit, D., Clemons, E., Benlian, A., Buxmann, P., Hess, T., Kundisch, D., Leimeister, J. M., Loos, P., & Spann, M. (2014). Business models: An information systems research agenda. *Business & Information Systems Engineering, 6*(1), 45–53. https://doi.org/10.1007/s12599-013-0308-y.

Von See, B. (2019). *Ein Handlungsrahmen für die digitale Transformation in Wertschöpfungsnetzwerken* (Dissertation). Technische Universität Hamburg. https://doi.org/10.15480/882.2513.

Weking, J., Stöcker, M., Kowalkiewicz, M., Böhm, M., & Krcmar, H. (2020). Leveraging industry 4.0 – A Business model pattern framework. *International Journal of Production Economics, 225*(2020), 107588. https://doi.org/10.1016/j.ijpe.2019.107588.

Development of a Trend Management Process for Supply Chain Management in the Context of Industry 4.0

Hendrik Birkel and Evi Hartmann

Abstract

Disruptive technologies in the context of Industry 4.0, such as the Internet of Things, Big Data Analytics, smart devices, or Artificial Intelligence are developing at a rapid pace with an increasing impact on global value creation. Companies are facing major challenges in maintaining an overview of these developments and linking them to other trends. Thus, the aim of this article is the development of a comprehensive trend management process for the structured collection and processing of Industry 4.0 trend information. The process is divided into the steps identification, analysis and evaluation, processing, and preparation and is supplemented by continuous monitoring and improvement through knowledge management. Special attention is paid to the development of Industry 4.0, which enables an automated collection of information through the application of web and text mining, which can significantly improve the preparation of information.

1 Introduction

Industry 4.0 tackles the management of today's complexity of global value chains, rising customer demands, and increasingly faster product life cycles with the help of technologies such as the Internet of Things, Big Data, Artificial Intelligence, or Augmented Reality. The extensive potentials enabled through Industry 4.0 change

H. Birkel (✉) · E. Hartmann
Chair for Supply Chain Management, Friedrich-Alexander University Erlangen-Nürnberg, Lange Gasse 20, 90403 Nürnberg, Germany
e-mail: hendrik.birkel@fau.de

K.-I. Voigt and J. M. Müller (eds.), *Digital Business Models in Industrial Ecosystems*, Future of Business and Finance, https://doi.org/10.1007/978-3-030-82003-9_2

the way how business is done, how companies interact, and how employees work (Birkel & Müller, 2021).

However, the breadth of technologies and the high speed of their development make it difficult for companies to maintain an overview. The challenges of managing trends can be summed up in three central issues (Fichter & Kiehne, 2006):

- Increasing complexity of forecasting future emergence, change, and disruption of trends.
- Lack of a foundation for early detection and forecasting requires company-specific knowledge integration, networking, and anchoring of trend research results within a company.
- Lack of recommendations and orientation for action as well as increasing complexity of merging trend data and parameters obtained.

Therefore, there is a fundamental need for research to manage the increasing complexity and to enable optimization potentials of new technologies for companies. To be able to recognize, analyze, and evaluate trends, a defined company-specific trend management process is required. This necessitates the early identification of current and emerging trends, the analysis, and evaluation as well as the processing of these trend developments to use them as a foundation for further innovation processes. The corresponding analysis and reaction are essential for the innovation success of a company and result in the discipline of operational trend management. Several approaches for trend management already exist in the literature, but the company-specific use of new types of tools and information sources for the systematic identification and derivation of strategic follow-up activities have been neglected. Therefore, the aim of this article is the conception of a methodology for the systematic identification, evaluation, and processing of emerging trends, especially in the context of Industry 4.0, which can be used as a foundation for coordination and adjustments of the digitization strategy and respective business models.

2 Theoretical Background

Trend management and the associated processes, such as trend analysis, do not pursue the goal of predicting trends. Rather, it is about diagnosing trends and the resulting activities. Thereby, a forecast can only be implemented by identifying development and opportunity areas (Kaiser, 2012). A trend refers to a direction in which a time series develops in a long-term and sustainable manner (Kaiser, 2012). In this context, the society, culture, or industry in which the trend is occurring is persistently influenced. Likewise, it can be an anomaly, in the sense of a deviation from the norm, which becomes increasingly significant over a period of time

(Raymond, 2014). Trends can be defined according to Müller-Stewens and Müller (2010) with the help of three characteristics:

- Scope: Trends are generally events that have a high range and influence several dimensions. They have an impact on ideals, lifestyles, and living conditions as well as consumer behavior of different socio-cultural milieus.
- Time: Trends generally last for several years (apart from short-term consumer and product trends as well as fashion trends). They are thus distinguished from hypes, which usually generate a high level of attention in a short period but may lose their impact and disappear in the longer run.
- Impact: Trends are highly stable on an ongoing basis and are, therefore, easy to predict once they have been identified and evaluated. Through this characteristic, they prove their strategic relevance for decisions about future actions.

Regarding their scope, trends can be divided into four categories: Metatrends, Megatrends, Macrotrends, and Microtrends (see Fig. 1).

Metatrends

A metatrend is a bundle of trends whose scope is either more comprehensive than that of a megatrend, or its reference is made to a complex, undifferentiated combination of trends which does not relate to a specific object or scope (Köpernik, 2009). Metatrends are also considered as a disturbance of existing systems and thus as the combination of a trend movement and the corresponding countermovement. An example of this is glocalization, the trend towards globalization and the simultaneous need for localness (Reich, 1998).

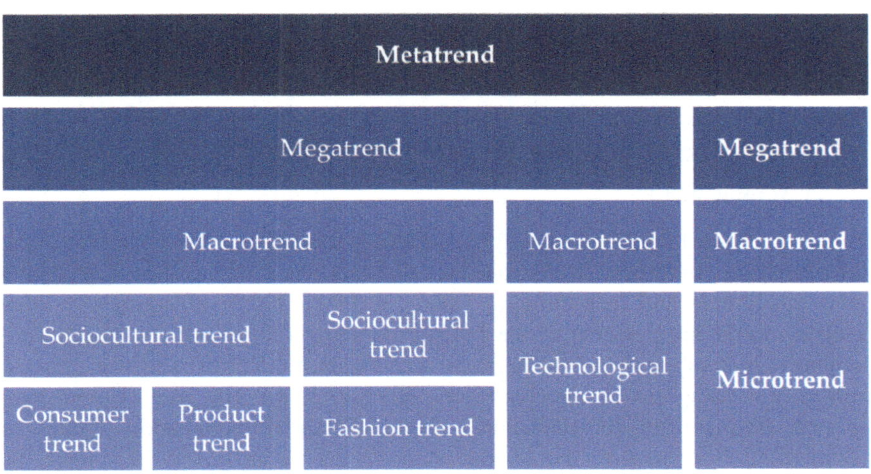

Fig. 1 Categorization of trends (own illustration based on Horx et al., 2007)

Megatrends

Megatrends describe far-reaching trends with a lifespan of about 30–50 years that cause holistic changes in society as well as on a technological and economic level. They can be observed globally, but their influence varies. Megatrends serve as a basis for strategic actions of a company, e.g., the orientation towards new products, new markets, or the research and development of new technologies (Horx et al., 2007). Examples include e-mobility, Artificial Intelligence, changes in the world of work, or new energy resources.

Macrotrends

Macrotrends are the subdivision of megatrends and usually last for 5 to 10 years. They have a direct impact on the company and require a strategic response from the management level (Peloso, 2020). The attitude that the company takes with regard to the macrotrend level determines its position in the competition, its future social significance, and whether the company pursues a future-proof design of its processes (Peloso, 2020). Macrotrends can be classified according to various dimensions, such as political, economic, social, technological, legal, or environmental. Examples comprise import tariffs in the context of political protectionism, the sharing economy, changes in communication behavior, emissions control regulations, or an increase in waste (Kalaitzi et al., 2021).

Microtrends

Microtrends are realizations of macrotrends, which thus have a verifying character for megatrends and are located at the level below the macrotrends (Peloso, 2020). Microtrends include technology trends, which include developments in the technological sector, and socio-cultural trends, which primarily affect consumption and product goods (Peloso, 2020). Companies need to identify such trends at an early stage and evaluate them. However, the successful application of new technologies, which are outside the field of vision of companies, can disseminate rapidly and thus have a decisive impact on a company's performance in the long run. Consumer trends, product trends and fashion trends are short-term as well as marketing-driven trends that usually exist for only one season or one year (Horx et al., 2007).

Trend Management

On a tactical level, trend management is used for strategic early recognition within enterprises. In contrast to market and environment research, trend management is rather qualitative and medium-term (Siebe & Fink, 2006). In contrast to trend research, trend management is the holistic handling of trends as a process in a company. It is subdivided into the steps identification, analysis, and evaluation as well as processing and monitoring (Siebe & Fink, 2006). The goal of trend management is, therefore, the detection, conversion, and dissemination of relevant information. Furthermore, the overall context has to be linked to support the strategic (innovation) process. Depending on the object of investigation, the discipline of trend management uses various methods, such as online research and databases, Delphi studies, expert knowledge, patents, and scientific publications, but also customer complaints and the venture capital market (Ena et al., 2016; Maier et al., 2016). Especially tools such as text and web mining can be used to automatically collect and process data from the Internet, as it became a hub for discoveries and inventions (Johnson & Gupta, 2012). The analysis of trends results in various follow-up activities where the generated and collected trend knowledge is further processed.

3 Conceptualization of an In-Depth Trend Management Process in the Context of Industry 4.0

3.1 Challenges

The increasing diversity of developments resulting from the digital transformation is intensifying the complexity of supply chains (Birkel & Hartmann, 2019). Due to the comprehensive nature of global value creation, it is extremely difficult to assess future developments. Changes in trends, trend breaks, and the probability of occurrence can significantly complicate its management (Ena et al., 2016). This complexity is composed of the increasing number of trend signals and thus the increase of possible relations among them as well as the degree of divergence (Thede, 2014). One example in the technological context is the Internet of Things, which collects data through a decentralized network of sensors, which are then processed through Big Data Analytics and/or Artificial Intelligence to describe, predict, and prescript future actions. Therefore, it is necessary to create an adequate comparison level or to sharpen the focus of the observation.

The purpose of the following developed concept for a trend management process is to reconcile a defined and structured approach while ensuring flexibility. For the development, the essential components from Siebe and Fink (2006) are applied and extended (see Fig. 2).

3.2 Trend Identification

Various sources can be used to identify trends for value creation in the context of Industry 4.0. A general distinction can be made between internal and external sources of information. Internal sources include, among others, the research and development department, the sales, or the purchasing department of a company. In turn, customers, universities, consultants, or even competitors can be used to collect information from external sources. Furthermore, with regard to external sources, the Internet offers a wide range of possibilities that can be implemented quickly and cost-effectively. These include, for example, access to research and technology portals, online business and trade journals, press releases, patent databases, and

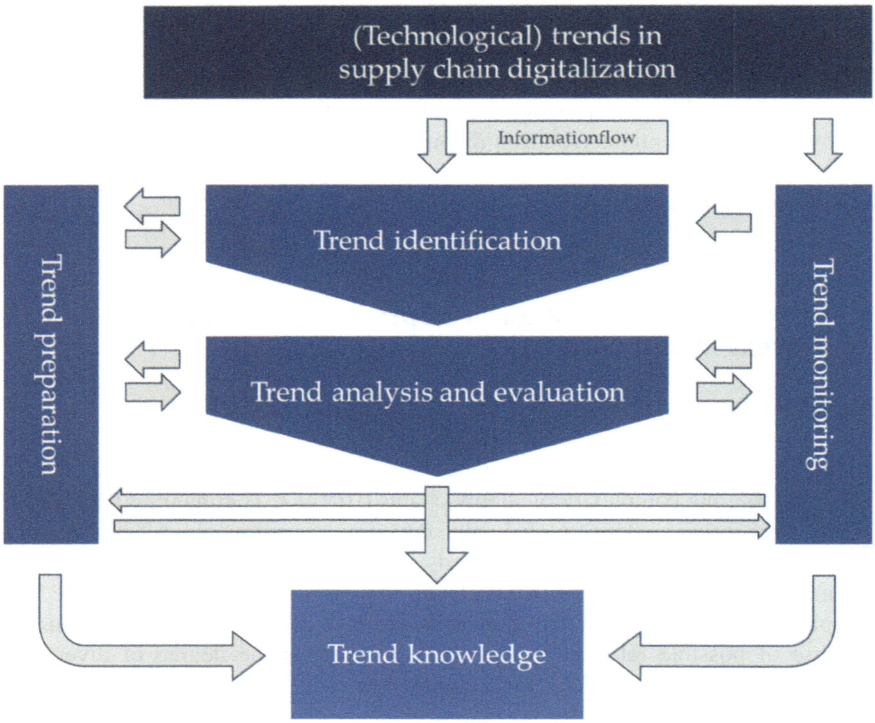

Fig. 2 Trend management process (own illustration adapted from Siebe & Fink, 2006)

business databases (e.g., Industry 4.0 platform, Industrial Internet Consortium, Made in China 2025, etc.).

Therefore, a four-step process is developed below as a foundation (see Fig. 3):

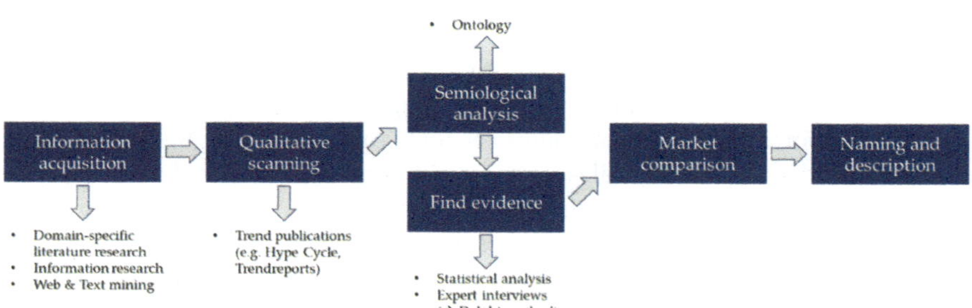

Fig. 3 Process of trend identification (own illustration)

Step 1—Information acquisition: First, the user of the trend identification process must acquire sufficient information about the domain, e.g., through a literature review, a desk research, or an automated approach through web and text mining. This is necessary to contextualize topics and technical terms and to grasp interrelationships.

Step 2—Qualitative scanning: The aim of this step is an initial derivation of possible trends from already known and frequently mentioned technologies. Therefore, a fixed period must be defined for the (first) scanning (e.g., the last three months or the last year). Qualitative and continuous scanning of additional information sources helps to access additional sources and to develop a feeling for recurring terms and technologies. At the same time, this enables the identification of trend signals.

Step 3a—Semiological analysis: By analyzing and evaluating trend sources, frequently recurring terms can be identified and collected. This form of quantitative content analysis is considered the most widespread method for identifying indications of trends (Thede, 2014). This can be used to collect time-series data regarding the frequency of mentioned terms and thus to identify emerging fields of technology. For an expanded search, a collection of search terms, associated synonyms, and translations can be defined, which can be incorporated into automated search algorithms with web and text mining.

Step 3b—Find evidence: Further quantitative (and qualitative) evidence is sought for the identified potential trends. For this purpose, statistical analyses similar to the quantitative content analysis mentioned in step 3a can be continued. In addition, databases (patents, publications, and press releases) can be analyzed based on their metatags. The goal is to identify time series developments or further indicators that confirm the hypothesis of the identified signals as a trend (Thede, 2014).

Evidence can also be found by using the tacit knowledge of employees. Thus, based on the findings of the previous steps, the discovered trends can be scrutinized and concretized within expert meetings (qualitative evidence). This ensures the relevance of the trend for the own company, involves employees in the process, and at the same time, enables feedback for the developers of the trend management.

Step 4—Market comparison: Based on the relevance check by the experts, a rough assessment can be made whether further indications of individual trends should be sought or whether individual trend developments can be neglected. For the remaining trends, best practice examples or case studies have to be identified. With increasing use in the industry, the user can optionally assess the maturity of the technology. In this way, the trends can be further classified according to their relevance for the user's own company as well as the industry in general.

Step 5—Naming and description: In the final step, the identified trends are named to achieve consensus for the further processes. Based on criteria, the trends can then be described and grouped into trend fields to provide employees in subsequent process steps with the most important information on the respective trend.

Table 1 Industry 4.0 trend fields and exemplary trends

Industry 4.0 trend fields	Exemplary trends
IT systems	Digital platforms, cloud logistics, multipurpose networks, quantum computing, edge computing, serverless computing
Data analytics	Big Data Analytics, predictive and prescriptive analytics (logistics and maintenance), data lakes, enterprise taxonomy and ontology management
Smart sensors and labels	Internet of Things, sensor technology in the supply chain, NFC, RFID, smart dust, digital labeling
Smart assistants	Driverless transport systems, drones, smart and collaborative robots, autonomous vehicles, conversational user interfaces, virtual assistants, smart workspaces
Communication networks	5G, next-generation wireless, machine-to-machine communication
Expanded reality and wearables	Augmented and virtual reality, mixed reality, volumetric displays, augmented data discovery, conversational AI platforms, exoskeleton
Decentralized databases	Blockchain, Internet of Value
Artificial Intelligence	Context-aware systems, deep reinforcement learning, cognitive computing, artificial curiosity, neuromorphic hardware, cognitive expert advisors
Digital twin	Telematics, versatile mounting system
Additive manufacturing	3D printing, 4D printing

In Table 1, the identified trend fields for Industry 4.0 and exemplary trends are shown.

3.3 Trend Analysis and Evaluation

Trend Analysis

Subsequently, the analysis of trends is necessary. The basic steps for the trend analysis are in line with a scenario analysis and include the following:

1. collection of time-series data,
2. extrapolation of further developments,
3. estimation of the probability of occurrence, and
4. classification of an interpreted scenario in the trend evaluation.

In the course of estimating the probability of occurrence, knowledge experts are required to assess the extent how future events will interrupt or redirect the developments of a trend and when which degree of maturity can be expected. Even if this assessment is subjective, it enables an efficient and quick evaluation of the identified trends.

Trend Evaluation

Trends can be individually evaluated for the company within the framework of a utility value analysis. These evaluations can subsequently be displayed visually to enable an efficient comparison. To be able to compare the trends with each other, it is essential to define evaluation criteria that can be quantitatively determined as precisely as possible or subjective assessments with a definite interpretation. For the development of an evaluation model in trend management, important factors arise from the literature, such as the relevance, strength and direction of the trend influence, the probability of occurrence, and the time horizon (Schatzmann et al., 2013).

Taking into account the categorization models from innovation and technology management, which are already established in practice and literature (e.g., Gartner Hype Cycle, the BCG matrix, or the technology portfolio by Pfeiffer), we developed a holistic portfolio for the evaluation of trends within a company. Our portfolio considers existing competencies within the company as well as the likelihood of occurrence/relevance for the company. The portfolio contains four fields, each of which represents a recommendation for action (see Fig. 4):

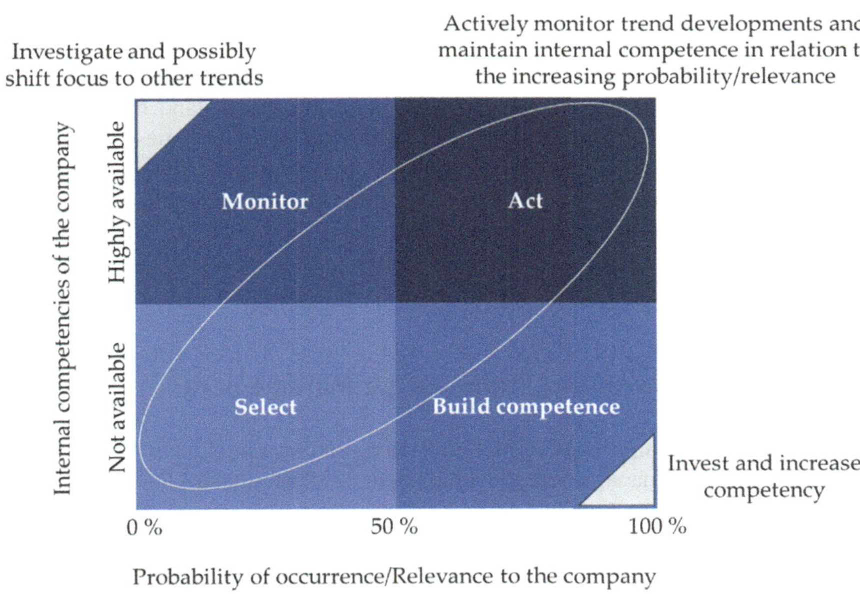

Fig. 4 Trend portfolio for the assessment of trends (own illustration)

- Select (low/low): For trends with low competency within the company but simultaneously low relevance, a selective approach and a deeper analysis of the trend and its impact are necessary.
- Observe (high/low): Trends in this area are characterized by a low probability of occurrence but can be easily managed due to high competencies. These trends should be closely reviewed with regard to their probability of occurrence and relevance for the company. If the monitoring shows an intensification of this trend, the company needs to shift the trend into the field Acting.
- Building up competence (low/high): Due to the high probability of occurrence of those trends, competencies in this area need to be built up quickly.
- Acting (high/high): Trends in this field should be the focus of attention for companies and respective technologies should be implemented.

Following the trend evaluation, a group of experts can agree on recommendations for actions based on the analysis and evaluation of the trends. This recommendation is optionally incorporated into the subsequent preparation form.

3.4 Trend Processing and Continuous Monitoring

Following the analysis and evaluation of trends, the results are processed and presented to enable the continuous generation of trend knowledge. Visualization is crucial to ensure that the findings of the trend management process are communicated intuitively to internal and external stakeholders (e.g., cross-departmental employees, customers, or suppliers) (Warschat, 2015). The content can only be grasped quickly and processed logically if it is easy to understand but has also a polarizing character (Thede, 2014). Especially for new technologies with a high degree of abstraction, using examples as well as a recurring structure is crucial. Trend monitoring incorporates the results of the previous steps and provides the foundation that initiates a new start of the process. Monitoring examines various factors and provides trend signals that are incorporated back into the trend management process.

3.5 Enhancement through Knowledge Management

For the continuous improvement of trend management, enrichment through connected knowledge management is fundamental. This enables the storage of knowledge, which contributes to its integration within a company. The aim is not only to handle the output of the process but also to support trend management in its individual phases. Consequently, data flow is crucial in all process steps. Within the previous trend management process, key personnel holds implicit knowledge, which is only revealed in the later stages (trend preparation, e.g., as a report). To make this knowledge explicit, trend processing based on knowledge management can be used. Therefore, a database structure is required that allows linking knowledge within a network (Bürgel, 1998), so that trend processing can serve as a comprehensive knowledge platform. This can be achieved by a process-supporting instance. In the context of knowledge management, a frequently pursued approach is the use of ontologies and semantics, which can be also applied in trend research and automated trend monitoring (Kim et al., 2017). Furthermore, utilizing so-called "extreme tagging systems," trend knowledge can be converted into a semantic network. Depending on the process step, Boolean search queries, paths, and data for regression analyses can subsequently be extracted based on the interconnections.

4 Summary and Implications

To meet today's challenges in the areas of production and logistics, an increasing number of manufacturing companies are pursuing a digitization strategy. However, many strategies lack a continuous management process for new trends and technologies, which are increasingly complex and at the same time volatile. Significant assessment difficulties in trend research and thus also in the management of trends result from the increasing complexity in three fields: (1) multi-layered business models and a rising number of product derivatives and their relations (due to, e.g., global action), (2) a wide range of new technologies, which increases the complexity of the solution approaches, and (3) the complexity on the level of the trends themselves due to the high number of trend signals.

The developed process for a company's trend management enables efficient and targeted management of technology trends from identification, analysis, and company-specific evaluation to knowledge integration and continuous monitoring. Supported by this, operational decision-makers can pave the way for a subsequent strategic innovation process. At the same time, it provides a concept for a technologically improved process that remains flexible and adaptable. The sub-process of trend preparation is a key starting point for information technology support. The interoperability of the data also benefits the other sub-processes, and trend management makes it possible to increase the overall efficiency. Expert assessment and subjective evaluation remain an integral part of trend management, but time-consuming steps such as information acquisition, information linkage, and trend monitoring can easily be automated to manage the complexity more effectively.

References

Birkel, H., & Hartmann, E. (2019). Impact of IoT challenges and risks for SCM. *Supply Chain Management: An International Journal, 24*(1), 39–61.

Birkel, H., & Müller, J. M. (2021). Potentials of industry 4.0 for supply chain management within the triple bottom line of sustainability—A systematic literature review. *Journal of Cleaner Production, 289*, 125612.

Bürgel, H. D. (1998). *Wissensmanagement: Schritte zum intelligenten Unternehmen. Edition Alcatel SEL Stiftung*. Berlin, Heidelberg: Springer.

Ena, O., Mikova, N., Saritas, O., & Sokolova, A. (2016). A methodology for technology trend monitoring: The case of semantic technologies. *Scientometrics, 108*(3), 1013–1041.

Fichter, K., & Kiehne, D. O. (2006). *Trendmonitoring im Szenario-Management – Eine erste Bestandsaufnahme informationstechnischer Unterstützungspotenziale*. Fraunhofer IRB.

Horx, M., Huber, J., Steinle, A., & Wenzel, E. (2007). *Zukunft machen: Wie Sie von Trends zu Business-Innovationen kommen. Ein Praxis-Guide. Business Backlist*. Frankfurt, New York: Campus.

Johnson, F., & Gupta, S. K. (2012). Web content mining techniques: A survey. *International Journal of Computer Applications, 47*(11), 44–50.

Kaiser, I. (2012). collaborative trend analysis using web 2.0 technologies. *International Journal of Distributed Systems and Technologies, 3*(4), 14–23.

Kalaitzi, D., Matopoulos, A., Fornasiero, R., Sardesai, S., Barros, A. C., Balech, S., & Muerza, V. (2021). Megatrends and trends shaping supply chain innovation. In: R. Fornasiero, S. Sardesai, A. C. Barros & A. Matopoulos (Eds.), *Lecture notes in management and industrial engineering. Next generation supply chains: A roadmap for research and innovation* (pp. 3–34). Cham, Springer.

Kim, Y., Ju, Y., Hong, S., & Jeong, S. R. (2017). Practical text mining for trend analysis: Ontology to visualization in aerospace technology. *KSII Transactions on Internet and Information Systems, 11*(8), 4133–4145.

Köpernik, K. M. (2009). *Corporate Foresight als Erfolgsfaktor für marktorientierte Unternehmen* (Dissertation). Freie Universität Berlin.

Maier, M. A., Hofmann, M., & Brem, A. (2016). Technology and trend management at the interface of technology push and market pull. *International Journal of Technology Management, 72*(4), 310–332.

Müller-Stewens, G. & Müller, A. (2010). Strategic Foresight—Trend- und Zukunftsforschung als Strategie instrument. In: M. Reimer & S. Fiege (Eds.), *Perspektiven des Strategischen Controllings: Festschrift für Professor Dr. Ulrich Krystek* (pp. 239–257). Wiesbaden, Gabler / Springer Fachmedien.

Peloso, A. (2020). Leveraging the power of micro-macro trends in contemporary organizations. *Journal of Applied Business and Economics, 22*(4), 168–174.

Raymond, M. (2014). *The trend forecaster's handbook (Reprint)*. King.

Reich, S. (1998). *What is globalization? Four possible answers* (No. 261).

Schatzmann, J., Schäfer, R., & Eichelbaum, F. (2013). Foresight 2.0—Definition, overview & evaluation. *European Journal of Futures Research, 1*(1), 1–15.

Siebe, A., & Fink, A. (2006). *Handbuch Zukunfts management: Werkzeuge der strategischen Planung und Früherkennung*. Campus.

Thede, J. T. (2014). *Ambient Data zur Trendforschung*. Technische Universität Berlin.

Warschat, J. (2015). *Technologien frühzeitig erkennen, Nutzenpotenziale systematisch bewerten: Methoden, Organisation, semantische Werkzeuge zur Informationsgewinnung und -speicherung; Ergebnisse des Verbundforschungsprojektes syncTech - synchronisierte Technologieadaption als Treiber der strategischen Produktinnovation*. Stuttgart, Fraunhofer.

Unlocking the Hidden, Data-Driven Potential of the Supply Chain

Stefan Asenkerschbaumer

Abstract

Even though a digitalized supply chain can be a veritable driver of performance, industry is still doing far too little to unlock the potential that is hidden in a data-driven supply chain. Yet for any company that seizes this opportunity and systematically exploits the wealth of supply-chain data, an enduring competitive advantage beckons. The game-changer is an end-to-end supply chain, based on standardization and data transparency, that permits largely automated, AI-assisted, and highly efficient planning processes. In this respect, supply-chain planning and production scheduling go hand in hand as building blocks of the factory of the future, whose operations are digitalized and highly flexible. There are four fundamental elements for achieving this:

- Leadership and associates—empowerment
- The design of end-to-end processes
- The use of digital interfaces to manage partners
- Data security

Combining cross-company and company-internal digitalization projects can play a major part in making processes more robust, conserving resources, enhancing flexibility, and making the supply chain future-proof.

S. Asenkerschbaumer (✉)
Robert Bosch GmbH, Robert-Bosch-Platz 1, 70839 Gerlingen-Schillerhöhe, Germany
e-mail: Stefan.Asenkerschbaumer@de.bosch.com

K.-I. Voigt and J. M. Müller (eds.), *Digital Business Models in Industrial Ecosystems*, Future of Business and Finance, https://doi.org/10.1007/978-3-030-82003-9_3

1 Introduction

"Data is the new oil"—first used by *The Economist* in 2017, this sentence is now more relevant than ever. Global data volumes are exploding: the International Data Corporation estimates that it will increase from 45 zettabytes, or 45 billion terabytes, in 2019 to 175 zettabytes in 2025 (Seagate, 2020).

Currently, users and companies have roughly an equal share in the production of this data. Over the next two years, the volume of company-generated data is expected to grow by more than 40% annually, and to make up as much as 80% of total data volume by 2025. Much of this data will come from automated manufacturing and connectivity among companies.

Faced with these data streams, the 64,000-dollar question is how companies can turn these huge data volumes to their advantage. Currently, just 32% of the data available to companies is actually used—the remaining 68% is neglected (Seagate, 2020).

Clearly, therefore, the effective use of the growing volumes of data is a source of huge potential. And in this respect, the supply chain has more opportunities to offer than ever before.

1.1 The Digitalized Supply Chain as a Driver of Performance

Indeed, the supply chain has the potential to be a true driver of performance. A landmark study suggests that companies that aggressively digitalize their supply chains can expect to grow their EBIT by an average 3.2% annually (McKinsey, 2017).

Within a company's organization, therefore, the supply chain is the area in which digitalization can contribute most to EBIT growth.

In addition, the companies that follow this path can expect to increase their sales revenue by 2.3% annually. This considerable potential also shows how supply-chain digitalization can be much more than just a tool for driving down logistics costs.

Artificial intelligence (AI) has a central role to play in preparing the ground for this, but a Deloitte study shows that it is still in its infancy when it comes to the supply chain (Deloitte, 2020).

1.2 The Objective of a Completely Digitalized, Self-regulating Supply Chain

If we want a largely autonomous, connected, and cross-company supply chain, we first of all have to completely digitalize it (Fig. 1).

Companies that are just starting to digitalize frequently complain about three drawbacks of working with digital tools. First, the data is unstructured and kept in

Fig. 1 Steps in the evolution of the supply chain

organizational silos, which prevents it from being shared across the company and meaningfully interpreted. Second, there is no clear line of sight from supplier to customer. And third, performance indicators are not available in real time, so that the supply chain can only be managed reactively.

Currently, even companies with a high level of maturity as concerns their supply-chain digitalization are still transitioning from using digital twins of their business processes to semi-automatic management on the basis of alert signals.

The final goal is autonomous systems that use AI to manage and control the supply chain, and to react to changes in real time. The companies in such a supply chain are tightly interconnected, and can be managed from a single source (within the bounds of the data sovereignty that has been agreed).

1.3 Companies are Still Insufficiently Prepared

Even though digitalization has accelerated considerably since the late 1990s, the level of uptake in many companies is still very low. Studies show that it is above all small and medium-sized enterprises (SMEs) that lack the digital basics (Hochschule Coburg & TMG Consultants, 2017).

According to a survey conducted by Bosch in collaboration with the Friedrich-Alexander University of Erlangen-Nuremberg (FAU), SMEs in particular are hesitant when it comes to digitalization.

Frequently, this is due to shortcomings in the level of automation, in connected, standardized value-creation processes, in the electronic exchange of data with partners, and in the use of cloud-based collaboration platforms.

On top of this, 81% of these companies identify lack of expertise as the main reason for not digitalizing their supply chains.

Companies that are insufficiently digitalized, and that lack even basic tools such as electronic data interchange, will have to make a huge effort to stay competitive.

The increasing globalization of supply chains, the customization and diversity of products and services, and the expectation of ever-shorter reaction times call for a targeted, cross-functional digitalization strategy.

2 Bosch's Path to Digital Excellence—Also in the Supply Chain

Bosch is successfully transforming itself into a leading company for the Internet of Things (IoT) and mobility solutions. As a supplier of technology and services, Bosch is accelerating the digitalization of its supply-chain processes in order to secure the company's strong development.

This will give it the basis it needs for supplying products and services that are "Invented for life"—improving quality of life in a connected world and conserving natural resources.

With a purchasing volume of 50% of total sales revenue and logistics costs coming to another roughly 5% of sales revenue, the Bosch supply chain is an increasingly digitalized global network of 800 warehouses, 280 plants, 30,000 suppliers, and 250,000 customers, as well as of several hundred million parts that are procured by these plants every day.

The necessity of managing such networks digitally, and to include all partners is also demonstrated by a recent survey by the German logistics association (BVL). It lists the digitalization of business processes, transparent value creation, and above all cross-company data exchange as the top trends in the industry (Bundesvereinigung Logistik, 2020).

2.1 Digital Interfaces with Suppliers

As early as 2000, Bosch joined with other companies to set up SupplyOn, one of the first digital B2B platforms. The platform provides a basis for digital transactions, and increasingly also collaboration, with the companies' respective suppliers.

Today, more than 100,000 companies and their locations worldwide, from a variety of industries, are linked in to the SupplyOn platform. They make use of the modules it provides for transactions relating to procurement, logistics, quality, and finance.

In the case of Bosch alone, some 85,000 suppliers' and service providers' locations and plants are part of SupplyOn, and exchange on average some 100,000 datasets with Bosch every working day.

For transactional platforms in the B2B sphere to be successful, it is essential that data formats are standardized, and that interface design is user-friendly and open. Increased efficiency as a result of improved processes has to be the prime objective, and evident for all partners.

At Bosch, SupplyOn has allowed the following processes to be improved:

- Inquiries and quotations
- Awarding contracts on the basis of electronic bidding
- E-procurement in the purchasing of indirect materials
- Electronic initial sample inspection reports, with interfaces to all common measuring tools
- Transmission of delivery and call-off schedules, and vendor managed inventory
- Electronic invoicing and overview of invoice status
- Logistical solutions such as transport management systems, empties management, and tracking and tracing applications
- Collaborative solutions in project management, change management, and surveys.

2.2 Digitalization of Intralogistics

Taking its lead from the Toyota production system, Bosch has been systematically digitalizing its in-house manufacturing operations for some 20 years now. It relies here on its Bosch production system (BPS) and a number of supplementary digitalization initiatives.

As a leading user and provider of Industry 4.0 solutions for connected manufacturing, Bosch relies on electronically controlled manufacturing supermarkets and on the employment of demand-driven milk runs and automated guided vehicles (AGVs). The company also uses RFID and scanner technologies, and flexible tools for production scheduling and management, various forms of which are running in its plants.

Over the years, this has allowed Bosch to systematically reduce costs and inventories and increase flexibility.

For example, automating incoming goods on the basis of an advanced shipping notification (ASN) in combination with a unique ID (on a label or using RFID) allowed the company to reduce operations in its German plants' incoming goods departments by one shift.

Moreover, the average return on investment (ROI) when using AGVs is 1.5 years. This efficiency potential means that the number of AGVs in use at Bosch is expected to double in 2021 alone.

To ensure a perfect match when using digitalized logistics solutions, Bosch has a "chapter book" that lists the digitalized solutions on offer in terms of benefit, implementation effort, interfaces, and prerequisites (such as API).

Bosch plants can use an internal service to order these logistics solutions and the necessary hardware. A corporate team of experts works with the plants to check requirements and ensure the standardized deployment of the solutions.

For each use case, for example, a catalogue can be consulted that contains all standardized AGVs with payloads between 200 and 5,000 kg. All of them can communicate with the company's ERP and MES systems.

2.3 Digitalizing Interlogistics

In the case of deliveries that are managed via the Bosch transport management center, the physical deliveries are mapped using a digital twin, the transport order (TO). In combination with an EDI interface to the shipper, or via Bosch's driver app, this allows Bosch to trace the status of the consignment and expected time of arrival on the company's InTrack platform. The TO and confirmed receipt of the goods serve as proof of delivery and trigger the automatic process of paying the shipper.

To link deliveries with materials and asset tracking in interlogistics, Bosch has developed a GPS-assisted transport data logger. This positioning sensor is used both within the company and for external customers that use a variety of applications in rail and truck freight services.

As Bosch products become increasingly integrated in the Internet of Things, the company will be able to seamlessly track its products and offer additional services. The Bosch Power Tools division provides one example of this. Here, the division applies the GS1 industry standard, in combination with a data matrix code (DMC), to give its appliances and packaging digital twins.

2.4 Forecast—The Huge Challenge Digitalization Faces in a VUCA World

One major focus for Bosch is to forecast customer call orders as precisely as possible, and to plan on that basis. The high level of volatility in a global customer and supplier structure presents considerable challenges to maintaining supply-chain integrity.

Especially in the current situation, Bosch can clearly see bottlenecks—for example, in the semiconductor industry—and dependencies—for example, on monopolistic and oligopolistic structures such as those found in the chemicals industry. On top of this, there are the challenges of profound technological change and rapidly changing customer behavior. Meeting these challenges also requires new forecasting models that take much more account of environment data, dependencies, and disruptive technological developments than is the case today.

In this context, AI-based forecasting models will play an increasingly dominant role: both in order to better reflect the increasing volatility and complexity of demand, and to identify disruptions in the supply chain in advance. Disruptions in globalized supply chains—whether because of Brexit, trade conflicts, or lockdowns resulting from the Covid-19 pandemic—have led many companies to put their supply chains on a more resilient footing.

2.5 Data and Sustainability as Drivers of the Development of the Digital Supply Chain

As the supply chain becomes digitalized, the traditional focal points of supply chain management—quality, costs, and logistics—are being joined by a new factor: data.

On the one hand, the supply chain generates data—such as about the movement of freight—to improve the accuracy of forecasting arrival times. On the other hand, data from external providers, such as the risk profiles of suppliers, is systematically adding to the data relevant for the supply chain. By analyzing this data, forecasts and decisions can be made with a higher degree of accuracy. However, the data can also be used to create new business models.

In addition, bought-in data about financial ratings and location risks (supplemented by the company's own data on changes in quality and delivery performance) allow Bosch to engage with suppliers early. In this way, solutions can be found to prevent delivery bottlenecks and the need for support programs.

When combined with data-driven risk management and corporate social responsibility (CSR) ratings (as a supplement to the conventional total cost of ownership, or TCO), this information provides a sound basis for purchasing decisions.

For Bosch, as one of the first industrial enterprises worldwide to have achieved climate neutrality in 2020, sustainability is very important in this context. Given that Bosch has set itself the target of a 15% reduction in emissions from upstream and downstream value chains by 2030, suppliers' ecological footprint and greenhouse gas emissions will also be a criterion for awarding contracts.

2.6 The Bosch "LOG 2025" Strategy

As part of the Bosch "LOG 2025" strategy, logistics will use the systems architecture of a connected logistic platform that links SAP and non-SAP supply-chain applications.

Through standardization and data transparency, Bosch will thus be gearing its supply chain to AI-assisted planning processes and greater reaction speeds. Any interventions will be alert-triggered only, and routine tasks will be automated.

Decision makers and logistics planners will in the future receive information via dashboards that act as a "single source of truth," providing an overview of all the relevant data. Drill-down functions in the various applications acting in the background will allow planners to access all relevant information without delay. Taking the need for agility into account, this potentially allows tasks to be consolidated within the organization.

In its manufacturing operations, Bosch wants to extend use of its "PROCON" planning tool, which is already in place in a number of plants. With the help of PROCON, interactive monitors can be used to change local manufacturing sequences. This information will be sent in real time to the warehouse, production preparation, and other interfacing units.

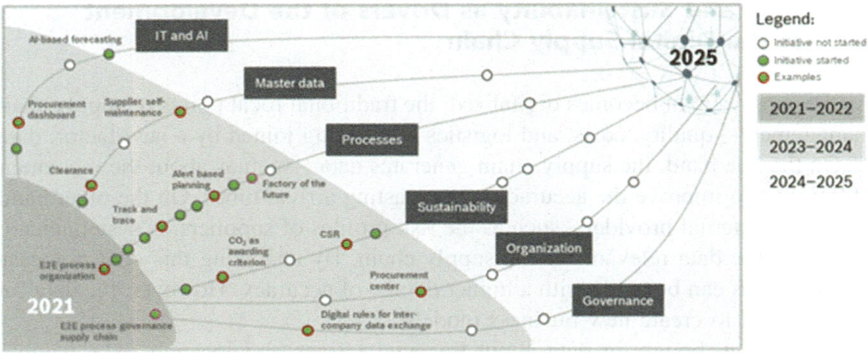

Fig. 2 Bosch connected logistics platform

As digitalization progresses further, it will decisively enhance sustainability in the supply chain by allowing improvements to be made jointly with the company's partners. In this way, it will help Bosch reach its climate and CSR targets (Fig. 2).

The supply chain is thus an integral part of Bosch's digital "factory of the future." The company's aim here is to achieve a perfect symbiosis of human skills, IT, machinery, and robots.

Putting the company's "LOG 2025" strategy into practice not only sets a high bar for the transparency of the supply chain and the digital integration of its partners, therefore. It also demands a lot of logistics associates' digital and end-to-end process competence. The task here is to prepare associates for their future functions as data analysts and process optimizers.

3 The Enablers of Successfully Digitalizing the Supply Chain

The "LOG 2025" strategy is based on four essential factors.

3.1 Leadership

Digitalizing the supply chain is a matter that concerns the entire company. Senior management has to know what digitalization can and cannot do, and devote itself fully to this challenge. It will only be possible to create a digitalization strategy that is right for the company if executives are familiar with the capabilities of supply-chain digitalization, and understand its benefits as well as its appropriate use.

Here, it is essential that they understand key technologies such as cloud computing, blockchain, and platform ecosystems, so that they can judge the effect they will have on the company. Executives have to be able to present their digital competence credibly to associates and external partners. This is crucial if they are to come to a joint understanding of the opportunities offered by digitalization, and to make a success of it in practice. As a supplier of technology and an aspiring AIoT company, Bosch is preparing its executives and associates for this challenge by offering customized training programs such as "Digitalization in a nutshell" as well as mandatory seminars in AI.

One thing that is clear is that a silo mentality hampers digitalization. Categorizing digitalization initiatives as "purchasing" or "logistics" projects means that they are frequently not sufficiently supported by their respective opposite numbers. If digital end-to-end processes are to be optimized effectively and rapidly, it is essential that they have cross-functional objectives with clear and quantifiable KPIs.

In addition, the above-mentioned joint study by Bosch and FAU Nuremberg showed that there are distinct regional differences. Executives in China, for example, are significantly more open-minded about digitalization in their own company, as well as about involving third parties such as customers, than their European counterparts.

The willingness to make the necessary human and financial resources available is also crucial. Many projects in the industrial sector, although they are carried out enthusiastically, are not equipped with sufficient resources, and thus never get beyond the pilot stage.

Furthermore, companies frequently focus on short-term ROI, which cannot do justice to the strategic importance of digitalization.

Executives should see digitalization as an opportunity to be pursued over the long term. At Bosch, this is ensured by means of what the company calls "enabling" projects.

3.2 Design of Digital End-To-End Processes

Roughly 50% of the companies polled in the above-mentioned BVL survey said they had no company-wide digitalization strategy. Another 50% said that while digital projects were in the pipeline, only few had been put into practice (Bundesvereinigung Logistik, 2020). The survey also showed that those companies that had made the most progress in digitalizing their supply chains proved to be more resilient in the Covid-19 pandemic. And while companies appreciate the importance of digitalization and IoT applications, there is a huge gap between theoretical approval and practical implementation.

In 2016, when structuring its end-to-end processes, Bosch defined strategic control points along the product life cycle, from start of design to end of life and services, and formulated a digitalization strategy for each of these control points.

The strategy encompasses all parts of the supply chain, from big data-assisted supply chain network design for new products, which allows the most cost-effective production location and logistics chain to be pinpointed, all the way through to spare parts procurement in the aftermarket. The aim of these strategic control points is to standardize processes as far as possible and to map physical processes with a digital twin.

To ensure the success of its digitalization projects, Bosch relies on extensive requirements engineering. This uses tools such as a matrix ("Zielkreuz") to define internal and external requirements, which then serves as the basis for project work. Such a matrix also has to consider the respective data architecture within the company.

Once this has been completed, existing processes are checked to see where they need to be changed, and shaped, so that they fit the requirements of the planned digitalization project and of the user interface. In doing so, end-to-end chains are created in order to ensure data and process consistency. For example, unique IDs are used to access order processes, incoming goods, the manufacturing supermarket, and payment transactions.

This also means taking account of national laws, as they can hamper global standardization in many areas and may require processes to be adapted to local conditions. For example, self-billing, settlement via consignment warehouses, and electronic bills of lading may not be permitted in every country, or only recordable by means of special processes.

In light of geopolitical risks and shifts, moreover, regionalizing the supply chain may make it more flexible and resilient, allow farther-reaching standardization, and shorten response times.

The key condition of any digitalization strategy, and one that is often underestimated in practice, is the existence of a "single source of truth." First of all, the management of master data requires the deployment of resources, permanent updates, user discipline at all times, and a robust IT with a clear-cut master data structure. All partners should grant it the priority it deserves. Clear responsibility for keeping data up to date is becoming a key factor for competitive success.

3.3 Using Digital Interfaces to Manage Partners

In cross-company digitalization projects, Bosch involves its partners as early as possible in the design of interfaces and processes.

This is especially important in light of the outdated IT systems that can often be encountered at many suppliers (especially the smaller ones). Such systems can only be adapted with difficulty to new and future challenges.

At some SMEs, the standards that apply between large companies on the basis of VDA recommendations or enhanced EDI notifications are only practicable with difficulty. In many cases, therefore, the highly integrated solutions that would be ideal for optimum process design are an impractical way of achieving the best possible consistency.

This is where the true potential of platform solutions such as SupplyOn is unlocked. These solutions make it possible for SMEs to fulfill the requirements of major Tier-1 suppliers and OEMs.

The focus here should always be on ensuring that all participants benefit. Cash flow and financing requirements for transformation work in industries such as automaking are just as important for suppliers as for their clients and customers. For this reason, the burden of digitalization must not be disproportionately borne by just one of the players. According to the Bosch/FAU Nuremberg study, consideration should also be given to monetary and non-monetary incentives, as long as the end result is process efficiency.

One further essential criterion here is rigid application of the agreed communication channel. Ideally speaking, the new process will be so stringent that it will not be possible to bypass it. For many associates, this is a challenge. And not least, it places considerable demands on leadership.

Depending on the scope, a digitalization project at Bosch can mean that thousands, if not tens of thousands, of suppliers are affected by its rollout. Here as well, the rollout effort and timescale are frequently underestimated. Expecting associates to conduct a rollout on top of their everyday tasks generally makes no sense. For this reason, the rollout should be done by dedicated teams with the requisite expertise.

In addition, a concept should also be developed for integrating the "long tails," the large share of smaller suppliers. They may need additional expert support or a simpler variant of the process. One example of this is the dispatch of invoices using standard formats. If EDI is not possible, these can be read out at Bosch using OCR (optical character recognition).

3.4 Data Security

The risk of data being misused, hacked, or passed on to third parties is still a cause of widespread concern. In a survey of 1,100 companies by the German Economic Institute (IW), roughly 82% cited data security as the factor inhibiting more data exchange and data trade with third parties (Institut der deutschen Wirtschaft, 2019).

This is why Bosch places great importance on standardized and secure protocols and the selection of certified platform providers. Above all, such providers give SMEs the confidence they need to communicate via these channels.

Companies in particular are very wary of passing on to third parties potential company value, proprietary know-how, or company information that could benefit competitors.

This is why it is important for Bosch not only to show companies how they can benefit from digital exchange with Bosch, but also to use confidentiality agreements to allay the concerns of companies supplying data.

4 Outlook

The future demands made of supply-chain legislation, end-to-end documentation of carbon emissions, the circular economy, and traceability will require that the players in the supply chain collaborate much more extensively with each other than they do today.

Cloud platforms such as the European GAIA-X initiative can offer a solution here, allowing all supply-chain partners to access a central data space. The keys to acceptance and success are the interoperability of already existing solutions with newly created platforms and block chains, data sovereignty, and standardized interfaces.

Combining cross-company and company-internal digitalization projects will play a major part in making processes more robust, conserving resources, enhancing flexibility, and futureproofing the supply chain. Systematic exploitation of the wealth of supply-chain data by means of analytics and AI will enduringly strengthen the competitiveness of all the companies that seize this opportunity.

References

BVL (2020). *Digitale Erfolgsfaktoren für resiliente Wertschöpfungsketten*. Retrieved from www.resiliente-wertschoepfungsketten.de.

Deloitte (2020). Lieferanten-Risikomanagement in der deutschen Automobilindustrie 2020.

Hochschule Coburg and TMG Consultants (2017). SCM 4.0. Marktumfrage 2017.

Institut der deutschen Wirtschaft (2019). Demand – Data, Economics and Management of data driven business. Cologne.

McKinsey (2017). The case for digital reinvention. *McKinsey Quarterly*.

Seagate and International Data Corporation (2020). *Rethink data*. Retrieved from https://www.seagate.com/de/de/our-story/rethink-data/.

Digital Business Models in Manufacturing

Digitalization as an Enabler of Subscription Business Models in the Manufacturing Industry

Günther Schuh, Jana Frank, Lennard Holst, Daniela Müller, Tobias Leiting, and Lukas Bruhns

Abstract

Subscription business models provide an important component for monetizing the potential of Industrie 4.0. Subscription business is based on a long-term and participative business relationship between customer and provider. However, only digitalization offers the necessary framework conditions to realize the characteristic recurring and performance-based billing, and to ensure the necessary transparency about the usage phase of products as well as continuous performance improvements in the customer process. Against this background, companies must not only recognize the much-cited potential that lies in the total dedication to the success of individual subscription customers. Rather, the central obstacles must be addressed, examined, and subsequently overcome in a targeted manner in order to successfully establish subscription business models and place them on the market.

1 Digitalization Paves the Way for Subscription Business Models

Digitalization is increasingly shaping our economy and society. In this world shaped by digitalization, the classic supply orientation is turning into a demand orientation that is largely driven by customer needs (Komor, 2019). In this context, digitalization means the transformation of business models through the optimization and increasing customer orientation of existing business processes with the help of

G. Schuh (✉) · J. Frank · L. Holst · D. Müller · T. Leiting · L. Bruhns
Rheinisch-Westfälische Technische Hochschule Aachen, Campus-Boulevard 30, 52074 Aachen, Germany
e-mail: G.Schuh@wzl.rwth-aachen.de

K.-I. Voigt and J. M. Müller (eds.), *Digital Business Models in Industrial Ecosystems*, Future of Business and Finance, https://doi.org/10.1007/978-3-030-82003-9_4

the intensive use of information and communication technologies (Heinrich, 2020). There is hardly a sector of the economy that is not affected by advancing digitalization (Bitkom, 2020).

In recent years, the traditional mechanical and plant engineering sector in particular, which is focused on products, has been attributed considerable economic potential through digitalization. In 2014, for example, a survey of 235 industrial companies revealed that these companies expect digitalized services for machines and plants to increase sales by an average of 12.5% by 2020 alone (Koch et al., 2014). A look at the current situation shows that Western European mechanical and plant engineering companies generate only 0.7% of their total revenue from digital business (Illner et al., 2020). The idea of using the potential of digitalization to generate new sales through digital offerings thus falls far short of expectations. The industry still predominantly sells products, machines and classic after-sales services (Moser et al., 2019).

However, the traditional product business in particular has been weakening increasingly in recent years, which is reflected, for example, in the lowest average capacity utilization in the German mechanical engineering sector in the recent past at 74% (Gushurst & Wolf, 2020). Companies in the sector are facing increasing stagnation in the sale of new machinery and equipment as well as an increase in the intensity of competition as products become increasingly interchangeable (Rieger & Wagner, 2019). To counteract the stagnating new business, manufacturers are making major investments in the development and implementation of product innovations to increase the efficiency and service life of their products (Gotsch et al., 2019).

However, the direct consequence of this is that customer demand can be met by a smaller number of products or via fewer repeat purchases (Teusch et al., 2019). As a result, demand for new products continues to fall. Although this phenomenon of stagnating new business has been observed for some time, only a few manufacturers have so far developed effective countermeasures (Bardt et al., 2019). So far, no real innovation or even transformation of the classic business models of manufacturing companies is apparent (Hoffmann & Bijedic, 2018).

Digitalization offers the opportunity to monetize sustainable competitive advantages by transforming the business model. It allows in-depth customer access and cross-customer networking, which makes it possible to achieve ever better quantitative mapping of customer relationships (Joecks-Laß & Hadwich, 2021). This lays the foundation for far-reaching automation of processes and production (Bouée & Schaible, 2015; Hermann, 2020). At the same time, a comprehensive benchmark is formed by aggregating the data on the use of the respective services in the utilization phase of all customers (Tzuo & Weisert, 2018). Based on this comprehensive data pool, the performance of the individual customer can be improved, for example, through the targeted parameter setting of the machines or the prediction of failures (Kaufmann & Servatius, 2020). These new opportunities for continuous learning and improvement must be translated into new business models that focus on revenue and growth with existing customers (Gerl, 2020). The goal of this type of business model is no longer to sell customers individual products or services. Rather, the goal is to offer them access to a constantly improving service (Busam, 2020). If the customer receives this access in return for regular payments, this is referred to as a subscription business model.

1.1 Subscription Business Models

The basic principle of industrial subscription business models, also known by numerous synonyms such as pay-per-use and pay-per-outcome models (Stoppel & Roth, 2017) or everything-as-a-service (Classen et al., 2019) as well as equipment-as-a-service offerings (Stojkovski et al., 2021), consists of the continuous provision of an agreed service by the provider in return for periodic payments by the customer (Uuskoski et al., 2020). In contrast to traditional, transactional product sales, the customer does not necessarily become the owner of the product system complemented by software and services. Instead, the subscription customer pays for the availability, usage, or outcome of a provided solution offering based on performance-based pricing metrics (Stoppel, 2016). To do this, the provider must build an ongoing, data-driven understanding of actual product usage and leverage digital technologies to predict potential outages and improve performance (Schuh et al., 2020). With an understanding of actual customer needs, subscription business models also make a key contribution to conserving resources by reducing over-engineering, i.e., keeping numerous functions ready "just in case they are needed" (Hermann, 2020, S. XIX) and replacing them with individual software or product releases, for example. This opens up opportunities for the provider to respond to customer usage and to align the solution package with individual demand by adapting it quickly. This helps to increase value creation on the customer side and, at the same time, to increase the provider's own economic success via the performance-based pricing metric (see Fig. 1).

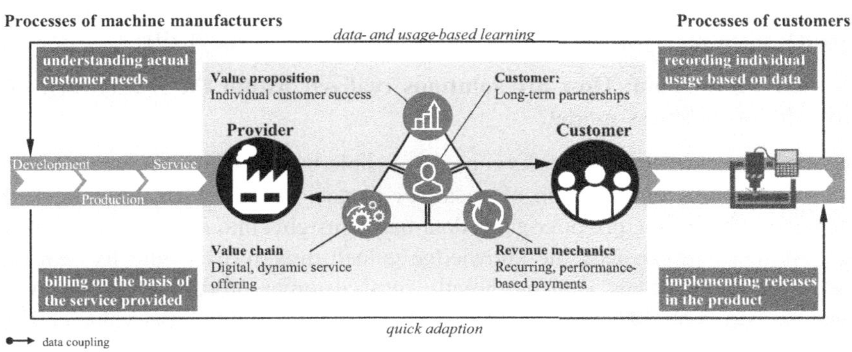

Fig. 1 Industrial subscription business models are based on a close provider-customer relationship (own illustration based on Harland, 2018)

1.2 Characteristics of Subscription Business Models

In the following, the characteristics of subscription business models are described based on the magic triangle (Schuh et al., 2020). The magic triangle describes the functioning of a business model through the interaction of four elements. At the center is the customer, who must be identified and whose wishes must be satisfied. The next dimension is the "value proposition". In the magic triangle, this dimension is identified by the key question "WHAT?". The value proposition dimension includes all the activities a company needs for delivering the value proposition to its customers. The fourth element describes the revenue mechanics, i.e., how a financial result is achieved in the business model (Gassmann & Frankenberger, 2016).

Element customer: Who are my subscription customers?

A subscription offer is generally only aimed at specific customer segments: in mechanical and plant engineering, where high-priced assets are often integrated into the customer's production process, the focus is mostly on potential customers for whom long-term success can be predicted from the use of the subscription service (Schuh et al., 2020). The focus in a subscription is on a long-term, positive "lock-in effect", i.e., the customer does not want to terminate the subscription offer due to an individual optimization of its performance—a win–win effect for all parties (Eldridge, 2018).

Element value proposition: What benefits are offered to the customer with a subscription business model?

Instead of the benefits from the purchase of products and services to be weighed up by the customer in advance, the customer is offered the successful use of a solution package in a subscription business model. This means that the customer is guaranteed individual success, e.g., maintaining or increasing a certain level of productivity (Jussen, 2019). Whereas in the past the customer had to bear the risks of failure or incorrect operation after purchase, in a subscription business model the provider increasingly assumes the customer risks (Ebi et al., 2019).

Element value chain: How are solutions realized within the framework of a subscription business model?

The assumption of customer risks is made possible by the intelligent networking of products and the digitalization of customer contact points. With the help of the Internet of Things, the provider gains data-based insights into actual product use by the customer and can feed the knowledge gained directly back into its own processes and products, as well as directly into customer processes via (software) releases (Hermann, 2020). This optimizes the customer's individual value creation (Schuh et al., 2019). Since the provider is interested in the best possible, long-lasting operation of the products and no longer in new business, both customer and provider pursue the goal of the highest possible performance of the services in the customer process. This results in a resource-saving alignment of the target systems of provider and customer (Classen et al., 2019).

Element revenue mechanics: How is revenue generated in a subscription business model?

A solution package consisting of products, software, and services is integrated into the customer's production process. Customers are no longer billed for individual products or services, but for a **productive state in the customer's process,** for example, on the basis of usage time or production results (Roth & Stoppel, 2014). Starting from a basic fee that covers the basic risk of availability as well as the services delivered by the provider, the customer only pays for what they actually use. This enables an often beneficial shift from one-off investments to recurring investments over the term of the investment (Sato & Nakashima, 2020).

2 Challenges for Providers of Subscription Business Models

The characteristics of subscription business models focus on the alignment of interests, long-term, participative economic success, and the associated win–win situation for customer and provider (Deutscher, 2019). However, the development and implementation of subscription business models is accompanied by key challenges that companies must overcome in the course of a business model transformation (Gudergan et al., 2021). Also based on the magic triangle, the central challenges are illustrated in the four dimensions.

Element customer: How are needs identified early in the sales process?

The defined goal in the as-a-service business is to get to know the individual customer and their needs in a way that was neither necessary nor desirable in transactional sales (Hermann, 2020). Right at the beginning of the customer journey, in contrast to previous marketing measures, it must be clear how potential customers can be identified and addressed (Binckebanck et al., 2020). In the following, sales is challenged to sell a continuous service, contrary to the previous transactional sale of a physical product (Wölfle & Leimstoll, 2019). To do this, sales must know the needs of individual customers in order to customize the service (Jussen, 2019).

Element value proposition: How can the close, trust-based collaboration be built?

From the value proposition of a subscription business model, the benefit to the customer from such a permanent business relationship must be apparent at first glance (Janzer, 2017). At the same time, initial trust in the provider is required, because in the case of a subscription, the provider must continuously deliver against the value proposition made (Sunyaev, 2020). The value for the customer is generated by a combination of various partial benefits, such as products, services, software, and in some cases even consumer goods (Schuh et al., 2020). This increases the complexity of the service internally on the provider side, while it must be reduced for the customer as part of the value proposition. The assumption of customer risks also increases dependency on the actual performance of the customer (Roth & Stoppel, 2014). The inclusion of physical assets, some of which are capital-intensive, in the subscription offering thus causes a shift in the distribution of risk toward the plant manufacturer.

Element value chain: How can the tension of service delivery be resolved?

In the meantime, further challenges arise in relation to the **value chain,** such as the reliability of the data-based coupling between the customer and provider processes (Joecks-Laß & Hadwich, 2021). Furthermore, especially in mechanical and plant engineering, there is no subscription without efficient technical service because a subscription business model only generates revenue if the customer can use a machine or plant at any time (Schuh et al., 2019). It is therefore essential to reduce downtimes and failures to a minimum. This is a particular challenge for companies whose plants are distributed around the world or to which they do not have access at all times. In this respect, providers are faced with the conflicting demands of providing high-quality service and keeping service costs as low as possible to keep the model viable. This is because the service is usually no longer paid for directly but is integrated into the subscription price (Glaser-Gallion, 2013). Component suppliers in particular do not see themselves in a position to set up such an innovative business model because of their "distance" from the end customer and their limited share of the customer's value chain (Staegemann et al., 2020).

Element revenue mechanics: How are the different and complex price factors weighted?

To achieve a win–win situation between customer and provider over time, it is necessary to link the **revenue mechanics** more closely to the service provided to the customer and the benefits it creates (Deutscher, 2019). This balanced pricing is individual and very demanding due to numerous variables, such as the time of use or the production result (Stoppel & Roth, 2017). The service is no longer billed as a one-time financial transaction, but as a recurring payment over the time of the subscription transaction (Jussen, 2019). However, many existing billing systems are not yet geared to these continuously billable services. When we talk about providers of high-priced machinery and plants, the first issue that usually comes up is that of financing. This is because a shift from one-off transactions to recurring, smaller payments results in an extensive delay in terms of operating cash flow (Huntley, 2018). Many companies shy away from taking this financing risk (Faß, 2019).

3 Success Factors for Subscription Business Models

According to Eisenhardt, conducting case studies is a suitable approach for developing an understanding of issues arising in practice in the subscription business, and formulating success factors (Eisenhardt, 1989; Eisenhardt & Graebner, 2007). It helps to discover underlying mechanisms and principles and thus to formulate new hypotheses. Moreover, case study research ensures that the results obtained are closely related to the practical reality of a company that is in the process of implementing subscription business models. In selecting the case studies, manufacturing companies of different sizes and purposes were included in order to obtain a diversified and holistic result. To select suitable case studies, an international questionnaire study was first conducted with 100 companies to identify particularly successful companies in the subscription business. Case studies were then prepared from the top 25 performers in the study using a semi-structured interview, on the basis of which overarching success factors could be identified. As a result of the case-based approach, six principles for a successful implementation of subscription business models in the manufacturing industry could be derived. These six principles can be assigned to the dimensions of the magic triangle.

Element customer: Know your customer!

A look at the creation of the 2013 Netflix series "House of Cards" shows what aligning movie content with actual customer interest can look like: By analyzing the usage data of its 30 million streaming customers at the time, Netflix knew that movies with director David Fincher are rarely canceled, that actor Kevin Spacey is considered a crowd favorite, and that an English political show generates particular interest among Netflix customers. In short, the US series was created on the drawing board and became a global success (Ströbele, 2019).

At this point, one may ask how well manufacturing companies actually know their customers and how they can react quickly and efficiently to latent changes in needs. In the subscription business, knowledge of individual, changing customer needs is a crucial success criterion (Moring & Deurloo, 2018). In the first instance, it is a matter of understanding the customer's business model and assessing their current business situation. Only those customers who also signal the potential for growth, increased performance and long-term partnerships are of interest to the provider. Because only if the customer really uses the offer consistently and derives a benefit for himself from it, does the pay-per-use/pay-per-part metrics inversely increase the profit for the provider (Classen et al., 2019; Stojkovski et al., 2021). Otherwise, contracts will be terminated, because this flexibility is one of the original reasons why customers decide to buy a subscription (Stoppel & Roth, 2017).

Companies that know their customers well use customer data from all phases of the customer lifecycle to align the entire process from product development to training for product users with customer needs (Schuh et al., 2020). Inventory changes in the provision of consumables are analyzed in some cases, as are production times, downtimes and fault messages from machines and plants (Picot et al.,

2018). In addition, the scope of technical functions used on the machine or software functions in the software solutions (customer portals and assistance systems, etc.) can provide information about the "state of health" of a customer (Engel & Hähnel, 2020). At the same time, according to an internal consortium study, over 80% of successful companies are able to combine the data from the various sources into meaningful and value-creating customer insights, both systemically and organizationally (Paproth & Leiting, 2020).

A case study from B2C for the professionalization of customer insight management is the company Vorwerk. With the Cookidoo platform, the company adds a digital customer interface to the best-selling Thermomix. Via recommender functions based on the cooked products, the platform offers customers additional creative cooking ideas, similar to the suggestion of new playlists and songs on Spotify. The usage behavior on the platform and the cooked products of the customers are correlated with each other via a self-learning algorithm. As a result, suggestions are consistently provided digitally. The platform is billed based on a subscription model. In this case, complete integration in the sense of the subscription logic presented, i.e., the merging of product, service, and software, has not yet been implemented due to the high margins of the core product.

Element customer: Customer success management for the subscription relationship

The customer is the center of attention and thus in the way. This motto applies in many manufacturing companies that propagate customer centricity to the outside world but criminally neglect existing customer management on the inside (Ziegler, 2017). In traditional product sales, this can go well for a while. In the subscription business, on the other hand, the customer must be nurtured as a strategic asset, cared for like a tender little plant, and supported as it grows, because the following applies here: customer success = supplier success (Schuh et al., 2019). This fact is one of the most formative changes from product to subscription provider. Only if the customer achieves its business goals, i.e., is successful in its target system and according to its target metrics (quality increased, productivity increased, costs reduced, etc.), only then can the provider generate long-term profits and grow together with the customers (Schuh et al., 2019). The revenue mechanics of recurring, performance-based payments are responsible for this dependency. In the revenue mechanics already shown, such as pay-per-use or pay-per-outcome, the provider assumes numerous risks from the customer. The provider interest increases to reduce risks such as process, quality, and productivity risks in the customer process through differentiated existing customer management (Ebi et al., 2019).

The good you do to others, you always do to yourself. —Leo Tolstoi

Customer success management (CSM) is the central organizational concept for these tasks and has been an indispensable part of the SaaS world for several years (Hochstein et al., 2020): "We now have more customer success managers than sales people," reports a marketing manager of a large cloud provider of customer relationship management (CRM) systems. "Sales has a natural limit, while expansion and growth with existing customers seems almost endless," says the product manager for cloud-based condition monitoring solutions at a leading manufacturer of rolling bearings.

of successful subscription providers **use** CRM systems to **manage** subscription contracts

The CSM is now entering the manufacturing industry and acts between the established functions of sales and service (Ulaga et al., 2020). It takes on tasks for which these roles have not previously been incentivized: the realization of the successful use of the subscription offer (Ulaga et al., 2020). At its core is the definition of a so-called customer health score, which carries out a continuous, data-based evaluation of defined success criteria such as target achievement, functional scope used, payment behavior, and so on (Hilton et al., 2020). This is the only way to enable the CSM to initiate proactive measures and make recommendations to customers, e.g., in so-called monthly or quarterly business reviews with all parties involved on the customer side (operators, internal maintenance, IT experts, buying center managers, etc.), to increase success with the subscription solution. In the long term, this reduces customer churn and increases usage intensity (Mehta & Steinman, 2016). As a result, the value received by the customer is successively increased over the period of the business relationship (Schuh et al., 2020).

Two important findings in conclusion:

1. Customer success does not equal customer satisfaction. Customer satisfaction is a feeling, a subjective evaluation by people on the customer side. Customer success is quantitative, measurable and linked to the specific achievement of the customer's business objectives (Hochstein et al., 2020).
2. CSM activities should be differentiated: So-called high-touch customers (high sales volume or low adaptation rates) receive short-cycle personal support, while low-touch customers (low sales or high adaptation rates) are provided with process improvement information relevant to them in an automated manner, similar to marketing automation (Jacobs, 2020). Basically, the CSM should be

free of charge or priced into the subscription fee so that the customer has no inhibitions to interact with the CSM, to open up and to solve challenges together.

In the software-as-a-service world, the role of the customer success manager is more in demand than ever. A leading CRM cloud provider relies on differentiated customer success management to guarantee customers an optimal customer success experience depending on their usage performance. If functions of the software are not used, the customer access manager can react immediately and proactively before the unpopular "churn" occurs.

Manufacturing companies such as Heidelberger Druckmaschinen have also recognized that there are gaps in customer support in the subscription business from sales and service alone. To ensure consistency and continuous performance tracking, a customer success management role was created. This role proactively addresses customer usage patterns, jointly discusses goals and roadmaps with customers, and explains new features, such as in software, as needed (Schmedding, 2019).

Element value proposition: First standardize, then individualize

Apple is often praised for its ability to innovate, but it is not widely known that, that the iPhone was inferior to comparable cell phones in almost all technical categories when it was launched in 2007 (Skibicki, 2020). Nevertheless, the iPhone also made Apple the most valuable company in the world. The recipe for success is simplicity and a focus on a few exceptionally good products (Raitner, 2019). When Steve Jobs set this course for Apple in 1997, the company was on the verge of insolvency and had over 100 different product variants on offer for every conceivable customer requirement (Otto et al., 2019). These were simplified to such an extent that in 2007 there were about 10 products left in the portfolio. Customization no longer takes place via the hardware, but rather via the software (Mohr, 2020). As a result, the cell phone does not simply remain a product, but becomes a platform that simplifies users' everyday lives with the help of an individually configured selection of digital apps (Otto et al., 2019).

The transfer to the much more complex manufacturing industry is not entirely straightforward. The manufacturing industry is characterized by much more complex offerings, consisting of hardware, services and software, and by lower unit volumes than the IT sector (Leimeister, 2020). Many solutions are cost-intensive and developed individually for one or a few customers. Nevertheless, the optimization goal here as well is to offer all customers a solution that is as cost-efficient and customized as possible (Leimeister, 2020). Modularization and digitalization in the subscription business offer potential, so that a high degree of individualization of the solution and the associated high added value do not have to be at odds with cost efficiency (Schuh & Riesener, 2018).

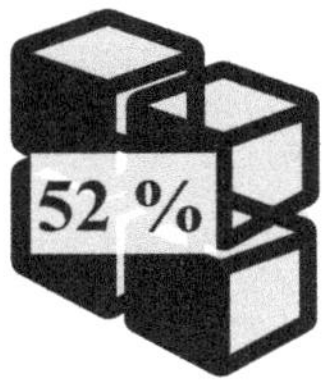

of successful subscription companies rely on **modularization** of services for individual customer segments

A success principle of successful subscription providers from the manufacturing industry is therefore "standardize first and then individualize over time through software" (Paproth & Leiting, 2020). Hardware provides the basis for long-term customer loyalty and creates a lock-in effect for the subscription business (Schuh et al., 2020). It provides a standardized platform for offering the subscription. Based on this, the offer is tailored to the customer's individual requirements over time with the help of services and digital solutions (Schuh et al., 2020). Successful subscription providers carry out end-to-end evaluations and adaptations of individual services for the customer twice as often as less successful providers (Paproth & Leiting, 2020).

One example of the successful implementation of this principle of standardization and individualization from the machine and plant engineering sector is TruConnect from the TRUMPF Group. The company has developed various components for its Smart Factory product in the categories of hardware, software, and classic services. These components allow modular adaptation to individual customer needs. Standardized machines or even entire manufacturing cells serve as hardware components. Building on this, six software components are offered to support and optimize the customer's operational work. These are supplemented by classic services such as training or implementation support. This modularity enables the customer to be provided with an individual service package (TRUMPF, 2020).

Element value chain: Cooperation in business ecosystems

As part of the evolution of the company's own business model, it is becoming increasingly crucial to enter into associations in the form of an ecosystem in which different players in a value network work together with the aim of boosting performance or realizing new business models (Dremel & Herterich, 2016).

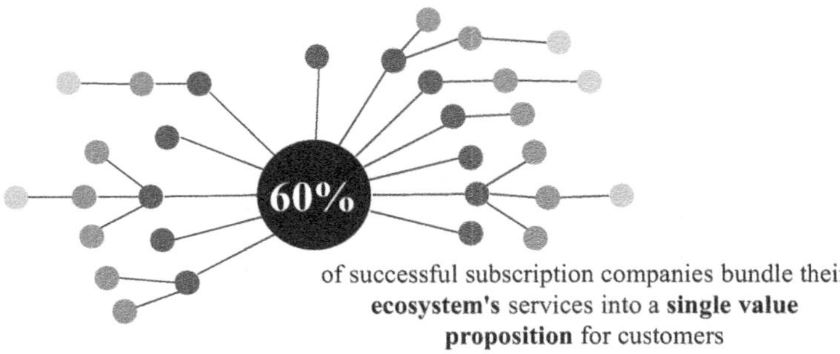

Today, well-developed specialist knowledge is worth a great deal. A wide range of skills and experience is needed to develop and implement new business models such as subscriptions on this basis (Schedler & Bolz, 2020). But today it is no longer necessary to acquire new skills and combine them in one company. After all, building up new competencies is often a lengthy process with high demands on capital and personnel (Farhadi, 2019). It is much more efficient to collaborate with other players who locate their expertise in the relevant areas needed. By joining forces, companies can grow faster because they can draw on the resources of partners (Farhadi, 2019). By aggregating resources and competencies, each company can add value to its own expertise through subscription offerings, and the customer is provided with a total solution (Farhadi, 2019).

For component manufacturers in particular, integration into a value-creating ecosystem has the advantage of reducing risk. Since ownership of components that have been permanently installed in a plant and are critical to its function is transferred by law to the plant owner, the provider cannot demand the return of the installed component, even though it has not been paid off, in the event of termination of the contract. As part of a business ecosystem, this risk can be mitigated (Krug, 2009).

As part of this, diverse, new ecosystems are developing in practice with players who assume the provider's financing risk. Intermediaries and insurers are visibly entering the market to build the financial bridges and reduce risks of non-payment by unproductive or insolvent customers (Demont & Paulus-Rohmer, 2016). It is important to note: Subscription business is much more than classic leasing! Leasing is exclusively about the financial allocation of a one-time price to periods and residual value calculations (Stanula et al., 2020). Subscription business is essentially about performance for the customer. Machinery and plant, consumables, software, service, and ultimately forms of financing are merely means to an end (Schuh et al., 2020).

An increased margin by building a business ecosystem and integrating the customer into the company's processes: Heidelberger Druckmaschinen AG has achieved this. A great deal of expertise is required to operate a printing press, both in terms of maintenance and in terms of setting up and operating the press and selecting consumables. This allows customers to concentrate on their core business again. The presses are intelligent and networked. Heidelberger has access to the usage data and can also intervene in the processes by controlling the press itself. This means that the presses are used in the best possible way and receive optimum maintenance, which helps to avoid unscheduled service calls. By including the manufacturers of consumables in the ecosystem, Heidelberger can realize volume discounts as a central partner and thus generate additional margins (Hermann, 2020).

Element value chain: Efficiency and optimal integration

"Every service call burns our margin. Without maximum service efficiency through predictive maintenance and remote technologies, no subscription model will pay off in the long run." A statement many of you have probably heard while developing a subscription business model. An unscheduled service call on the customer's machine suddenly no longer brings in additional revenue but only incurs costs. A paradigm shift in the process of work delivery is therefore necessary. To increase efficiency, subscriptions in particular offer the practical opportunity to extend one's own company boundaries to the surrounding value network as well as to the customer (Kreutzer, 2016).

Optimal integration of the customer into own processes can create a common, efficient system with smooth communication and end-to-end data exchange (Bouée & Schaible, 2015). 60% of successful subscription providers therefore integrate their solution into the customer's value chain via multiple interfaces (Paproth & Leiting, 2020). For customer and provider processes to be intertwined in this way, the customer must be equipped with intelligent networked systems and enable the provider to intervene in usage processes and access usage data (Joecks-Laß & Hadwich, 2021). These processes require a stable basis of trust between customer and provider (Demont & Paulus-Rohmer, 2016). Accordingly, integrating the customer into your own corporate sphere requires intensive cultivation of the customer relationship by sales and product management. Particularly through subscriptions, with appropriate design, a stronger bond between customer and provider can be achieved through a comprehensive alignment of interests (Schuh et al., 2019). The service is no longer aimed at maximizing the customer's liquidity and willingness to pay, but at providing the service promised to the customer with the highest quality at lower cost (Schuh et al., 2020).

of successful subscription companies use **cloud services** for better **connectivity**

The alignment of interests can be strengthened by the risk assumption and design already described. This also includes the design of an appropriate connectivity concept to enable a high level of service without the physical presence of the provider (Herterich et al., 2016). Particularly in the case of globally deployed plants, there is the challenge of limited or protracted accessibility (Dispan & Schwarz-Kocher, 2018). This requires not only a dense network of trained service technicians; rather, digital technologies (e.g., condition and predictive monitoring) must be used and customer contact points (e.g., by means of AR or service platforms) must be consistently digitized (Appelfeller & Feldmann, 2018). Self-help must also be provided as part of this.

A first level of integration and efficiency is already being implemented by many companies through predictive maintenance and condition monitoring with a high level of connectivity and an end-to-end data flow (Appelfeller & Feldmann, 2018). This is because the optimal time for appropriate maintenance measures can be determined on the basis of a data-based determination of the condition of the plants or components (Appelfeller & Feldmann, 2018). This leads to the greatest possible utilization of related resources and thus to high efficiency. In the process, the company boundaries are extended to include the customer and their machine as well as potential service providers and spare parts suppliers (Kreutzer, 2016).

The Dieffenbacher company sells wood processing plants all over the world. Despite a worldwide service network, service calls can be expensive and involve long travel times, depending on the location. The plants are crucial for the customer's productivity, which is why it is particularly important to achieve the highest possible availability and thus keep downtime and costs as low as possible. A remote service solution with condition monitoring and a ticket system with seamless integration of the customer's employees enables a large number of malfunctions to be resolved remotely. The system enables direct communication between Dieffenbacher and the user on site. Any language barriers are overcome by implemented translation software. As a result, Dieffenbacher can solve more than 9 out of 10 inquiries remotely, reduce downtime and save travel costs (Dieffenbacher, 2020).

Element revenue mechanics: Risk-taking as a baseline

"If the user is having a problem, it's our problem" (Carla, 2019). As Steve Jobs recognized early on, customer problems in a customer-centric business model are also the provider's problems (Carla, 2019). Through offering a solution in the form of a subscription, there is a shift in the distribution of risk (Lenart & Horst, 2019). In particular, this assumption of risk establishes the value proposition of the service for the customer (Ebi et al., 2019).

of successful subscription providers **manage and monitor the risks** they take with their subscription model.

The risks assumed depend on the maturity of the subscription business model (see Fig. 2). According to Roth and Stoppel, this already starts from an availability-oriented maturity (Roth & Stoppel, 2014). In this case, the equipment manufacturer assumes the risk of plant availability. The manufacturer must maintain this at least at the agreed level through appropriate service, development and planning services. In addition, the manufacturer assumes the investment risk (Roth & Stoppel, 2014). This means that the financing of the plant is provided or organized by the manufacturer. Any downtime is borne by the manufacturer. In a **usage-based** subscription business model, the usage intensity is the quantifiable reference variable (Roth & Stoppel, 2014). Here, market risks arise in relation to the customer's market (Roth & Stoppel, 2014). A lower order situation at the customer's site reduces the utilization of the machine and thus its utilized capacity, which forms the billing basis for the provider. Furthermore, process risks are transferred, which exist in the case of incomplete or error-prone processes (Roth & Stoppel, 2014). It therefore makes sense for the provider to support its customer in optimizing its processes. If a **result-oriented** promise is made within the subscription business model, the reference variable is often the number of well-produced units (Roth & Stoppel, 2014). Accordingly, the provider also assumes the **quality risk** of the products produced with the machine. From this maturity at the latest, the manufacturer also assumes the **productivity risk**, which is why they are well advised to raise the performance of the machine to as high a level as possible, since they profit directly from this. Here, the provider benefits both from the manufacturer's know-how and often also from the network effect (Lechler & Schlechtendahl, 2016). The network forms the connected base of the manufacturer, which continuously provides data on performance and settings (Lechler & Schlechtendahl, 2016). Digitalization is a necessary prerequisite here. The supplier thus has the necessary knowledge to maximize the productivity of the individual plant. The customer themselves do not have the opportunity to do this due to the lack of information Picot et al., 2018). If the provider refers to the economic success of the customer as the basis for billing in his subscription business model, i.e., if it is **success-oriented**, there is usually a share in economic variables such as profit or reduced costs. This results in a **value risk** in relation to the valuation of the measurement variable, which can fluctuate over time. For example, a product unit may lose value as a result of a competitive price war, reducing the concrete

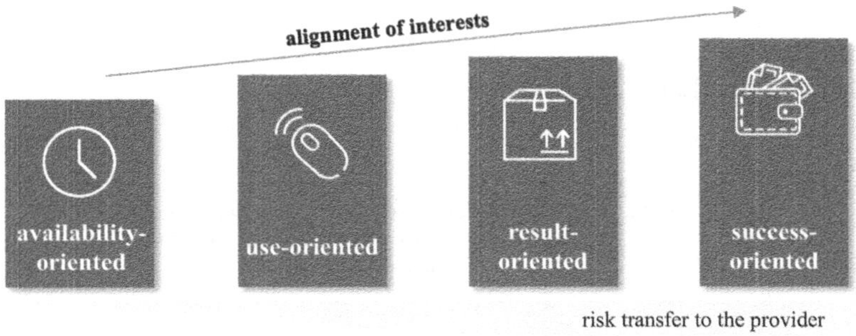

Fig. 2 The added value of the subscription is achieved with increasing risk (own illustration, based on content from Roth & Stoppel, 2014)

economic success of the customer and thus also the profit of the supplier (Schuh et al., 2019).

For plant manufacturers, the anticipation of risks can already lead them to shy away from entering an innovative value proposition. However, these same risks form the potential for value creation and thus, thanks to increasing **alignment of interests,** the basis of a participative business model (Deutscher, 2019). However, risks can often be mitigated or reduced. For example, before submitting an offer, the customer's business model should be reviewed to determine whether it is suitable for a subscription offer. One indicator here is the growth ambitions and opportunities of the potential customer (Jodlbauer, 2020). Other risks can be distributed among various players according to their competencies through cooperation in the form of a business ecosystem (Farhadi, 2019).

An example of risk sharing is provided by the TRUMPF Group's new "pay-per-part" business model. It is designed to make laser-cut sheet metal parts available for purchase by customers. Thanks to full automation, the need for action by the customer is to be eliminated, so that the customer receives a part manufactured according to plan at the push of a button. The customer should thus be able to concentrate on his core business in the future, since the operation of the laser cutting machine is outsourced and he can procure the required components easily and at low cost. By involving the partner Munich Re and its subsidiary relayr, an overall solution with calculated risks is to be designed. While relayr develops the data analysis for the pricing, Munich Re as a company for reinsurance and risk solutions takes over the financing of the machines and bears the investment risk. Thus, a part of the risks associated with the subscription is to be absorbed by a cooperation partner (Munich, 2020).

4 Conclusion

The proliferation of subscription business models has increased continuously in recent years, not only in the software sector, but also in the manufacturing industry due to the increasing networking of machines and systems (Dispan, 2021; Stich & Hicking, 2019). The focus of a subscription is on a long-term, positive "lock-in effect" resulting from the mutually beneficial cooperation (Schuh et al., 2020). The customer no longer obtains its service through a transactional product sale, but pays on the basis of performance-based price metrics for the availability, use, or result of a solution offering provided (Stoppel, 2016). The prerequisite for this is that the customer is understood throughout the entire usage phase and the individual benefit from the solution package offered is presented transparently (Schuh et al., 2019). To do this, it is necessary for the manufacturer to build a continuous, data-based understanding of the actual usage of the products, and to apply digital technologies to predict potential failures and improve performance. The insights gained are used to optimize the customer's value creation, which results from the provider's guarantee of successful use of the solution package (Stich & Hicking, 2019).

The path to successful implementation of subscription business models is full of challenges (Paproth, 2020). However, companies that have already taken this route can draw conclusions about success factors that successful providers of subscription business models have in common. They do not just look at usage data selectively and performance-related, but create transparency across all phases of the customer life cycle in order to be able to optimally align the entire process with customer needs in a targeted manner (Schuh et al., 2020). They do not achieve this individualization of their services through a large number of different product variants, but rather exploit the possibilities of modularization combined with the potential of digitalization (Schuh & Riesener, 2018). Standardized hardware is complemented by individualized software that adapts more and more to the customer's needs over time. In this context, their central position at the heart of a wide customer network is very valuable. Within the network, a large amount of data from individual customers is available to the provider (Lechler & Schlechtendahl, 2016). The insights gained from the data of all customers can subsequently be used again to increase the productivity of the individual plant. However, the customers' activities are also becoming increasingly complex or are developing into areas that are no longer part of the provider's area of expertise (Farhadi, 2019). For this reason, another success factor is that companies bundle their services together with other providers (Paproth & Leiting, 2020). Joint service provision within the ecosystem enables providers to offer the required competencies without having to build them up themselves (Farhadi, 2019). But even when providing services in an ecosystem, success criteria must be defined and monitored and evaluated on a data basis. Successful companies use customer success management systems (Paproth & Leiting, 2020), which are the starting point for deriving proactive measures and recommendations to increase the performance of the solution package.

References

Appelfeller, W., & Feldmann, C. (2018). *Die digitale Transformation des Unternehmens: Systematischer Leitfaden mit zehn Elementen zur Strukturierung und Reifegradmessung*. Springer Gabler.

Bardt, H., Beznoska, M., & Demary, M. (2019). Konjunktur tritt auf der Stelle: IW-Konjunkturprognose und Konjunkturumfrage Winter 2019. *IW-Trends - Vierteljahresschrift Zur Empirischen Wirtschaftsforschung, 46*(4), 3–37.

Binckebanck, L., Hölter, A. K., & Tiffert, A. (2020). *Edition Sales Excellence. Führung von Vertriebsorganisationen: Strategie - Koordination - Umsetzung* (2nd ed.). Springer Fachmedien.

Bitkom (2020). *Last Call: Germany!: Die Bitkom-Digitalstrategie 2025*. Retrieved from https://www.bitkom.org/sites/default/files/2020-01/200113_bitkom_digitalstrategie.pdf.

Bouée, C. E., & Schaible, S. (2015). *Die Digitale Transformation der Industrie*. Retrieved from https://bdi.eu/media/presse/publikationen/information-und-telekommunikation/Digitale_Transformation.pdf.

Busam, T. (2020). *Kontinuierliche Verbesserung mittels Prescriptive Analytics* (Dissertation), Technische Hochschule Aachen.

Carla, S. (2019). *Why user research is crucial for successful mobile app development*. Retrieved from https://www.business2community.com/mobile-apps/why-user-research-is-crucial-for-successful-mobile-app-development-02169762.

Classen, M., Blum, C., Osterrieder, P., & Friedli, T. (2019). Everything as a service? Introducing the St. Gallen IGaaS Management Model. *2nd Smart Services Summit,* Zürich.

Demont, A., & Paulus-Rohmer, D. (2016). Industrie 4.0-Geschäftsmodelle systematisch entwickeln: Eine strategiegeleitete Vorgehensweise für den Maschinen- und Anlagenbau. In: D. Schallmo, A. Rusnjak, J. Anzengruber, T. Werani & M. Jünger (Eds.), *Schwerpunkt. Digitale Transformation von Geschäftsmodellen: Grundlagen, Instrumente und Best Practices* (pp. 97–126). Springer Fachmedien.

Deutscher, R. (2019). *Subscription based services: Innovative business-modelle*. Billwerk.

Dieffenbacher (2020). *Service Dieffenbacher*. Retrieved from https://dieffenbacher.com/de/holzwerkstoffe/service.

Dispan, J., & Schwarz-Kocher, M. (2018). *Digitalisierung im Maschinenbau: Entwicklungstrends, Herausforderungen, Beschäftigungswirkungen, Gestaltungsfelder im Maschinen- und Anlagenbau*. Hans Böckler Stiftung.

Dispan, J. (2021). Digitale Transformation im Maschinen- und Anlagenbau. Digitalisierungsstrategien und Gestaltung von Arbeit 4.0. In: E. A. Hartmann (Ed.), *Digitalisierung souverän gestalten* (pp. 118–132). Springer.

Dremel, C., & Herterich, M. (2016). Digitale Cloud-Plattformen als Enabler zur analytischen Nutzung von operativen Produktdaten im Maschinen- und Anlagenbau. *HMD Praxis Der Wirtschaftsinformatik, 53*(5), 646–661.

Ebi, M., Tittel, J., Doelle, C., & Schuh, G (2019). Generic Description of service-related business models in the field of machinery and plant engineering. In: R. Schmitt & G. Schuh (Eds.), *Advances in Production Research: Proceedings of the 8th Congress of the German Academic Association for Production Technology (WGP)* (pp. 763–775). Springer International.

Eisenhardt, K. M. (1989). Building theories from case study research. *The Academy of Management Review, 14*(4), 532–550.

Eisenhardt, K. M., & Graebner, M. E. (2007). Theory building from cases: Opportunities and challenges. *Academy of Management Journal, 50*(1), 25–32.

Eldridge, C. (2018). *The subscription economy and why it's a win win for you and the company*. Retrieved from https://medium.com/@chris.eldridge0/the-subscription-economy-and-why-its-a-win-win-for-you-and-the-company-dd7947a6d0b1.

Engel, M., & Hähnel, D. (2020). *Data analytics: So machen Sie aus Masse Klasse: Wie Big Data auch Ihrem Unternehmen Wettbewerbsvorteile verschafft*. Retrieved from https://www2.deloitte.com/de/de/pages/trends/data-analytics.html.

Farhadi, N. (2019). *Cross-industry ecosystems: Grundlagen, Archetypen, Modelle und strategische Ansätze*. Springer Gabler.

Faß, T. (2019). *Capex vs OpEx – Zwei finanzielle Ansätze für Technologie-Ausgaben*. Retrieved from https://alter-solutions.de/allgemein/capex-vs-opex-zwei-finanzielle-ansaetze-fuer-technologie-ausgaben/.

Gassmann, O., & Frankenberger, K. (2016). *Geschäftsmodellinnovationen: Vom Trend zum Geschäftsmodell*. Springer Gabler.

Gerl, S. (2020). *Innovative Geschäftsmodelle für industrielle Smart Services*. Springer.

Glaser-Gallion, P. (2013). *Risikoorientiertes Pricing industrieller Leistungssysteme* (Dissertation). Universität Stuttgart.

Gotsch, M., Jäger, A., & Jackwerth, T. (2019). *Industrielle Produktinnovationen für mehr ökologische Nachhaltigkeit - Ausprägungen und wirtschaftlicher Erfolg: Mitteilungen aus der ISI-Erhebung Modernisierung der Produktion Nr. 74*. Mitteilungen aus der ISI-Erhebung-Modernisierung der Produktion.

Gudergan, G., Müller, J., Senderek, R., Kuntz, J., Kwiatkowski, A., & Krechting, D. (2021). Digitale Transformation durch die Entwicklung datenbasierter Dienstleistungen – Erforschung von Transformationsmustern und Merkmalen datenbasierter Dienstleistungen für die Ableitung des Smart Service Engineerings als Handlungsleitfaden für Unternehmen. In: D. Beverungen, J. H. Schumann, V. Stich & G. Strina (Eds.), *Dienstleistungsinnovationen durch Digitalisierung: Band 1: Geschäftsmodelle – Methoden – Umsetzungsbeispiele* (pp. 49-105). Springer Gabler.

Gushurst, K. P., & Wolf, T. (2020). *PwC Maschinenbau-Barometer Q2/2020: Maschinenbau in Zeiten digitaler Transformation & Corona-Pandemie*. Retrieved from https://www.pwc.de/de/industrielle-produktion/pwc-maschinenbau-barometer-q2-2020.pdf.

Harland, T. (2018). Chancen und Risiken durch Subscription-Modelle im Maschinenbau (Dissertation-Vortrag.) Technische Hochschule Aachen.

Heinrich, S. (2020). Digitalisierung bedeutet, Kundenverhalten und Geschäftsmodelle besser zu verstehen. In: S. Heinrich (Ed.), *Edition Sales Excellence. AkquiseB2B: Neukundengewinnung im digitalen Zeitalter* (pp. 29–49). Springer Fachmedien.

Hermann, U. (2020). *Die Chancen der digitalen Ökonomie der Dinge erkennen, entwickeln und erfolgreich umsetzen*. Apprimus.

Herterich, M. M., Uebernickel, F., & Brenner, W. (2016). *Industrielle Dienstleistungen 4.0: HMD Best Paper Award 2015. essentials*. Springer Vieweg.

Hilton, B., Hajihashemi, B., Henderson, C. M., & Palmatier, R. W. (2020). Customer success management: The next evolution in customer management practice? *Industrial Marketing Management, 90*, 360–369.

Hochstein, B., Rangarajan, D., Mehta, N., & Kocher, D. (2020). An industry/academic perspective on customer success management. *Journal of Service Research, 23*(1), 3–7.

Hoffmann, M., & Bijedic, T. (2018). *Digitale Geschäftsmodelle - Chancen und Herausforderungen für den Mittelstand*. Retrieved from https://www.researchgate.net/publication/333995609_Digitale_Geschaftsmodelle_-_Chancen_und_Herausforderungen_fur_den_Mittelstand.

Huntley, S. (2018). *Operating expenditures vs capital expenditures in a SaaS model*. Retrieved from https://www.hubstor.net/blog/operating-expenditures-vs-capital-expenditures-in-a-saas-model/.

Illner, B., Konjustic, R., Birkmeyer, J., & Breunig, M. (2020). *Kundenzentrierung als Chance für den digitalen Durchbruch: Was sich die Endkundenindustrien vom Maschinenbau bei digitalen Plattformen und Mehrwertdiensten wünschen*. Retrieved from https://www.mckinsey.de/~/media/McKinsey/Locations/Europe%20and%20Middle%20East/Deutschland/News/Presse/2020/2020-09-18%20Maschinenbau/VDMA_McKinsey_Broschre_Digitale%20Plattformen_DEUTSCH.pdf.

Jacobs, M. (2020). *Low-touch vs. high-touch customer success models*. Retrieved from https://blog.totango.com/2020/08/low-touch-vs-high-touch-customer-success-models-fc/.

Janzer, A. H. (2017). *Subscription marketing: Strategies for nurturing customers in a world of churn* (2nd ed.). Cuesta Park Consulting.

Jodlbauer, H. (2020). *Geschäftsmodelle erarbeiten: Modell zur digitalen Transformation etablierter Unternehmen*. Springer Gabler.

Joecks-Laß, D., & Hadwich, K (2021). Wollen, Können und Dürfen der Kunden – Digitale Souveränität durch Kundenentwicklung. In: E. A. Hartmann (Ed.), *Digitalisierung souverän gestalten* (pp. 74-85). Springer.

Jussen, P. (2019). Mit Industrie 4.0 Beute machen. *Tec4u*(1), 66–67.

Kaufmann, T., & Servatius, H.-G. (2020). *Das Internet der Dinge und Künstliche Intelligenz als Game Changer*. Springer Fachmedien.

Koch, V., Kuge, S., Geissbauer, R., & Schrauf, S. (2014). *Chancen und Herausforderungen der vierten industriellen Revolution*. Retrieved from https://www.strategyand.pwc.com/de/de/studien/2014/industrie-4-0-chancen/industrie-4-0.pdf.

Komor, R. H. (2019). Agiler B2B-Vertrieb im Zeitalter der Digitalisierung. In: P. Buchenau (Ed.), *Chefsache Interim Management: Praxisbeispiele für den erfolgreichen Einsatz in Unternehmen* (pp. 115–139). Springer Fachmedien.

Kreutzer, R. T. (2016). Treiber und Hintergründe der digitalen Transformation. In: D. Schallmo, A. Rusnjak, J. Anzengruber, T. Werani & M. Jünger (Eds.), *Schwerpunkt. Digitale Transformation von Geschäftsmodellen: Grundlagen, Instrumente und Best Practices* (pp. 33–58). Springer Fachmedien.

Krug, A. (2009). *Die Verweisung von Bau- und Anlagenbauverträgen in das Kaufrecht durch § 651 BGB*. (Dissertation). Julius-Maximilians-Universität Würzburg.

Lechler, A., & Schlechtendahl, J. (2016). Steuerung aus der Cloud. In: B. Vogel-Heuser, T. Bauernhansl & M. ten Hompel (Eds.), *VDI Springer reference. Handbuch Industrie 4.0 Bd.1: Produktion* (2nd ed., pp. 61–74). Springer.

Leimeister, J. M. (2020). *Dienstleistungsengineering und -management: Data-driven service innovation* (2nd ed.). Springer Gabler.

Lenart, M., & Horst, C. (2019). Time to subscribe? Subscription-Geschäftsmodelle im Maschinenbau. *Unternehmen Der Zukunft, 1*, 12–16.

Mehta, N., & Steinman, D. (2016). *Customer success: How innovative companies are reducing churn and growing recurring revenue*. John Wiley & Sons.

Mohr, T. (2020). *Der Digital Navigator: Ein Modell für die digitale Transformation*. Springer Gabler.

Moring, A., & Deurloo, S. (2018). *Binäre Innovation – Kreativität und Geschäft für digitale Märkte*. Springer Fachmedien.

Moser, B., Frank, J., & Faulhaber, M. (2019). *Digitale Geschäftsmodelle in der produzierenden Industrie: Status quo der Industrie – Von digitalisierten Prozessen bis zu digitalen Geschäftsmodellen*. Retrieved from https://www.fir.rwth-aachen.de/fileadmin/publikationen/whitepaper/cluster-whitepaper-digitale-geschaeftsmodelle-produzierende-industrie.pdf.

Munich, Re (2020). *Pay-per-Part: TRUMPF und Munich Re planen neues Geschäftsmodell für die produzierende Industrie*. Retrieved from https://www.munichre.com/de/unternehmen/media-relations/medieninformationen-und-unternehmensnachrichten/medieninformationen/2020/2020-10-14-pay-per-part.html.

Otto, K. S., Rösler, S., & Teucher, T. (2019). Denken und Handeln in Ökosystemen – ein strategischer Ansatz für Wirtschaft und Gesellschaft. In: M. Englert & A. Ternès (Eds.), *Nachhaltiges Management: Nachhaltigkeit als exzellenten Managementansatz entwickeln* (pp. 183–209). Springer

Paproth, Y. (2020). *Industrielle As-a-Service-Geschäftsmodelle: Potenziale und Herausforderungen subscriptionsbasierter Geschäftsmodelle im Maschinen- und Anlagenbau. FIR-Flash*. Retrieved from https://www.fir.rwth-aachen.de/fileadmin/newsroom/newsletter/fir-fir-newsletter-2020-01-leitartikel.pdf.

Paproth, Y., & Leiting, T. (2020). *Online-event: Subscription business*. Retrieved from http://darwin.bth.rwth-aachen.de/cgi-bin/lik.pl?sigel=011.

Picot, A., Berchthold, Y., & Neuburger, R. (2018). Big Data aus ökonomischer Sicht: Potenziale und Handlungsbedarf. In: B. Kolany-Raiser, R. Heil, C. Orwat & T. Hoeren (Eds.), *Technikzukünfte, Wissenschaft und Gesellschaft / Futures of Technology, Science and Society. Big Data und Gesellschaft: Eine multidisziplinäre Annäherung* (pp. 309–416). Springer.

Raitner, M. (2019). *Wider die Überregelung des Miteinander*. Retrieved from https://fuehrung-erfahren.de/2019/10/wider-die-ueberregelung-des-miteinander/.

Rieger, V., & Wagner, M. (2019). Digitale Geschäftsmodelle treiben Industry Rebuilding. *Lünendonk Magazin, 04*, 27–28.

Roth, S., & Stoppel, E (2014). Preissysteme zur Gestaltung und Aufteilung des Service Value. In: M. Bruhn & K. Hadwich (Eds.), *Service Value als Werttreiber: Konzepte, Messung und Steuerung Forum Dienstleistungsmanagement* (pp. 183–204). Springer Gabler.

Sato, K., & Nakashima, K. (2020). Optimal pricing problem for a pay-per-use system based on the Internet of Things with intertemporal demand. *International Journal of Production Economics, 221*, 107477.

Schedler, K., & Bolz, U. (2020). Innovative Geschäftsmodelle: Staat und Wirtschaft. *Swiss Yearbook of Administrative Sciences, 11*(1), 25–37.

Schmedding, D. (2019). Heidelberg goes digital!: Subscription – ein neues Geschäftsmodell der Heidelberg Druckmaschinen AG. *22. Aachener Dienstleistungsforum*.

Schuh, G., Frank, J., Jussen, P., Rix, C., & Harland, T. (2019). Monetizing industry 4.0: Design principles for subscription business in the manufacturing industry. In *IEEE International Conference on Engineering, Technology and Innovation*, Valbonne Sophia-Antipolis.

Schuh, G., & Riesener, M. (2018). *Produktkomplexität managen: Strategien - Methoden - Tools* (3rd ed.). Hanser.

Schuh, G., Wenger, L., Stich, V., Hicking, J., & Gailus, J. (2020). Outcome economy: Subscription business models in machinery and plant engineering. *Procedia CIRP, 93*, 599–604.

Skibicki, K. (2020). *Das DJ-Prinzip des Managements: Handlungsorientiertes Wissen für Führen und Entscheiden im digital vernetzten Zeitalter*. Springer Gabler.

Staegemann, D., Volk, M., & Turowski, K. (2020). Mobile procurement management. In: T. Kollmann (Ed.), *Handbuch Digitale Wirtschaft* (pp. 241–254). Springer Gabler.

Stanula, P., Praetzas, C., Kohn, O., Metternich, J., Weigold, M., & Buchwald, A. (2020). Stress-oriented, data-based payment model for machine tools. *Procedia CIRP, 93*, 1526–1531.

Stich, V., & Hicking, J. (2019). Smartifizierung von Maschinenbauprodukten mittels einer zielorientierten Methode. *HMD Praxis Der Wirtschaftsinformatik, 56*(3), 542–556.

Stojkovski, I., Achleitner, A. K., & Lange, T. (2021). *Equipment as a service: The transition towards usage-based business models*. Retrieved from https://papers.ssrn.com/sol3/papers.cfm?abstract_id=3763004.

Stoppel, E. (2016). *Nutzungsabhängige Preissysteme auf industriellen Märkten*. Springer Fachmedien.

Stoppel, E., & Roth, S. (2017). The conceptualization of pricing schemes: From product-centric to customer-centric value approaches. *Journal of Revenue and Pricing Management, 16*(1), 76–90.

Ströbele, C. (2019). *Die unendlichen Geschichten*. Retrieved from https://www.zeit.de/kultur/film/2019-12/tv-serien-netflix-streaming-2010er-jahre-rueckblick/komplettansicht.

Sunyaev, A. (2020). Cloud-Dienst-Zertifizierungen zur Schaffung von Vertrauen in und Transparenz von digitalen Diensten. In: A. Hentschel, G. Hornung & S. Jandt (Eds.), *Mensch - Technik - Umwelt: Verantwortung für eine sozialverträgliche Zukunft: Festschrift für Alexander Roßnagel zum 70. Geburtstag* (pp. 149–166). Nomos.

Teusch, C. D., Prakash, S., & Gailhofer, P. (2019). *Verlängerung der Produktnutzungs- und -lebensdauer mittels Durchsetzung von Verbraucherrechten* (No. 76). Retrieved from https://www.umweltbundesamt.de/sites/default/files/medien/1410/publikationen/2019-07-17_texte_76-2019_verbraucherrechte.pdf.

Trumpf (2020). *Smart Factory – viele Wege, ein erfahrener Partner*. Retrieved from https://www.trumpf.com/de_DE/loesungen/smart-factory/.

Tzuo, T., & Weisert, G. (2018). *Subscribed: Why the subscription model will be your company's future - and what to do about it*. Portfolio Penguin.

Ulaga, W., Eggert, A., & Gehring, A. (2020). Customer Success. In: M. Bruhn, C. Burmann & M. Kirchgeorg (Eds.), *Marketing Weiterdenken: Zukunftspfade Für eine Marktorientierte Unternehmensführung* (2nd ed., pp. 357–373). Springer Fachmedien.

Uuskoski, M., Kärkkäinen, H., & Menon, K. (2020). Rapid sales growth mechanisms and profitability for investment product manufacturing SMEs through Pay-Per-X business models. In F. Nyffenegger, J. Ríos, J. Ríos, L. Rivest, & A. Bouras (Eds.), *Product Lifecycle Management Enabling Smart X: 17th IFIP WG 5.1 International Conference, PLM 2020, Revised Selected Papers* (pp. 402–415). (IFIP Advances in Information and Communication Technology; Vol. 594). Springer.

Wölfle, R., & Leimstoll, U. (2019). *Digitalisierung im Vertrieb an Konsumenten. Eine qualitative Studie aus Sicht der Anbieter*. Retrieved from https://irf.fhnw.ch/handle/11654/32098.

Ziegler, W. (2017). *Der Kunde steht im Mittelpunkt und damit jedem im Wege*. tredition.

Digital Business Models for Industrial Suppliers—The Case of Schaeffler OPTIME

Philipp Jussen, Martin Meinel, and Tim Hosenfeldt

Abstract

Today more than ever, industrial suppliers are facing existential challenges. The ever-faster pace of technological change, the emergence of innovative business models, and the increase of servitization are threatening the very existence of entire industries. In view of these challenges, the question arises as to how established companies in the supplier industry can develop strategies and generate innovations that can ensure the long-term survival of these companies. This article answers this question by examining a current practical case in the rotating machinery market. Using Schaeffler OPTIME, a digital condition monitoring solution, the challenges and benefits of digital business models for traditional industrial suppliers are highlighted. Thus, the article provides a valuable contribution to a better understanding of new digital business models in changing ecosystems. At the same time, the article provides a best practice for those responsible for innovation in industrial companies.

P. Jussen (✉)
Schaeffler Monitoring Services GmbH, Kaiserstr. 100, 52134 Herzogenrath, Germany
e-mail: philipp.jussen@schaeffler.com

M. Meinel · T. Hosenfeldt
Schaeffler AG, Industriestraße 1-3, 91074 Herzogenaurach, Germany
e-mail: martin.meinel@schaeffler.com

T. Hosenfeldt
e-mail: tim.hosenfeldt@schaeffler.com

K.-I. Voigt and J. M. Müller (eds.), *Digital Business Models in Industrial Ecosystems*, Future of Business and Finance, https://doi.org/10.1007/978-3-030-82003-9_5

1 Introduction

1.1 Opportunities and Challenges for Industrial Suppliers Through Digital Technologies and Digital Business Models

Today more than ever, industrial suppliers, i.e., manufacturing companies in the supplier industry, are facing existential challenges (Veile et al., 2019). The ever-faster pace of technological change, the emergence of innovative business models, and the increase of servitization are threatening the very existence of entire industries (Baden-Fuller & Haefliger, 2013; Baines et al., 2009). In view of these challenges, the question arises as to how established companies in the supplier industry can develop strategies and generate innovations that can ensure the long-term survival of these companies (Schiele, 2006). This article aims to answer this question using an example from corporate practice.

One of the most important megatrends manufacturing companies currently face is digitalization (Bogner et al., 2016; Ghobakhloo, 2018). Digitalization, i.e., "the changes associated with the application of digital technology in all aspects of human society" (Stolterman & Fors, 2004), is not only changing the way we as humans communicate, live, and work with each other but also the value creation of companies (Amit & Han, 2017; Matt et al., 2015). Surprisingly, seven of the world's ten most valuable companies, including Microsoft, Amazon, and Facebook, are companies whose business model is already based, to a large extent, on digital technologies (PwC, 2020).

The digitalization of companies is particularly challenging for established companies that so far focus on analog technologies because digitalization changes or accelerates fundamental market mechanisms (Paulus-Rohmer et al., 2016). In particular, companies that are able to adapt digital technologies share three key advantages. First, digital technologies enable faster market access and scalability than analog technologies because the physical transportation of goods is reduced or eliminated (Stampfl et al., 2013). For example, apps can be installed and used on an existing smartphone in seconds. Second, digital technologies enable faster rollout of product improvements. For example, performance improvements can be downloaded and installed through Over The Air (OTA) technology in the form of software updates or new releases (Nilsson & Larson, 2008). This functionality means that, unlike physical products, product improvements can be rolled out even after purchase and during use by the customer. Third, digital technologies enable the creation of new knowledge and services based on mass data (Berman, 2012; Ives et al., 2016). For example, data generated during product use can serve as a starting point for further product improvements, whereas data collection with analog products involves comparatively high costs and an enormous amount of time. These three starting points give companies that rely on digital technologies a significant competitive advantage.

Nevertheless, the underlying technology is only one of many components of a successful business model (Baden-Fuller & Haefliger, 2013). Over the past 20 years, scientists have developed the understanding that successful business model concepts, i.e., the organizational and financial architecture of a firm (Teece, 2010), consist of the following building blocks in addition to the central value proposition: value creation including resources, activities, and partners; value delivery including customer relationships, customer segments, and channels; and value capturing including cost structure and revenue streams (Osterwalder & Pigneur, 2010; Zott et al., 2011). As a result, digital business models are not only characterized by relying heavily on digital technology or software alone but rather use this technology to create a fast scaling business which is built on the use of data as well as frequent releases of new functions to provide customer value (Al-Debei & Avison, 2010).

In addition, companies benefit from the design options offered by digital business models. One type of business model that uses these technological capabilities and combines them with smart design choices to generate decisive competitive advantages is the subscription business model (Schuh et al., 2019). The subscription business model differs from other business models in that users are allowed to use a company's offering on a continuous and self-determined basis and pay the company a uniform fee on a regular schedule, such as monthly or annually (Schuh et al., 2020). Although subscription business models are by no means a novelty, newspaper subscriptions were already available in the 1800s, the concept of this business model became very popular only recently with the rise of the digital age. Typical examples of digital subscription business models from the B2C context are Netflix, Amazon Prime, or Spotify. Increasingly, examples can also be found from within the B2B sector such as in the use of licensed software solutions or fleet management services.

Although a recurring service fee for a constant or unlimited access to the service offering is widely considered the main characteristic of these business models, there are a few other important characteristics of subscription business models. Subscription business models are radically customer-centric and often integrate many channels of service provisioning into a holistic customer experience. Convenience and the ease of consumption of a service play an important role for the service provisioning in subscription business models. Consequently, the costs of service are very transparent and easy to calculate for the customer.

The digital subscription business model has further competitive advantages over other types of business model. For the provider, it has the decisive advantage of being able to scale quickly with a uniform range of services and generate continuous revenue without having to constantly negotiate prices (Stampf et al., 2013). Likewise, this form of business model has decisive advantages for users. Users enjoy a very simple way of using or applying the service, usually via digital access, and they also do not have to deal with price negotiations or developments because the price is transparent and the same or constant for all users (Schuh et al., 2020). Maybe the most important factor regarding the long-term success of a subscription business with its customers is the ability to constantly innovate and provide new features, functions, and services that are a better fit to the customer needs than those of the competition. For example, Netflix started by changing its business model from a subscription-based DVD rental company to a subscription-based streaming provider that integrates the offerings of many TV series and movie production studios and makes them consumable with any end-consumer device for a fixed monthly fee. In order to be successful in the long-run, Netflix realized that it needed to start producing its own series, movies, and documentaries based on a unique understanding of what consumers wanted to watch. Thereupon, they targeted what new content to develop by leveraging the data it had collected during their 2nd generation existence.

Having said this, manufacturing companies which, in particular, previously pursued a strategy of technology leadership, are now facing decisive challenges in product development. First, a combination of physical products, services, and digital services fundamentally promises additional benefits for the customer compared to a pure product business (Schuh et al., 2020). In addition, integrated digital services can build much stronger and more long-term customer relationships than a pure product business. Secondly, a possible innovation head start from technology leaders with purely physical products can be quickly made up by a comparatively simple update of digital products/services of a follower. Thirdly, companies with digital products/services may have the advantage of owning the usage data, which in turn can be a starting point for further solutions that optimally fit the customer needs.

These challenges are putting many manufacturing companies to the test, and they are reinforced by the fact that companies cannot switch from selling purely physical products to digital solutions in the blink of an eye (Rachinger et al., 2019). For establishing digital business models, new competencies must be built up compared to established product-based business models, especially in agile IT development and deployment (Mezger, 2014). Other competencies that have been built up over decades, such as physical logistics, are becoming less important. Nevertheless, technological and business model developments also open up new opportunities for the further development of established industrial companies in terms of a sustainable competitive advantage (Tallman et al., 2018).

For the time being, it can be summarized that there will undoubtedly be a need for physical components (hardware) in the future. However, the question will be which providers will succeed in generating decisive competitive advantages with digital components (software) in the future, and how these providers will change the value chain in established industries and thus shape new digital ecosystems (Weill & Woerner, 2013).

1.2 Course of Contents

Against this backdrop, it can be seen that, more and more, established companies are addressing the question of what value they want to create in a digitized world. The global automotive and industrial supplier Schaeffler has also addressed this issue in order to actively seize the opportunities offered by digital technologies and digital business models. This article will explain how Schaeffler is succeeding in doing this in the market for rotating machinery.

To this end, the existing ecosystem and current developments in the market for rotating machinery are first presented. The authors also discuss Schaeffler's particular motivation for developing digital solutions for this market. Subsequently, a digital innovation for predictive maintenance in rotating machinery is presented using the concrete example of Schaeffler OPTIME. Here, the special features in the design of the business model, compared to the classic product business model, will be addressed. Finally, the challenges and opportunities that have emerged over the course of the development of OPTIME will be explained.

With this article, the authors show, on the one hand, the possibilities for manufacturing companies to gain a competitive advantage in the digital age with innovative, digital solutions, and business models. On the other hand, the authors provide concrete assistance for decision-makers and developers in companies by sharing exclusive insights from a highly topical case study that has only recently appeared in the market.

2 Ecosystems Around Rotating Machines

2.1 Value Chain in the Ecosystem for Rotating Machines

With the rapid development of technology and science, mechanical equipment in modern industry becomes more and more functional and complex. In particular, rotating machinery is among the most important equipment in modern industrial applications (Muthanandan & Nor, 2019). The typical value creation within the ecosystem around rotating machinery is shown in Fig. 1.

There are companies that use rotating machines in their production facilities. These are called machine operators. The machine operators buy their machines

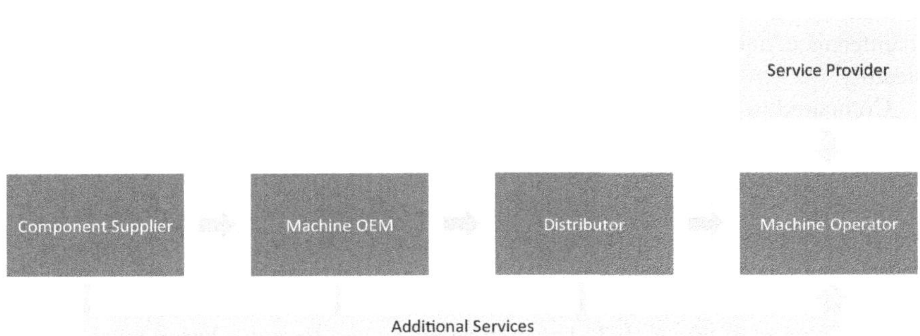

Fig. 1 Typical value chain for the rotating machinery market

from machine Original Equipment Manufacturers (OEMs). The shipping and assembly of the machines is either done by the OEMs themselves or by distributors. The machine OEMs, in turn, usually purchase components for the machines they design and assemble from various component suppliers. In addition to the production and logistics of the machines and systems, there are service providers who offer various services for rotating equipment. These include services such as repair and maintenance, spare parts management, and condition monitoring (CM) (Muthanandan & Nor, 2019).

As rotating machinery has a very wide range of applications, the market for rotating machinery is a continuous economic driver worldwide. Due to the extremely high functionality and complexity of machines and systems, all companies along the value chain typically have a very profound understanding of the complete rotating machine and its application (Baharom & Zahir, 2019). Accordingly, it is not uncommon for companies to limit themselves to their core task in the value chain (e.g., component supplier) but also to offer corresponding services themselves. In this way, a complex ecosystem has emerged over the decades in which players across the individual phases of value creation in this market attempt to create value and generate market share.

2.2 Trends in the Ecosystem Around Rotating Machines

The ecosystem around rotating machinery is continuously evolving. In particular, fault diagnosis and management of rotating machinery have become one of the most critical aspects in this context. Therefore, some of the latest trends on this topic are explained below.

Since the 1990s, a wide market has developed for different technology and service providers focusing on CM (see Tavner, 2008 for a review). CM is an umbrella term for the collection and analysis of physical measured data with the aim of evaluating the condition of machines and systems (Schaeffler Monitoring Services GmbH, 2019). Depending on the type of machine, there are different approaches and technologies for CM, which shall not be explained in detail here. Driven by steadily increasing demands on machine availability, optimization of maintenance, and life cycle costs or safety requirements, the CM market is growing steadily.

Compared to the first developments, the CM market has evolved into a complex system (Tavner, 2008). From a technological perspective, traditional wired CM systems exist that provide very accurate data. The goal of these systems is to provide accurate, high-quality insight, and analysis about the health of complex machinery. However, analyzing this data often requires deep expertise. Since technology providers usually focus only on either hardware and sensors or analytics and services, but do not typically offer end-to-end solutions, the integration of the various internet of things (IoT) layers to create an end-to-end solution must be done by the asset owner or a service provider. Typically, CM systems are tailored to specific machine component types, which further limits the scaling of their use in other environments. As a result, the combination of the cost of cabling and infrastructure as well as the vast expertise required has often made CM systems expensive to deploy.

At the same time, new players are entering the CM market. Driven by emerging data analytics and predictive technologies such as machine learning and artificial intelligence (AI), these new providers promise a new level of insight from existing data. These services are typically offered under the term predictive maintenance (PM) and promise to not only detect the current state of a machine or system but to go beyond and predict its future state and, more importantly, to predict failures (Crowder & Lawless, 2007; Hashemian, 2010). However, the providers of these services require mass data as a basis for machine learning and AI technology and rarely offer a solution for collecting this mass data (Susto et al., 2014).

Finally, a trend towards a combination of CM and other services can also be identified. Typically, manufacturing companies and machine operators are not interested in the machine condition itself but are rather looking to use that information to optimize their productivity. Increasing the availability of machines while at the same time reducing maintenance and spare parts costs have benefitted service providers which are able to combine information about the condition of a machine with additional services which guarantee, for example, specific productivity results. These often called (full) performance contracts include a range of services from consulting to condition monitoring to maintenance (Kim et al., 2007). The service provider is either fully payed on the basis of the machine's performance or on a bonus or penalty system which rewards certain results of the service. Such contracts have the customer benefit of transferring the risk of the productivity of the machine to the service provider and guaranteeing a certain performance level is delivered by the service (Selviaridis & Wynstra, 2015).

2.3 Motivation for Schaeffler to Invest in Digital Technology and Business Models for CM

Having said this, CM is an integral part of modern production facilities. However, due to the significant cost and expertise required, current CM systems lack the scalability and affordability necessary to be widely deployed. Typically, only the three most important machines for a given production process are monitored, which rarely accounts for more than five to ten percent of the total machines in a production facility. Occasionally, additional manual hand measurements are used for another 20–40% of the machines. Overall, it can be concluded that the condition of most of the machines and equipment in a production facility is unknown to maintenance and production managers for a large portion of the time. In asset-intensive industries, this approach leads to frequent unplanned downtime and production losses corresponding to costs in the millions.

In the existing CM market, Germany-based Schaeffler can be qualified as a full-range supplier. Schaeffler is an important innovator and manufacturer in the field of high precision and high-performance bearings and therefore has an in-depth knowledge of rotating machinery and equipment. At the same time, Schaeffler offers a global portfolio of CM measurement equipment as well as various CM services such as remote monitoring or on-site assessments including hand measurements and endoscopies (Schaeffler, 2021).

Due to this breadth of offerings, Schaeffler not only possesses first-class know-how for the production of individual components but also the corresponding knowledge about the behavior of the components over the course of their life cycle. With regard to the costs along the life cycle, studies have shown that approximately half of the costs of a machine component are not incurred until operation, support, and service (Ahmed, 1996). This situation opens previously unexploited potential, especially for established market players. As an established player in the CM market and against the backdrop of emerging opportunities through digital technologies and business models (Tallman et al., 2018), Schaeffler was looking for opportunities to further develop its service portfolio.

3 Schaeffler OPTIME

3.1 OPTIME as an Innovative Approach to CM/PM

In order to design a next level condition monitoring solution, Schaeffler approached the topic as a service design challenge and not primarily from a technological perspective. Even though it was clear from the beginning that the new condition monitoring solution should utilize state-of-the-art technology, in order to identify the key requirements towards Schaeffler's new solution, it was decided to design it as a service based around customer needs.

The first step in designing the new condition monitoring solution was to identify the customer pain points with current solutions. More specifically, Schaeffler started working with lead customers to find out why they were not monitoring most of their machines even though the technology needed was already available. From a pure technological view, the measurement systems to monitor almost every rotating machine in production has been available for more than 10 years. Still, depending on the industry, up to 95% of machines are not monitored. This lack of monitoring means that besides a few bottlenecks or high priority machines, the condition of most of the production and auxiliary equipment in a production plant is unknown to the operators and maintenance staff. The absence of monitoring leads to significant inefficiencies in the form of unexpected breakdowns including not only downtime but production losses. It is also common that machines which are still in good condition get inspected, maintained, or even replaced on a regular basis.

Via in-depth interviews and workshops with lead customers, the Schaeffler analysis team established a common understanding of the customers' view of condition monitoring, its value, and obstacles customers experienced with current solutions. Schaeffler's analysis identified that despite the obvious factor of the cost of the solution, other enablers were also missing for customers to engage in monitoring of machines at large scale. For example, the installation process of the solution had to be fast and require no training or configuration so that the solution could be installed on hundreds or even thousands of machines in a very short time. Also, the use of the solution should require only little training and especially be independent of existing condition monitoring know-how. The new solution had to provide automated but still reliable alarms and recommendations without requiring expert knowledge from the user.

Based on this analysis, Schaeffler OPTIME was designed as a service instead of as a measurement system. Typically, a condition monitoring solution is designed based on technical parameters from the application resulting in technical requirements such as measurement frequency, sample rate, etc. Schaeffler developed OPTIME as a digital service with a mobile first approach starting from the situations and decisions for which the customer would use the solution. Technological requirements and decisions were taken subsequently. The result of this user-centered innovation approach towards condition monitoring is a next level condition monitoring solution which enables users to monitor rotating machines on an unprecedented scale.

The condition monitoring solution, OPTIME, is an easily expandable system and consists of wireless, battery-powered vibration sensors, a gateway, and an app for visualizing the analysis results (see Fig. 2). The data collected by the sensors is analyzed using specially developed algorithms, and the algorithms are based on Schaeffler knowledge, physical models that have been further developed over decades, and condition monitoring experience. With a lead time of several weeks, OPTIME detects damage to the respective components of, for example, electric motors, fans, and pumps, as well as imbalance, misalignment, or lubrication issues. The app displays trend curves and the severity of incidents by means of traffic light colors, alarms, and other information. Concrete recommendations for action make it easy for in-house maintenance staff or even service companies to plan maintenance measures, personnel deployment, and spare parts procurement in a timely and cost-efficient manner. Maintenance personnel do not require any condition monitoring knowledge for installation and commissioning, and the vibration sensors are screwed or glued to the aggregates and activated via near field communication (NFC) using the app. All sensors independently connect to each other and to the gateway to form an independent mesh network. Here, the sensors transmit raw vibration and temperature data as well as KPIs of the aggregates via the gateway to the Schaeffler Cloud. There, the data is analyzed, and the results are sent to the app for output to a wide variety of end devices used by maintenance staff and plant operators.

Using this service-based innovation approach and combining it with state-of-the-art digital technology like cloud or machine learning, Schaeffler was able to generate significant USPs for their solution and an upside for their customers. The installation time per sensor was reduced from several hours to just a

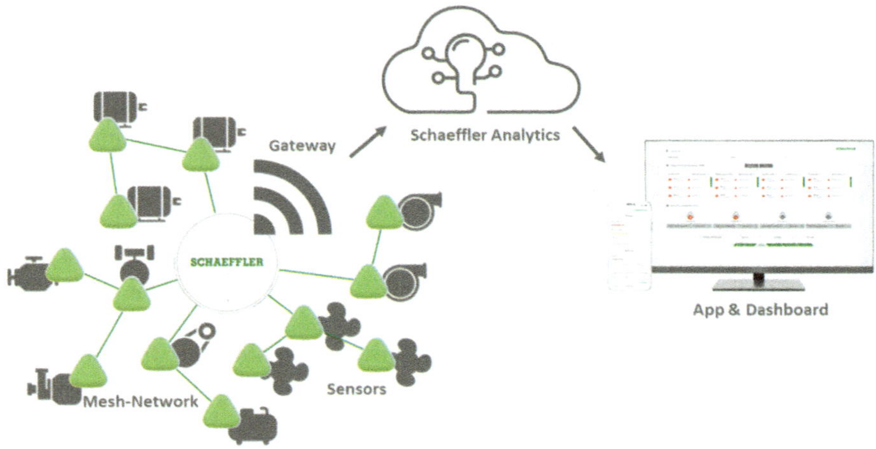

Fig. 2 Operating principle of Schaeffler OPTIME

few minutes. The solution requires almost no training and no condition monitoring expertise from the customer in order to analyze the condition of a machine and generate recommendations. Compared to monthly offline measurements with handheld devices, significant cost savings of over 50% can be realized with OPTIME.

3.2 OPTIME as a Digital Business Model

The business model of OPTIME is based on a simple and an easy-to-use approach resulting in great scalability of the solution for the customer. Creating scalability, therefore, was also the main goal of the design of the business model. Besides scalability, the following requirements were defined for the design of the business model:

- The business model should reflect the service characteristics of OPTIME in the sense that it provides constant value to the customer, and new functions and features of the solution are continuously developed
- The business model should make OPTIME easy-to-buy for customers and support the buying decision for OPTIME by being transparent and economical.

Based on these requirements, it was decided that the business model of OPTIME should follow the design principles of subscription business models as presented above.

Because of a technical architecture which heavily relies on cloud and software components, the OPTIME solution is very easy to update. Compared to solutions which only include firmware in measurement systems and which are installed on-premise at the customer site, the actual costs of any updates for OPTIME are minimal. Therefore, the strategy for Schaeffler OPTIME is to offer the customer continuous innovation and new functions at zero extra cost.

In order to reach the required scalability of the business model, there was one other key aspect to consider. Purchasing processes in industrial or B2B settings are often fundamentally different from B2C buying processes. Industrial purchasing processes, especially in large companies, follow a very formal approach and incorporate many stakeholders and decision makers including technical and commercial decision makers, purchasing agents, and lawyers. In order to be able to scale the OPTIME solution quickly with many customers, the typical aspects of the purchasing processes of these customers, such as purchasing categories, purchasing budgets, decision limits, etc., had to be considered as well.

As a result, the business model of OPTIME was defined accordingly. The OPTIME hardware components of the solution (sensors, gateways) are bought by the customer. The digital service is purchased in an as-a-service business model with a monthly subscription based on the number of monitored machines and includes all functions of the OPTIME App and Cloud such as access for multiple users, analytics and recommendations, data hosting, etc. Updates to the functionality of the OPTIME digital service (e.g., increased analytics capabilities) are provided without extra cost to the customer. With this business model, the customers can make a simple lifetime cost calculation of the complete OPTIME solution which is provided to them by Schaeffler, and there are no hidden or additional cost or multiple options from which to choose. The business model fits well with the existing purchasing categories of most industrial companies and is at the same time transparent and easy to explain.

4 Managing and Integrating Digital Business Models as an Industrial Supplier

4.1 Opportunities from Digital Business Models

The business model of industrial suppliers is usually product or component driven. Industrial suppliers gain competitive advantages by acquiring technological capabilities that create technical USPs of their components or by creating cost advantages. Industrial suppliers typically try to form strategic partnerships with their customers (OEMs) to strengthen their position and identify their needs first. This strategic position has several disadvantages for industrial suppliers. Because they often do not have direct access to the end customers or even the OEM's customers, they must rely on the OEMs to correctly identify market trends and changes. Even though the industrial supplier might have significant application know-how which is relevant for the entire lifecycle of a component or a machine, they often have difficulty leveraging this know-how into offerings, service, or otherwise, because they lack the end-customer access. Therefore, the main revenue source for industrial suppliers is component or product sales.

In this situation, digital business models offer several opportunities for industrial suppliers in general. First, digital business models can be a door opener for the industrial supplier to a new customer group. By offering services which help to optimize the lifecycle of a component or product, industrial suppliers can gain access beyond their typical OEM customer group. This access enables them to identify market trends and technological requirements sooner and more precisely; therefore, this insight significantly reduces the risk to the core business of the industrial supplier. In addition to the positive effect on the core business, industrial suppliers can use digital business models to enter into long-term service relationships with customers and create additional recurring revenue streams alongside traditional component or product sales.

By incorporating an open technological approach using a flexible and agile cloud architecture, industrial suppliers can not only create a direct service offering but also engage in partner models. This approach has the advantage that, even though industrial suppliers also provide their services to the OEM's customers, they can create an offering which allows the OEM or any other partner to benefit from that offering, thus reducing the strategic tension between the OEM and the industrial supplier. Through this platform approach, the industrial supplier significantly strengthens its position in the entire ecosystem by creating service offerings for multiple partners and allowing the entire ecosystem to benefit from the service and the service provider's expertise.

In order to tackle these opportunities, Schaeffler used an open platform approach for its condition monitoring solution. For example, OPTIME provides standard interfaces that enable third parties to access their data and analysis results with their own software or cloud solution and create their own service offerings based on OPTIME data. These interfaces enable not only OEMs but also industrial service providers to use the OPTIME solution and integrate it into service offerings for their own customers.

4.2 Challenges from Digital Business Models

From the perspective of industrial suppliers, digital business models also pose specific challenges. Of course, industrial suppliers experience the same challenges as any company that offers digital business models (e.g., mastering digital technology). Yet, a number of these challenges are specifically demanding for industrial suppliers due to their existing business model.

The biggest difference to the existing component or product-based business model of an industrial supplier is that, with a digital business model, you are constantly connected to the customer. This difference implies that the entire innovation approach needs to change from that of identifying and fulfilling technical parameters to, instead, identifying and fulfilling user requirements. For successful digital business models, the user's needs must be understood relative to the user's processes, decisions, and even emotional requirements. In order to fully capture the benefits of digital offerings, the innovation approach must change into an agile approach that is able to constantly provide new releases and functions based on the continuous feedback the organization gets from the users.

In addition to the innovation approach, other parts of the organization must also be transformed in order to successfully offer digital business models. As explained above, digital business models typically target a different customer group than the one an industrial supplier serves in his core business. Likewise, the sales approach for the digital business needs to change from a technology-driven to a value-based sales approach. This shift requires new roles, such as customer success managers, and new competencies within the organization.

5 Summary

Against the backdrop of increasing digitalization, industrial suppliers worldwide are facing major challenges. Nevertheless, technological change also holds enormous opportunities for adapting traditionally grown industrial business models. This article has used the example of Schaeffler OPTIME, a modern CM solution, to illustrate in a practical way how traditional industrial suppliers can expand their portfolio with new digital services to ensure the long-term survival of the company.

The impact of the adaptation of the business model does not only affect the company itself but also the entire digital ecosystem. The new OPTIME service offers changes the way industrial suppliers work with key partners in the market and with customers. The latter benefit from the new subscription business model in multiple ways, which significantly strengthens the customer relationship.

References

Ahmed, J. U. (1996). Modern approaches to product reliability improvement. *International Journal of Quality & Reliability Management, 13*(3), 27–41.

Al-Debei, M. M. (2010). Developing a unified framework of the business model concept. *European Journal of Information Systems, 19*, 359–376.

Amit, R., & Han, X. (2017). Value creation through novel resource configurations in a digitally enabled world. *Strategic Entrepreneurship Journal, 11*(3), 228–242.

Baden-Fuller, C., & Haefliger, S. (2013). Business models and technological innovation. *Long Range Planning, 46*(6), 419–426.

Baharom, M. B., & Zahir, M. A. N. B. (2019). Turnaround activities of rotating machinery for mechanical engineers. In S. A. Sulaiman (Ed.), *Rotating machineries: Aspects of operation and maintenance* (pp. 23–42). Singapore.

Baines, T. S., Lightfoot, H. W., Benedettini, O., & Kay, J. M. (2009). The servitization of manufacturing: A review of literature and reflection on future challenges. *Journal of Manufacturing Technology Management, 20*(5), 547–567.

Berman, S. J. (2012). Digital transformation: Opportunities to create new business models. *StrateGy and Leadership, 40*(2), 16–24.

Bogner, E., Voelklein, T., Schroedel, O., & Franke, J. (2016). Study based analysis on the current digitalization degree in the manufacturing industry in Germany. *Procedia CIRP, 57*, 14–19.
Crowder, M., & Lawless, J. (2007). On a scheme for predictive maintenance. *European Journal of Operational Research, 176*(3), 1713–1722.
Ghobakhloo, M. (2018). The future of manufacturing industry: a strategic roadmap toward Industry 4.0. *Journal of Manufacturing Technology Management, 29*(6), 910–936.
Hashemian, H. M. (2010). State-of-the-art predictive maintenance techniques. *IEEE Transactions on Instrumentation and Measurement, 60*(1), 226–236.
Ives, B., Palese, B., & Rodriguez, J. A. (2016). Enhancing customer service through the internet of things and digital data streams. *MIS Quarterly Executive, 15*(4), 279–297.
Kim, S. H., Cohen, M. A., & Netessine, S. (2007). Performance contracting in after-sales service supply chains. *Management Science, 53*(12), 1843–1858.
Matt, C., Hess, T., & Benlian, A. (2015). Digital transformation strategies. *Business & Information Systems Engineering, 57*(5), 339–343.
Mezger, F. (2014). Toward a capability-based conceptualization of business model innovation: insights from an explorative study. *R&D Management, 44*(5), 429–449.
Muthanandan, S., & Nor, K. A. B. (2019). Condition monitoring and assessment for rotating machinery. In S. A. Sulaiman (Ed.), *Rotating machineries: Aspects of operation and maintenance* (pp. 23–42). Singapore.
Nilsson, D. K., & Larson, U. E. (2008). Secure firmware updates over the air in intelligent vehicles. In *IEEE International Conference on Communications Workshops*, Beijing.
Osterwalder, A., & Pigneur, Y. (2010). *Business model generation: A handbook for visionaries, game changers, and challengers*. Hoboken, Wiley.
Paulus-Rohmer, D., Schatton, H., & Bauernhansl, T. (2016). Ecosystems, strategy and business models in the age of digitization - How the manufacturing industry is going to change its logic. *Procedia CIRP, 57*, 8–13.
PwC (2020). *Global Top 100 companies by market capitalization*. Retrieved from https://www.pwc.com/gx/en/services/audit-assurance/publications/global-top-100-companies.html.
Rachinger, M., Rauter, R., Müller, C., Vorraber, W., & Schirgi, E. (2019). Digitalization and its influence on business model innovation. *Journal of Manufacturing Technology Management, 30*(8), 1143–1160.
Schaeffler monitoring services GmbH. (2019). *Condition monitoring praxis*. Vereinigte Fachverlage.
Schaeffler (2021). *Vibration analysis with condition monitoring for more transparency*. Retrieved from https://www.schaeffler.de/content.schaeffler.de/en/products-and-solutions/industrial/industry-4.0/digital-services/index.jsp.
Schiele, H. (2006). How to distinguish innovative suppliers? Identifying innovative suppliers as new task for purchasing. *Industrial Marketing Management, 35*(8), 925–935.
Schuh, G., Frank, J., Jussen, P., Rix, C., & Harland, T. (2019). Monetizing industry 4.0: Design principles for subscription business in the manufacturing industry. In *IEEE International Conference on Engineering, Technology and Innovation*, Valbonne Sophia-Antipolis, France.
Schuh, G., Wenger, L., Stich, V., Hicking, J., & Gailus, J. (2020). Outcome economy: Subscription business models in machinery and plant engineering. *Procedia CIRP, 93*, 599–604.
Selviaridis, K., & Wynstra, F. (2015). Performance-based contracting: A literature review and future research directions. *International Journal of Production Research, 53*(12), 3505–3540.
Stampfl, G., Prügl, R., & Osterloh, V. (2013). An explorative model of business model scalability. *International Journal of Product Development, 18*(3–4), 226–248.
Stolterman, E., & Fors, A. C. (2004). Information technology and the good life. In B. Kaplan, D. P. Truex, D. Wastell, A. T. Wood-Harper, & J. I. DeGross (Eds.), *Information systems research* (pp. 687–692). Boston.

Susto, G. A., Schirru, A., Pampuri, S., McLoone, S., & Beghi, A. (2014). Machine learning for predictive maintenance: A multiple classifier approach. *IEEE Transactions on Industrial Informatics, 11*(3), 812–820.

Tallman, S., Luo, Y., & Buckley, P. J. (2018). Business models in global competition. *Global Strategy Journal, 8*(4), 517–535.

Tavner, P. J. (2008). Review of condition monitoring of rotating electrical machines. *IET Electric Power Applications, 2*(4), 215–247.

Teece, D. J. (2010). Business models, business strategy and innovation. *Long Range Planning, 43* (2–3), 172–194.

Veile, J. W., Kiel, D., Müller, J., & Voigt, K.-I. (2019). Lessons learned from Industry 4.0 implementation in the German manufacturing industry. *Journal of Manufacturing Technology Management, 31*(5), 977–997.

Weill, P., & Woerner, S. L. (2013). Optimizing your digital business model. *MIT Sloan Management Review, 54*(3), 71–78.

Zott, C., Amit, R., & Massa, L. (2011). The business model: Recent developments and future research. *Journal of Management, 37*(4), 1019–1042.

Digital Industrial Platforms

German B2B Platforms' Contribution Towards a Resilient Economy

Dieter Kempf and Steven Heckler

Abstract

The Corona pandemic has highlighted the necessity for enterprises resilience, i.e. the ability to withstand systemic discontinuities and adapt to new risk environments. Companies can adjust to these challenging circumstances by constantly reinventing themselves. German industry is world-renowned for its engineering of technical products and services. Due to the success of US-American and Chinese consumer-oriented platform-based business models, the question arises if German companies' approaches to develop industrial business-to-business platforms can enhance their resilience in light of challenges such as the digital transformation, or systemic shocks, such as global trade conflicts and the Corona pandemic. Based on a categorisation of Germany's B2B landscape into data-centric and transaction-centric platforms, the paper draws on recent quantitative studies to analyse the potential of German B2B platforms for augmented enterprise resilience in industry and industry-related services. The paper showcases that B2B platforms are a cornerstone for implementing Industry 4.0 and thus the digital transformation from a product-centric economy to a model that smartly combines physical engineering with data-based, digital value-added services. At the same time, digital B2B platforms help to minimise CO_2 emissions, to cut back on production and logistics costs and to maximise the efficient utilisation of R&D, production and transport capacities.

D. Kempf (✉) · S. Heckler
Bundesverband der Deutschen Industrie e.V., Breite Straße 29, 10178 Berlin, Germany
e-mail: d.kempf@bdi.eu

K.-I. Voigt and J. M. Müller (eds.), *Digital Business Models in Industrial Ecosystems*, Future of Business and Finance, https://doi.org/10.1007/978-3-030-82003-9_6

1 Introduction: Germany's Flourishing B2B Platform Landscape

Digital platforms are the dominant business model of the digital age. Online marketplaces, booking platforms and app stores are all based on the principles of the platform economy. Today, seven out of the ten companies with the highest market capitalisation worldwide operate at least one digital platform as an integral part of their business model (PWC, 2020). As most of these business-to-consumer (B2C) platforms originate either from Silicon Valley or China, one might argue that Europe overslept the trend towards digital platform-based business models.

This analysis, however, would ignore significant developments in recent years. German industrial companies, which contributed about 27% to GDP in 2019 (Statista, 2020), increasingly develop their own B2B platforms. However, while US-American and Chinese companies are predominantly developing platform-based business models for consumers, German companies' focus lies mainly on platforms for business users, i.e. business-to-business (B2B) platforms (BDI, 2020a). In many cases, the development of B2B platforms does not result in a strategy shift from a product-centred to a digital business model, but rather in offering digital value-added services based on platforms on top of their existing portfolio.

German enterprises perceive digital platforms as an opportunity (Bitkom, 2020). Thus, already 70% of German companies in the industry and industry-related services utilise or even operate a digital platform (vbw, 2019). Consequently, 6.8 per cent of value creation in German industry and the industry-related service sector substantially depends on platforms, corresponding to a gross value added of 112 billion euros (Ibid.).

While the above-cited figures illustrate that digital platforms are increasingly of integral importance both for the single company as well as for the entire economy, the question arises how exactly B2B platforms contribute to more resilient enterprises and economy. Based on a brief discussion in Chapter two of German B2B platforms' characteristics and typology and against the backdrop of an outline of the concept of "resilience" in Chapter three, this paper analyses how five types of digital B2B platforms operated by German companies contribute to enhanced resilience (Chapter four). The article shows that Germany will not win the digital race only based on its B2B platforms, but that it cannot win this race without these platforms. B2B platforms are a central pillar for the implementation of Industry 4.0, i.e. the intelligent networking of machines, sensors, cloud services and platforms.

2 German B2B Platforms Explained

"Digital platforms are intermediaries which connect two or more market participants via a digital technology and thereby, either simplify interactions, or even make new interactions possible" (BDI, 2020a). They orchestrate an ecosystem of supply, demand and digital services by making use of data and bridging media gaps (BMWi &

Plattform Industrie 4.0, 2019). The following sub-chapters briefly discuss Germany's evolving platform landscape by providing a typology of German B2B platforms (2.1) and major characteristics of B2B in comparison to B2C platforms (2.2).

2.1 Typology

The term "digital platforms" refers to various types of digital business models reducing transaction costs and facilitating (business) interactions among large numbers of (physically dispersed) possible users or participants. Typical platform-based B2C business models are marketplaces, booking platforms, app stores, social networks and search engines. Likewise, various types of digital platform-based B2B business models exist. The literature on B2B platforms identifies two approaches when differentiating between B2B platforms: The structural approach differentiates platforms according to technological and organisation characteristics (Plattform Industrie 4.0 & BMWi, 2019; VDMA & Roland Berger, 2019) whereas the functional approach focuses on the transactions facilitated by platforms (BDI, 2020a; BMWi, 2019; Evans & Gawer, 2016; Falck & Koenen, 2020). Like BDI (2020a), this paper follows the functional approach and differentiates between two main categories, which can be divided into five sub-types (Fig. 1).

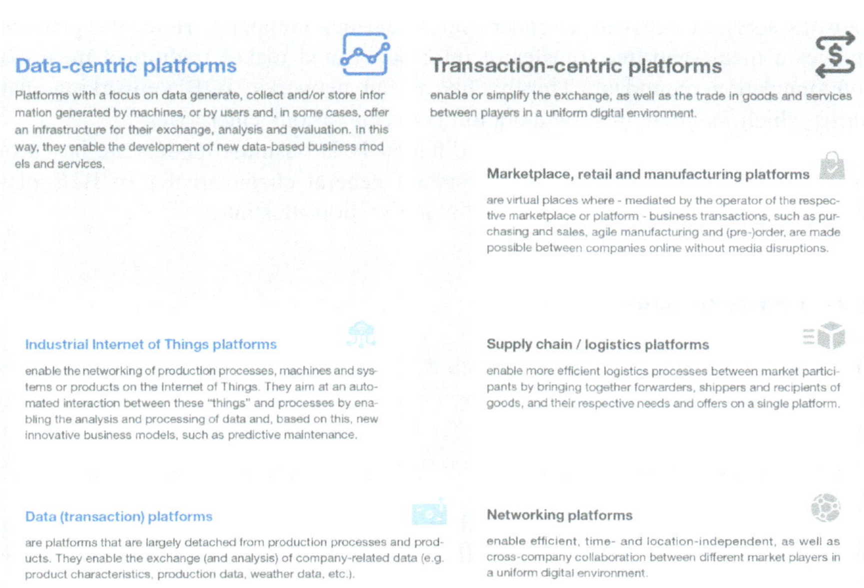

Fig. 1 Typology of German B2B platforms (BDI, 2020a)

The first category consists of data-centric platforms, i.e. platforms that offer an infrastructure for the storage, exchange, analysis and evaluation of data originating from various sources (BDI, 2020a; Haucap, Kehder & Loebert, 2020). These platforms can be differentiated into two sub-types: Firstly, Industrial Internet of Things (IIoT) platforms enable the networking of production processes, machines and systems or products on the Internet of Things. Based on the processing and analysis of data generated by various types of machines, insights into formerly analogue business processes can be generated and new services, such as condition monitoring, can be offered. Secondly, so-called data (transaction) platforms—which are also referred to as data marketplaces (BMWi, 2020b; Falck & Koenen, 2020)—are neutral intermediaries facilitating the exchange of data between actors. As the figure showcases, a neat classification of data (transaction) platforms into one of these two categories is not possible since—depending on the specific platform—either their data- or their transaction-focus prevails.

The second category comprises transaction-centric platforms which focus on facilitating transactions, such as purchasing, logistics or networking, among enterprises (BDI, 2020a; Haucap, Kehder & Loebert, 2020). Three different sub-types have been identified: Firstly, digital marketplaces which "are virtual places where—mediated by the operator of the respective marketplace or platform—business transactions, such as purchasing and sales, agile manufacturing and (pre-)order, are made possible between companies online without media disruptions" (BDI, 2020a). Secondly, supply chain and logistics platforms which facilitate logistics services between a sender and a logistics company. Here, the platform enables a media-gap-free transfer of information and makes traditional means of communication redundant. Thirdly, like social networks, B2B networking platforms which facilitate the collaboration between various enterprises.

This overview illustrates that very different B2B business models are based on the platform economy. Nonetheless, certain general characteristics of B2B platforms have been identified, as the following section illustrates.

2.2 Characteristics

Digital B2B platforms are different from B2C platforms, as their respective areas of use and particularly the actors engaging on these platforms differ immensely (Haucap, Kehder & Loebert, 2020). To facilitate the following discussion, this section briefly summarises key findings of a study by Falck and Koenen (2020), which is one of the first analysing the characteristics of B2B platforms.

The differences between B2C and B2B platforms consist of structural as well as functional aspects. Firstly, while on B2C platforms asymmetrical market players interact with each other (large, often multinational companies and individual consumers), on B2B platforms, more symmetrical market players interact. At times, even the operator of a B2B platform possesses a smaller market power in comparison to the platform's users. This provides users of B2B platforms with a greater market power, inter alia, allowing them to negotiate customer-individual contracts. (Falck & Koenen, 2020).

Secondly, the German B2B platform landscape is characterised by a high degree of competition. This competition is taking place between platforms offering similar solutions and platform-based versus traditional business models. To win new customers, operators of B2B platforms differentiate their platforms not only based on price and costs, but also by providing new, innovative functionalities, offering customer-specific adaptations, such as tailoring a marketplace to the customer's purchasing processes, and by remaining open towards new user groups (Falck & Koenen, 2020).

Thirdly, in contrast to B2C platforms, which often address a very large group of potential users, many B2B platforms specialise in certain industries (BDI, 2020a). Based on the know-how of a certain industry, operators of B2B platforms aim to tailor their platform to the requirement of their potential customers (Falck & Koenen, 2020). For example, specialised marketplaces exist for various industry sectors (BDI, 2020a). However, a recent study suggests (VDMA & McKinsey, 2020) that, in future, we are likely to see the development of one major B2B platform or the integration of existing industry-specific platforms to allow the necessary scaling-up. The development of a sector-specific platform, benefitting from sector-specific know-how, might be appropriate as a First Mover and with a high degree of scalability and compatibility.

Fourthly, network effects are what causes the "power of the platform" (Parker, Van Alstyne & Choudary, 2016). Network effects can be defined as the "impact that the number of users of a platform has on the value created for each user" (Ibid.). Consequently, network effects are among the main drivers of growth for platforms. However, especially on B2B platforms, network effects are not only positive, since a rise in providers can lead to increased price pressure and prolonging the time until a user finds a specific offering (Falck & Koenen, 2020).

This section introduced a typology of B2B platforms and their characteristics. Before analysing the contribution, the five sub-types of B2B platforms can have for enhanced business and regional resilience, the next chapter discusses the concept of resilience.

3 A Resilient Economy: Conceptual Remarks

The Corona pandemic made—at least temporally—certain economic activities obsolete. Similarly, natural disasters, regulatory measures and long-term changes, such as digital transformation, all have significant implications for the economic development path of an entity. When businesses and regions are confronted with such "'system-wide' shocks" (Martin, 2012), they have to react to this changed situation. Both in business management studies (Hamel & Välikangas, 2003; Starr et al., 2003) and in economic geography (Martin, 2012; Martin & Sunley, 2015), scholars argue that the resilience of a company or region is detrimental to how it emerges from such a crisis. This paper takes the concept of "resilience" as an analytical background to discuss how B2B platforms can contribute to the resilience of an entity.

Martin and Sunley (2015) define resilience as "the capacity of a regional or local economy to withstand or recover from market, competitive and environmental shocks to its developmental growth path, if necessary, by undergoing adaptive changes to its economic structures [...] so as to maintain or restore its previous developmental path, or transit to a new sustainable one". In recent years, "a new imperative of 'constructing' or 'building' regional and urban economic resilience is gaining currency" (Ibid.). For example, at least since 2015, the political debate in Germany and the European Union is fuelled by considerations of how Europe, in light of an increasing dominance of tech companies headquartered in the US and China, could regain its digital and technological sovereignty (e.g. BDI, 2020b; BMBF, 2020; BMWi, 2015; BUSINESSEUROPE, 2020; European Commission, 2020) or even "strategic autonomy" (Michel, 2019)—two concepts strongly linked to resilience.

However, resilience should not only be discussed with regards to regions, but each single economic entity must be resilient and will thereby contribute to a region's resilience. Starr et al. (2003) define enterprise resilience as "the ability and capacity to withstand systemic discontinuities and adapt to new risk environments". In the globalised world, companies are—e.g. due to globally integrated value chains and the just-in-time production—exposed to a high degree of "interdependence risk" (Ibid.), meaning that a single company cannot control all potential risk vectors on its own. Hamel and Välikangas (2003) stress that companies need to be in times of crisis "as efficient at renewal as they are at producing today's products and services". Henceforth, companies following the resilience-paradigm have to be able to constantly adjust to changing circumstances by possessing the willingness to accept the necessity to change, quickly innovate and even adapt the entire business model.

4 B2B Platforms' Contribution to a Greener, More Resilient and Future-Proof Economy: Five Case Studies

The capacity to renewal and change is crucial for both regions and enterprises to economically prosper. Based on an analysis of studies on B2B platforms, the following sub-chapters discuss how the five types of B2B platforms introduced in Sect. 2.1, namely IIoT platforms (Sect. 4.1), data transaction platforms (Sect. 4.2), marketplaces (Sect. 4.3), logistics and supply chain management platforms (Sect. 4.4) and B2B networks (Sect. 4.5) contribute to the resilience of platform operators and platform users.

4.1 From Condition Monitoring to Predictive and Remote Maintenance—How Platforms Can Help in Time of Crises

The different types of production machines and logistic devices at manufacturing sites are generating a huge amount of data that until recently—and in many companies still today—remains unused. This, however, needs to change as the analysis of data can help to reduce production rejects, costs and downtime. For example, unplanned downtimes in the process industry alone cost around 20 billion US dollars annually worldwide (VDMA & Roland Berger, 2018). To this end, Industrial Internet of Things (IIoT) platforms have been developed.

Industrial Internet of Things (IIoT) platforms "enable the networking of production processes, machines and systems or products on the Internet of Things" (BDI, 2020a). The data generated by machines, such as error codes, movements and temperature, are recorded and transferred to the cloud, where algorithms analyse it. Thereby, the current condition of a machine or the status of an entire production process can be monitored—even remotely (condition monitoring). Thereby, maintenance staff can—even during a pandemic—monitor the uninterrupted operation of an entire production site. Based on Artificial Intelligence (AI) applications, the likely wear of components, and thereby, the probability of machine downtime can be predicted. To avoid downtime, IoT platforms inform maintenance staff of required interventions so that maintenance takes place before a defect occurs (predictive maintenance). (BDI, 2020a; Bender et al., 2020) Consequently, IIoT platforms are the basis for Internet-based services, as they serve both as the basis on which new services and products are developed and the channel through which services and products are made available (Bitkom, 2018).

Besides remote condition monitoring and the reduction of downtime, IIoT platforms generate significant advantages for both platform users and operator. Sixty per cent of companies operating on an IIoT platform experience an increase in productivity and revenues, combined with cost reductions within three months (IDG, 2020). Moreover, companies utilising IIoT platforms can save up to 20% of production and quality costs, can reduce complexity costs by up to 60% and can even save 20 to 30% on maintenance costs (Bitkom, 2018). Operators of IIoT platforms, on the other hand, strengthen their customer relations, since they no longer only sell a machine but rather a machine together with a plethora of associated digital services via the IIoT platform. Thereby, they can generate additional revenues. (Haucap, Kehder & Loebert, 2020) Furthermore, by using the data generated by their customers' machines, manufacturers can also improve the engineering of these machines (VDMA & Roland Berger, 2018).

Based on these data, IIoT platforms can help companies to build and run a digital twin of their production process, which allows the virtual simulation of the real business processes and functionalities of products and systems. Thereby, they facilitate business decisions, ideally for all stages of the product life cycle (DETECON, 2019).

However, the usage of IIoT platforms will only increase if currently existing challenges can be overcome. Studies suggest that data and IT security protection concerns, the fear of lock-in effects, a shortage of qualified personnel and a myriad of data protocols impede a speedy uptake of IIoT platforms (Bitkom, 2018; IDG, 2020). Consequently, operators of IIoT platforms should refrain from over-engineering their IIoT platform and rather ensure scalability, usability, reliability and compatibility (Bitkom, 2018; IDG, 2020; VDMA & McKinsey, 2020).

In economically challenging times, cost reductions, means to digitalise business processes and an attractive, future-oriented product portfolio are paramount to ensuring a company's competitiveness. Industrial Internet of Things (IIoT) platforms currently account for revenues totalling three billion Euros in Western Europe annually; a figure forecasted to grow by an average of 10% per year until 2024 (VDMA & McKinsey, 2020), as one in five companies is planning to invest in IoT platforms over the coming two years (IDG, 2020). Consequently, German manufacturing companies, which are globally renowned for their excellent, state-of-the-art machines, plants, cars and other products, should—in addition to their manufacturing portfolio—offer data-based value-added services on collaboratively developed IIoT platforms (Bender et al., 2020; VDMA & McKinsey, 2020). Moreover, they also need to make their own business processes smarter by utilising platform-based digital IoT services. Thereby, they can enhance their competitiveness and resilience.

4.2 Utilising Industry's Data Treasure

"As the raw material for the acquisition of information, data is considered to be of great importance for the (sustainable) economic success of a company" (Spiekermann, 2019). However, currently, four in five enterprises fail to monetise their data (Accenture, 2018). This hesitance to exchange and monetise data results from fears that competitors could gain valuable insights into the data provider's business processes, legal uncertainties emanating from discussions on data security and data protection, as well as problems in defining the monetary value of data (BMWi, 2020; Falck & Koenen, 2020; Spiekermann, 2019; Trauth et al., 2020). Data marketplaces, with strong and reliable data usage controls, can help augmenting the usage and monetisation of data.

Data marketplaces are digital platforms that provide the operational and organisational framework for simplifying or enabling the exchange of business-related data beyond organisational boundaries (BDI, 2020a; BMWi, 2020; Deichmann et al., 2016; Meisel & Spiekermann, 2019). The operator of a data transaction platform functions as a (neutral) intermediary between those possessing and those interested in data (BMWi, 2020; Deichmann et al., 2016; Falck & Koenen., 2020). In addition, the operator provides a governance structure that minimises, for both data providers and data buyers, transaction costs for trading data as well as legal uncertainty (BMWi, 2020; Meisel & Spiekermann, 2019; Spiekermann, 2019).

Moreover, by applying blockchain technology, the accuracy of data exchanged on these platforms can be ensured, as it provides potential buyers with authorised and unalterable information concerning the data on offer as well as transaction integrity (Accenture, 2018). Furthermore, enterprises but also regional authorities lacking the necessary resources for analysing and interpreting data, such as AI or data specialists, can generate value from their data as many data transaction platforms offer such services (Falck & Koenen, 2020; Meisel & Spiekermann, 2019).

Since 70% of companies regard their own data as insufficient to remain competitive, an increasing uptake in the usage of B2B data transaction platforms, such as data marketplaces, can be expected (Accenture, 2019). Consequently, operating a data transaction platform can develop into a promising business model, if the above-stated hurdles are overcome, especially since many companies are in search of high-quality data generated by other organisations. Estimates suggest that by 2030, the market value of data transacted on data marketplaces will rise to 3.6 trillion US Dollars (Accenture, 2018). Therefore, by exchanging data across with other market actors, companies can monetise a so far not monetised good. In addition, by collecting, aggregating, processing and utilising both internal and external data, companies can optimise and even develop new business models (Meisel & Spiekermann, 2019).

4.3 Marketplaces' Contribution to Reducing Costs, Winning New Customers and Increasing Margins

In Germany alone, B2B e-commerce accounted for 1.3 trillion Euros in 2018 (Statista, 2019) and is estimated to grow by 15% annually (Haucap, Kehder & Loebert, 2020). While many companies still order by fax (38%) or phone (34%), increasingly they opt—at least in addition—also for online channels. However, only 23% order via dedicated B2B platforms and 14% on B2C marketplaces. Wittmann et al., (2019) These figures are surprising, since applying a fully digitalised order process based on a digital marketplace integrated into a company's purchasing process can result in cost savings of up to 41% in comparison to a standardised manual process (Mercateo, 2017).

Marketplaces, retail and manufacturing platforms are virtual places where—mediated by the operator of the respective platform—business transactions, such as purchasing, sales and (pre)ordering, are made possible online without changing between different means of online and offline communication. In contrast to online shops, on which one seller offers its products, on marketplaces, the products of various sellers can be ordered. In recent years, many B2B marketplaces have been established by German companies, mainly of two types, those which offer a cross-sectoral stock of goods ranging from screws to forklifts and those dedicated to the requirements of certain industries, such as chemics and textiles (BDI, 2020a).

While 55% of companies regard a partial loss of direct business contacts and 48% reduced revenues as a downside to the utilisation of platforms (Bitkom, 2020), buyers, sellers and operators can massively benefit from B2B marketplaces. Buyers can simplify and standardise their purchasing process for certain product groups when utilising marketplaces (Haucap, Kehder & Loebert, 2020). This is the case, since operators of B2B marketplaces provide users with tailored interfaces in order to facilitate purchasing processes, for example, by integrating a company's authorisation processes into the marketplace (Falck & Koenen, 2020). Sellers benefit from marketplaces as they do not have to invest in their own (digital and or online) sales channel while simultaneously gaining access to new customers groups (Wittmann, Seidenschwarz & Pur, 2019). Operators, on the other hand, benefit from the above-stated growth potential of German B2B e-commerce.

4.4 Reducing CO_2-emissions, Augmenting Resource Efficiency in B2B Logistics

Ambitious targets to reduce CO_2 emissions, changing customer demands caused by just-in-time production, a shift from high street to online shopping, as well as increased costs require freight forwarders to adapt their business accordingly. Logistics processes are very complex. Thus, freight forwarders have to permanently match loads and capacities in light of changing external conditions, such as traffic jams or new bookings (Haucap, Kehder & Loebert, 2020). Today, logistics processes are still very inefficient, as 20% of all road-freight transports in the EU are run empty (Eurostat, 2020) and even 30% of the volume-based and 42% of the kilo-based capacity, respectively, remain unused in the air freight sector (Clive, 2020; IATA, 2020).

Since logistic processes are well standardised and thus easily available for algorithmic analysis, digital logistics platforms are suitable to optimise utilisation of loading capacity and quality while reducing costs (Haucap, Kehder & Loebert, 2020). B2B logistics platforms are transaction-centred B2B platforms that bring together forwarders, shippers as well as recipients of goods—with their respective needs and offers—on a single digital platform (BDI, 2020a). On these platforms, enterprises can indicate their shipping requirements without having to call several freight forwarders. The freight forwarders can then make an offer, from which the sender can choose its preferred one. In addition, freight forwarders can also market empty loading capacities on these platforms, which potential senders can book on-demand. As these platforms often integrate payment processes, logistics-related transaction costs are significantly reduced (BDI, 2020a).

By networking logistics processes, supply and shipping chains become more transparent, transport chains less vulnerable, and thus, the entire supply chain management can be optimised for both shippers and forwarders (Haucap, Kehder & Loebert, 2020). The combined usage of digital platforms and sensors can result in a truck-capacity-utilisation of 95% (Tagesspiegel, 2015). This ultimately reduces logistics costs and the amount of CO_2 emitted by the logistics sector (BDI, 2020a). Finally, since the European logistics sector is experiencing enormous growth rates (Schwemmer, 2019), the speedy uptake of digital tools can help to fulfil customers' requirements despite a shortage of qualified truck drivers amounting to 60,000 in Germany alone in 2018 (Spiegel, 2019).

4.5 Creating Networks to Enhance Resilience

The Corona pandemic illustrated that matching supply and demand is difficult in times of major supply chain disruptions. While some companies had unused production, development or transport capacities, others were desperately looking for exactly these services. Because of this mismatch, both sides missed vital business opportunities.

Mirroring the experiences from social networks, business interactions can be facilitated if companies engage in digital B2B networks. Digital B2B networking platforms enable efficient, time- and location-independent collaboration between different market players in a uniform digital environment (BDI, 2020a). B2B networking platforms already existed before the pandemic (Ibid.). The COVID-19-induced disruption of global supply chains though led to the establishment or increased use of digital B2B networks by German industrial enterprises. Many of these platforms have a regional focus (BMWi & Plattform Industrie 4.0, 2019; Leipzig vernetzt, 2020; Wirtschaftsförderung Region Stuttgart GmbH, 2021) and thereby facilitate business interactions especially in times of geographically dispersed crises. By interacting in a uniform digital environment, companies can significantly save transactions costs and quickly identify new business contacts according to their requirements.

When long established and trusted supply chains suddenly collapse—for example, due to a natural disaster, political upheavals or a health emergency—companies operating a just-in-time production process quickly experience disruptions. B2B networks, in which spare parts are exchanged, testing and certification capacities are offered or new business relations can be forged, are of outstanding importance to mitigate these disruptions and help to maintain continuous business processes. Besides the positive implications for each business, networks—in particular, those with a regional focus—can help mitigate economic shocks at the regional level, and thereby, support employment and economic development.

5 Conclusion: Competitiveness, Eco-Sustainability and Ingenuity: Digital B2B Platforms' Contribution to Europe's Resilience

Germany and Europe will not gain the required digital sovereignty only with B2B platforms "Made in Germany". However, without them, any aspirations for resilience are destined for failure, since B2B platforms are a cornerstone for implementing Industry 4.0 and thus the digital transformation from a product-centric economy to a model that smartly combines physical engineering with digital value-added services. Hence, platform operators have to integrate themselves into value-creating networks by offering products and services together with partners and simultaneously face competition (Schnittler & Zollenkop, 2019). While platformisation has previously been a major trend in B2C markets, in recent years, a considerable number of German companies, ranging from start-ups to SME and internationally operating large companies, are increasingly developing and operating their own platforms for business-to-business use cases (BDI, 2020a).

Building on their in-depth (sectoral) know-how, many German industrial enterprises—especially in the manufacturing sector—maintain their traditional business model, i.e. the production of machinery and physical goods. Increasingly, however, they are enriching their product portfolio by offering services and applications based on digital B2B platforms. In light of shorter product cycles, a fast-paced digital transformation and the arrival of new competitors, companies have to exploit the potentials of digitalisation if they want to remain competitive. Especially in times of (prolonged) crises, companies have to continuously innovate and even completely change their business model.

The five types of digital B2B platforms analysed in this paper all contribute to an increased resilience of Germany's companies—both for operators and users of digital B2B platforms. The COVID-19 pandemic demonstrates that companies that had already invested in the development of digital competencies as well as products and services found it much easier during the pandemic to serve customer needs, coordinate logistics processes, conduct remote condition monitoring and maintenance and continue purchasing and selling processes (VDMA & McKinsey, 2020).

The potentials of various types of platforms for cost savings as well as for additional revenues make the speedy uptake of these platforms by all companies of paramount importance. However, German companies should not wait too long before investing in the development and usage of digital B2B platforms, as high-tech companies from Silicon Valley and China are increasingly investing in the development of digital B2B platforms. As developing one's own platforms is quite costly, German industrial companies need to conduct an in-depth market survey before venturing into the platform economy in order to foster the company's resilience and not its economic downturn. (Schnittler & Zollenkop, 2019). Finally, companies should not underestimate the ecological dimension of utilising or developing digital B2B platforms. They can help companies to meet politically set ambitious climate targets and also reduce unnecessary waste of costly raw materials.

As Martin (2012) argues that regional economic resilience results from how both companies and political institutions react and adjust to a crisis. "Europe's political leaders must support innovative platform-based business models to strengthen Europe's economic resilience, make their industrial basis future-proof and harness the potentials for reduced CO_2 emissions". Consequently, the European Commission as well as member states' governments should strive for targeted policy measures that support the development of a flourishing platform ecosystem in Europe. Otherwise, regulators could "blight" the development of platforms in Europe and thereby threaten Europe's resilience.

References

Accenture (2018). *Value of data: The dawn of the data marketplace*. Retrieved from https://www.accenture.com/t20180904T113809Z__w__/us-en/_acnmedia/PDF-85/Accenture-Western-Digital-Value-of-Data-Dawn-of-the-Data-Marketplace.pdf#zoom=50.

BDI (2020a). *German digital B2B platforms*. Retrieved from english.bdi.eu/publication/news/German-Digital-B2B-Platforms.

BDI (2020b). *Strengthening Europe's digital sovereignty sustainably: Promoting technologies, developing skills, building a holistic ecosystem in a targeted manner*. Retrieved from https://english.bdi.eu/publication/news/strengthening-europes-digital-sovereignty-sustainably/.

Bender, B., Lass, S., Habib, N., & Scheel, L. (2020). Plattform-Bereitstellungsstrategien im Maschinen- und Anlagenbau: Strategien deutscher Unternehmen im Industrie 4.0-Kontext. *HMD Praxis der Wirtschaftsinformatik* (pp. 1–16).

Bitkom (2018). *IoT-Plattformen – aktuelle Trends und Herausforderungen: Handlungsempfehlungen auf Basis der Bitkom Umfrage 2018. Faktenpapier*. Retrieved from https://www.bitkom.org/sites/default/files/file/import/180424-LF-IoT-Plattformen-online.pdf.

Bitkom (2020). *Digitale plattformen: Chartbericht*. Retrieved from https://www.bitkom.org/sites/default/files/2020-02/bitkom_digitaleplattformen_2020.pdf.

BMBF (2020). *Karliczek: Mit vertrauenswürdiger und nachhaltiger Elektronik technologisch souverän in die Zukunft*. Retrieved from https://www.bmbf.de/de/karliczek-mit-vertrauenswuerdiger-und-nachhaltiger-elektronik-technologisch-souveraen-in-13051.html.

BMWi (2015). *Leitplanken Digitaler Souveränität*. Retrieved from https://www.de.digital/DIGITAL/Redaktion/DE/Downloads/it-gipfel-2015-leitplanken-digitaler-souveraenitaet.pdf?__blob=publicationFile&v=1.

BMWi (2019). *Die volkswirtschaftliche Bedeutung von digitalen B2B-Plattformen im Verarbeitenden Gewerbe*. Retrieved from https://www.de.digital/DIGITAL/Redaktion/DE/Digital-Gipfel/Download/2019/digitale-b2b-plattformen-im-verarbeitenden-gewerbe.pdf?__blob=publicationFile&v=3.

BMWi (2020). *Datenmarktplätze in Produktionsnetzwerken*. Retrieved from https://www.bmwi.de/Redaktion/DE/Publikationen/Industrie/industrie-4-0-impulspapier-datenmarktplaetze-in-produktionsnetzwerken.pdf?__blob=publicationFile&v=10.

BMWi & Plattform Industrie 4.0 (2019). *Germany's evolving platform landscape*. Retrieved from https://www.plattform-i40.de/PI40/Redaktion/DE/Downloads/Publikation/Germanys-evolving-platform-landscape.pdf?__blob=publicationFile&v=4.

BMWi & Plattform Industrie 4.0 (2019). *B2B-Plattformen in Zeiten der Corona-Krise*. Retrieved from https://www.bmwi.de/Redaktion/DE/Publikationen/Industrie/industrie-4-0-b2b-plattformen-in-zeiten-der-corona-krise.pdf?__blob=publicationFile&v=10.

Businesseurope (2020). *Smart technological sovereignty: How it could support EU competitiveness*. Retrieved from https://www.businesseurope.eu/sites/buseur/files/media/position_papers/iaco/2020-06-25_pp_technological_sovereignty.pdf.

Clive (2020). *Clive data services*. Retrieved from https://www.useclive.com/clive-data-services.html.

Deichmann, J., Heineke, K., Reinbacher, T., & Wee, D. (2016). *Creating a successful internet of things data marketplace*. Retrieved from https://www.mckinsey.com/business-functions/mckinsey-digital/our-insights/creating-a-successful-internet-of-things-data-marketplace.

Detecon (2019). *Digitale Zwillinge: Wegbereiter für Ökosysteme von morgen*. Retrieved from https://www.detecon.com/drupal/sites/default/files/2019-10/ST_Digitaler_Zwilling_final_online_091019_0.pdf.

European Commission (2020). *Europe: The keys to sovereignty*. Retrieved from https://ec.europa.eu/commission/commissioners/2019-2024/breton/announcements/europe-keys-sovereignty_en.

Eurostat (2020). *Freight transport statistics*. Retrieved from https://ec.europa.eu/eurostat/statistics-explained/index.php/Freight_transport_statistics#Road_transport.

Evans, P., & Gawer, A. (2016). *The rise of the platform enterprise: A global survey*. Retrieved from https://www.thecge.net/app/uploads/2016/01/PDF-WEB-Platform-Survey_01_12.pdf.

Falck, O., & Koenen, J. (2020). *Industrial dgital economy - B2B platforms. Study commissioned by Bundesverband der Deutschen Industrie e.V.* Retrieved from https://english.bdi.eu/publication/news/Industrial-digital-economy-B2B-platforms.

Hamel, G., & Välikangas, L. (2003). The quest for resilience. *Harvard Business Review, September*, 1–13.

Haucap, J., Kehder, C., & Loebert, I. (2020). *B2B-Plattformen in Nordrhein-Westfalen: Potenziale, Hemmnisse und Handlungsoptionen*. Retrieved from https://www.wirtschaft.nrw/sites/default/files/asset/document/gutachten_b2b-plattformen.pdf.

IATA (2020). *Air Cargo market analysis: Air cargo volumes picked up for another month*. Retrieved from https://www.iata.org/en/iata-repository/publications/economic-reports/air-freight-monthly-analysis—october-2020/.

IDG (2020). *Studie internet of things 2019/2020*. Retrieved from https://www.tuvsud.com/de-de/-/media/de/cyber-security/pdf/allgemein/marketing/studie_internet-ofthings_2019_2020.pdf?la=de-de&hash=A7B2170BE5F8474914E1458F94D9EF76.

Leipzig vernetzt (2020). *Digitale Initiative "Leipzig vernetzt"*. Retrieved from https://www.leipzig-vernetzt.de/.

Martin, R. (2012). Regional economic resilience, hysteresis and recessionary shocks. *Journal of Economic Geography, 2012*(12), 1–32.

Martin, R., & Sunley, P. (2015). On the notion of regional economic resilience: Conceptualization and explanation. *Journal of Economic Geography, 15*(1), 1–42.

Meisel, L., & Spiekermann, M. (2019). *Datenmarktplätze: Plattformen für Datenaustausch und Datenmonetarisierung in der Data Economy. Fraunhofer ISST-Bericht.* Retrieved from https://www.isst.fraunhofer.de/content/dam/isst-neu/documents/Publikationen/Datenwirtschaft/2019-2_ISST-Bericht_Datenmarktplaetze-ISSN-0943-1624.pdf.

Mercateo (2017). *Indirekter Einkauf im Fokus: Zwischen Einsparpotenzial und Zukunftschancen.* Retrieved from https://www.mercateo.com/corporate/wp-content/uploads/2017/03/Mercateo-Studie_Indirekter-Einkauf-im-Fokus.pdf.

Michel, C. (2019). *The digital in a fractious world: Europe's way: Speech at the FT-ETNO Forum.* Retrieved from https://www.consilium.europa.eu/en/press/press-releases/2020/09/29/the-digital-in-a-fractious-world-europe-s-way-speech-by-president-charles-michel-at-the-ft-etno-forum/.

Parker, G. G., Van Alstyne, M. W., & Choudary, S. P. (2016). *Platform revolution: How networked markets are transforming the economy and how to make them work for you*. New York, London: W.W. Norton Company.

PwC (2020). *Global Top 100 companies by market capitalisation*. Retrieved from https://www.pwc.com/gx/en/audit-services/publications/assets/global-top-100-companies-june-2020-update.pdf.

Rumscheidt, S. (2020). Die Bedeutung von Marktplätzen/Plattformen für den deutschen Groß- und Einzelhandel. *ifo Schnelldienst, 73*(1), 64–69.

Schnittler, V., & Zollenkop, M. (2019). Chance plattform: Plattformökonomie im B2B-Bereich. *Next Industry, 2019*(2), 24–31.

Schwemmer, M. (2019). *TOP 100 in European transport and logistics services: Executive summary*. Retrieved from https://www.scs.fraunhofer.de/content/dam/scs/DE/publikationen/studien/maerkte-standorte-logistik/TOP100_2019_ExecutiveSummary_english.pdf.

Spiegel (2019). *Fehlende Lkw-Fahrer: Spediteure warnen vor "Versorgungskollaps"*. Retrieved from https://www.spiegel.de/karriere/lkw-transporte-in-deutschland-fehlen-60-000-fahrer-a-1267387.html.

Spiekermann, M. (2019). Data marketplaces: Trends and monetisation of data goods. *Intereconomics, 54*(4), 208–216.

Starr, R., Newfrock, J., & Delurey, M. (2003). Enterprise resilience: Managing risk in the networked economy. In R. Rothenberg (Ed.), *Enterprise resilience: Risk and security in the networked world – A strategy+business reader* (pp. 58–69). Booz Allen Hamilton.

Statista (2019). *Umsatzvolumen im B2B-E-Commerce in Deutschland im Jahr 2018*. Retrieved from https://de.statista.com/statistik/daten/studie/254040/umfrage/b2b-e-commerce-umsaetze-nach-marktteilnehmern/#: ~ :text=Ums%C3%A4tze%20im%20B2B%2DE%2DCommerce%20in%20Deutschland%202018&text=Insgesamt%20wurden%20im%20B2B%2DE,Online%2DShops%20und%20Marktpl%C3%A4tze%20erwirtschaftet.

Statista (2020). *Anteile der Wirtschaftssektoren am Bruttoinlandsprodukt (BIP) in den wichtigsten Industrie- und Schwellenländern im Jahr 2019*. Retrieved from https://de.statista.com/statistik/daten/studie/37088/umfrage/anteile-der-wirtschaftssektoren-am-bip-ausgewaehlter-laender/.

Tagesspiegel (2015). *"Ein Viertel aller Lkw fährt leer durch die Gegend"*. Retrieved from http://www.tagesspiegel.de/wirtschaft/logistik-ein-viertel-aller-lkwfaehrt-leer-durch-die-gegend/12505110.html.

Trauth, D., Bergs, T., Gülpen, C., Maaß, W., Mayer, J., Musa, H., et al. (2020). Monetarisierung von Fertigungsdaten. In T. Bergs, C. Brecher, R. H. Schmitt, & G. Schuh (Eds.), *Internet of production - turning data into value: Statusberichte aus der Produktionstechnik* (pp. 340–364). Aachen.

Vbw (2019). *Plattformen – Infrastruktur der Digitalisierung*. Retrieved from https://www.vbw-bayern.de/Redaktion/Frei-zugaengliche-Medien/Abteilungen-GS/Wirtschaftspolitik/2019/Downloads/Plattformen-Infrastruktur-der-Digitalisierung_final.pdf.

VDMA & Roland Berger (2018). *Plattformökonomie im Maschinenbau: Herausforderungen – Chancen – Handlungsoptionen*. Retrieved from https://www.vdma.org/documents/15012668/26471342/RB_PUB_18_009_VDMA_Plattform%C3%B6konomie-06_1530513808561.pdf/f4412be3-e5ba-e549-7251-43ee17ec29d3.

VDMA & McKinsey (2020). *Kundenzentrierung als Chance für den digitalen Durchbruch: Was sich die Endkundenindustrie vom Maschinenbau bei digitalen Plattformen und Mehrwertdiensten wünschen*. Retrieved from https://www.mckinsey.de/ ~ /media/McKinsey/Locations/Europe%20and%20Middle%20East/Deutschland/News/Presse/2020/2020-09-18%20Maschinenbau/VDMA_McKinsey_Broschre_Digitale%20Plattformen_DEUTSCH.pdf.

Wirtschaftsförderung Region Stuttgart GmbH (2021). *B2B Region Stuttgart*. Retrieved from https://b2b.region-stuttgart.de/.

Wittmann, G., Seidenschwarz, H., & Pur, S. (2019). *B2B-E-Commerce 2020 – Status quo, Erfahrungen und Ausblicke*. Retrieved from https://ibi.de/veroeffentlichungen/B2B-E-Commerce.

Digital Logistics Platforms—Initial Approaches to Market Segmentation in Light of Traditional and New Providers

Wolfgang Stölzle and Ludwig Häberle

Abstract

Thanks to comprehensive networking possibilities and improved information flow, platforms present themselves as catalysts of the logistics industry's digital transformation. Providing a (digital) infrastructure enables the value-creating exchange of information, goods, or services between several players, the basis for the emergence of a functioning two-sided market. It is often startups that appear as new players in the digital logistics market, not infrequently from outside the industry and with a pronounced affinity for ICT. Digitization makes it significantly easier for new providers to enter the market, as entry barriers in the form of capital-intensive investments in vehicle fleets or warehouse capacity are eliminated. The market for digital logistics platforms is developing dynamically and offers a heterogeneous range of services that cannot be clearly defined and delimited. In addition, there is no meaningful overview of the provider structure. Platform users are faced with the question of which platform is best suited with its range of services for specific performance characteristics. This paper addresses these challenges and aims to segment the service spectrum of digital logistics platforms. This approach forms the basis for providing shippers, logistics service providers, platform operators, and investors with a market overview of the logistics' digital platform landscape.

W. Stölzle · L. Häberle (✉)
Institute of Supply Chain Management, University of St. Gallen,
Dufourstrasse 40a, 9000 St. Gallen, Switzerland
e-mail: ludwig.haeberle@unisg.ch

W. Stölzle
e-mail: wolfgang.stoelzle@unisg.ch

K.-I. Voigt and J. M. Müller (eds.), *Digital Business Models in Industrial Ecosystems*,
Future of Business and Finance, https://doi.org/10.1007/978-3-030-82003-9_7

1 Introduction

In the context of Industry 4.0, logistics is an industry that is fundamentally affected by digitization. In a narrower sense, digitization in logistics raises all players' questions about which business processes can be changed and how to realize efficiency improvements (Sucky & Asdecker, 2019). Due to the advancing networking and the resulting improved flow of information, platforms present themselves as catalysts of digital transformation in the logistics industry. They are often startups that appear as new players in the digital logistics market, not uncommonly from outside the industry and equipped with a pronounced affinity for ICT. This development is because digitization makes it significantly easier for new providers to enter the market, as entry barriers in the form of capital-intensive investments in vehicle fleets or warehouses no longer apply.

Different groups of market players meet on digital logistics platforms. By providing a (digital) infrastructure, platform operators enable the value-creating exchange of information, goods, or services between two or more players, thus laying the foundation for the emergence of a functioning two-sided market. This includes enabling and facilitating transactions via a platform which, as a central point of contact, serves the supply of or demand for logistics services depending on the market player and thus reduces transaction costs. On one side of the market, shippers are the demanders of logistics services. On the supply side, this demand is served by carriers and forwarders. Very often, independent entrepreneurs with only one truck and SMEs with a few transport units are to be found, which together represent the majority of freight carriers in Europe. While both the air and ocean freight markets have consolidated from the supply side, the European road freight transport market, in particular, is considered highly fragmented given a large number of small market players with over 300,000 carriers (Riedl et al., 2018). This opens up the potential to link a large number of individual players and consolidate transports across companies. Platforms fulfill the individual actors' different and overlapping needs through the accompanying bundling of supply and demand. Even though this article focuses on transport platforms in road freight transport, conclusions can also be drawn for other modes of transportation and logistics services.

In Germany alone, the logistics industry's market volume was around 285 billion euros in 2019 (BVL, 2021). Accordingly, the market for digital logistics platforms is developing dynamically and offers a heterogeneous spectrum of services. This ranges from automated market price determination for logistics services based on artificial intelligence to transaction-centered freight exchanges that optimize the utilization of transport capacities by matching freight carriers and forwarders at the network level, to tendering platforms that increase process efficiency in the awarding of contracts for logistics services and thus reduce transaction costs. If logistics service providers continue to adhere to their established business models and neglect digital trends, there is a risk of losing competitiveness in the medium to long term. Since traditional logistics service providers face the challenge of dealing with future-oriented technologies in a competitive market environment and integrating new technologies into their business model, the logistics industry's digital platform landscape is highly relevant for both shippers and service providers. The range of services offered by the market for digital platforms cannot be clearly defined and delimited. Also, there is no meaningful overview of the provider structure. Platform users—i.e., shippers and logistics service providers—face the question of which platform is best suited with its range of services for specific performance features.

This article addresses this challenge and aims to segment the range of services offered by digital logistics platforms. This is the prerequisite for providing shippers, logistics service providers, platform operators, and investors with an overview of the market. For this purpose, a schematic approach to market segmentation of digital logistics platforms is derived using the methodology of a morphological box. The basis for this is the outline of trends in Logistics 4.0 to the evolution of digital platforms in logistics (Sect. 2). Subsequently, criteria for the segmentation of digital logistics platforms are defined for platform markets in general (Sect. 3), which form a basis for the morphological box. Section 4 focuses on describing transaction mechanisms between the different market players in the various market segments. The formation of market segments for digital logistics platforms opens the door to allocating corresponding business models.

2 Evolution of Digital Platforms in Logistics

2.1 Development Traits of the Platform Economy

By providing a corresponding digital infrastructure, digital platforms act as intermediaries between multiple actors and enable interactions between platform actors (BMWI, 2016). While bilateral business relationships—whether physical or virtual —can be associated with high transaction costs, the bundling of supply and demand on digital platforms, combined with standardized handling of interactions, offers the opportunity to make processes more efficient and thus reduce transaction costs for all actors (Haller & Wissing, 2018). The central challenge in two-sided markets is not necessarily the technical implementation (van Alstyne & Schrage, 2016), but rather the targeted addressing of market needs. For digital platforms, the generation of positive direct and indirect network effects is the critical success factor (Becker et al., 2019). These are defined by the fact that the benefit of a platform for its users increases directly with the number of other platform participants on both sides of the market. A freight exchange, for example, becomes more attractive for the individual carrier the more players simultaneously place loading space or loads on a platform, as more choices for load consolidation mean better optimization potential. Suppose additional economies of scale accompany the positive direct and indirect network effects. In that case, platforms can develop monopolistic tendencies at the expense of other platforms following the "winner takes it all principle" (Haucap,

2020). This circumstance has not yet been observed on the market, given various platforms in the logistics sector.

In the logistics sector, electronic freight exchanges emerged as early as the 1990s, which can be regarded as the "ancestors" of today's platforms in logistics. The technological design options have evolved over the last 20 years thanks to new basic technologies (Kress, 2018). Thanks to standardized processes, digital platforms aim at generating bundling effects and minimizing transaction costs for all actors. Since the trouble-free and efficient control of goods flows is at the heart of logistics activities, the establishment of digital platforms promises considerable potential, especially in logistics. A roughly sketched application from practice illustrates this: A digitally handled tendering process initially reduces the effort involved in the initial search process for potential service providers for shippers. As the tendering process progresses, both shippers and service providers benefit from efficient data exchange and information via the platform, thanks to standardized offer formats.

With regard to the selection process, shippers benefit from a more straightforward comparison of offers, ideally supported by analysis options on the platform, which enable an in-depth comparison of individual performance features. In this way, digital platforms also contribute to an increase in transparency in logistics. New basic technologies play a central role here, as they enable the creation of innovative service offerings and business models through appropriate linking (Klötzer & Pflaum, 2015). The industry is currently focusing on new market players entering the market with innovative services, given the diverse application potential in logistics and challenging established providers with their primarily ICT-driven business models. Logistics 4.0 is proving to be a vital driver of this development.

2.2 Megatrend Logistics 4.0

Benefiting from digitization, the provision of logistics services is now more than ever characterized by individuality, flexibility, and cooperation. This is accompanied by new communication and data exchange requirements, for example, to react proactively to deviations by ensuring real-time-based visibility across logistics chains. To ensure the smooth management of goods flows under these conditions, platforms are positioning themselves in favor of the market players by providing adequate services. Their extensive use of digital technologies such as Big Data, mobile and cloud computing, blockchain, or the application of artificial intelligence can help to cope with the increase in complexity (Winkelhaus & Grosse, 2020). These digital technologies form the foundation of the platform economy and are also a core component of what is known as Logistics 4.0. As a cross-cutting function for other business areas, Logistics 4.0 plays a central role in implementing Industry 4.0 by creating the necessary foundations (BDI, 2017).

Logistics 4.0 can be understood as digitally supported networking of value creation within and between companies (Stölzle & Burkhardt, 2016). The focus here is on real-time-based data use and interface-free communication within value creation networks to simplify coordination and accelerate information flow. The lack of timely and correct information transmission is currently a weak point, especially in cross-company logistics processes. It is often only possible to react to process deviations at concise notice because information on critical events is transmitted with a time delay. In view of the large number of ICT systems involved, the system-side connection via interfaces is the key to value creation networks in order to enable the flow of information between logistics systems in a secure and real-time-based manner. The transparency created by permanent visibility enables the implementation of adequate measures, thanks to early intervention options in ongoing processes, so that cross-company logistics processes become more flexible and their robustness increases. Since logistics service providers can now integrate themselves deeply into the value creation processes of their customers on the system side (Kersten et al., 2017), supplementary planning and analysis methods are indispensable in order to master the complexity in the provision of logistics services. Here, digital platforms can contribute to exploiting the opportunities of Logistics 4.0.

Strandhagen et al. (2017) assume that individual trends of Logistics 4.0 represent drivers for the transformation and emergence of new business models. Since the realization of further efficiency potentials at the level of individual players is becoming ever smaller, the focus is shifting to the higher-level network level in the light of Logistics 4.0. In this context, the emergence of 4PL service providers is a development trend toward digital logistics platforms. Neutral 4PL service providers serve the planning, integration, and control of a client's cross-company value creation activities (Saglietto, 2013) without using their own assets. For 4PL providers, the focus has always been on ICT-based optimization of customers' logistics systems. By commissioning suitable ("best of breed") logistics service providers in each case, 4PL service providers address a central objective of Logistics 4.0—the realization of efficiency gains at the network level. Digital logistics platforms can make a significant contribution to this. Through the cross-company integration of logistics processes via a platform that all players can access into a logistics solution, traditional interface problems of different TMS or ERP systems can be overcome, and processes simplified and partly automated. Thus, 4PL service providers and digital logistics platforms are united by their focus on cross-company integration, resulting in efficiency gains and reduced transaction costs for all players in the logistics chain. This places digital platforms in logistics at the center of the implementation of Logistics 4.0.

2.3 Development Paths of Digital Logistics Platforms

The considerations that have so far been driven more by concepts need to be compared with phenomena in logistics practice in order to identify the development paths of digital logistics platforms. The technological possibilities of digital platforms are said to have disruptive potential in transportation and logistics. Consequently, the discussion about digital logistics platforms and their establishment has gained momentum in recent years (Baron et al., 2017). Big Data Analytics is particularly relevant for improving the route and load space optimization performed by freight exchanges and digital freight forwarders in the transportation sector. The complementary use of artificial intelligence facilitates predictive analyses, such as forecasting transport prices on selected routes. Across all logistics services (see Sect. 3.1), the use of cloud and mobile computing enables access to data regardless of location. Accordingly, investments in Logistics 4.0 are increasing sharply. According to Riedl et al. (2018), between January 2012 and September 2017 alone, more than US$3.3 billion flowed into startups in the digital transportation and logistics sector. Among many platform companies, three groups of players can be identified, shaping the market for digital logistics platforms with different approaches (Obermaier & Mosch, 2019). First, digital technology companies with existing platform knowledge primarily from the B2C environment. Second, industry-established companies are driving digitization in order to survive on the market themselves. Thirdly, startups with new and often specialized service features.

The range of services on offer reveals various market trends. In the tradition of electronic freight exchanges, marketplaces as transaction platforms usually aim to generate efficiency benefits, for example, by optimizing route utilization. Tendering platforms already start in contracting services from customers to logistics service providers and aim to improve the transaction process, focusing on reducing transaction costs between the players. In recent years, digital freight forwarders have established themselves on the market by founding numerous startups, which position themselves in direct competition with traditional freight forwarders. In most cases, not equipped with their own assets, these platforms themselves access a network of transport companies made up of a large number of market players who themselves often operate only a few transport units. The example of the European market leader in freight exchanges, Timocom, can be used to show development paths over a longer time horizon. The company, which today has more than 135,000 users, was founded in 1997, and initially focused purely on an electronic freight exchange on the brokerage of cargo and freight space on the spot market, each posted for specific routes at a specific time. Today, digital freight exchanges have long since become an established way for logistics service providers to facilitate the cross-company optimization of transports. With the growing number of users, the range of services has expanded to include more than just the pure exchange function, which more than 20 years after its founding also includes the brokerage of warehouse locations. Besides, numerous other services have been established through big data analyses, such as a tool for calculating transport costs or a transport barometer, which shows the supply situation on the transport market via the ratio of freight and loading space capacities. In addition to the spot market, the contract market is also addressed so that recurring transports can be awarded via a tendering tool. Startups in the market usually pursue a radical technology focus and aim to use predictive analytics with the use of artificial intelligence and Big Data analytics. This tendency can be seen in all logistics objects, starting with full loads, partial loads, and general cargo.

Even though Rauen et al., (2018) expect the digital platform market to consolidate into a few large providers over the next few years, it is still highly fragmented in the logistics sector today. Dominant market players have not yet emerged (Obermaier & Mosch, 2019). In view of the high market dynamics due to newly emerging players and constantly evolving service offerings, many (potential) customers lack an overview of the market segments covered and the functioning of individual platforms. Whether shippers or logistics service providers—for users, the ideal platform's question is often (still) associated with question marks because no systematic, recognized clustering of offerings and market segments is available. Platform operators would also benefit from market segmentation in order to gain an overview of their positioning on the market and to be able to evaluate the range of services offered. Ultimately, financial investors should also have a great interest in forming comprehensive performance profiles of individual platforms to better assess the opportunities and risks of their investments.

3 Market Segmentation of Digital Logistics Platforms

Market segmentation requires criteria that can be used to distinguish digital logistics platforms' services from one another. Based on existing digital platform segmentation approaches in other areas, developing a framework geared explicitly to digital logistics platforms for their market segmentation is on the agenda. Initially, the focus will be on traditional logistics services, the quasi-corresponding object of the platforms from the real goods economy's perspective.

3.1 Segmentation of Logistics Services

Because of its cross-sectional nature and system-relevant function, logistics serves various industries, customer segments, and requirements. Accordingly, the logistics market is characterized by a significant heterogeneity of service features. Segmentation allows market players to gain a transparent overview of market segments by forming individual homogeneous submarkets. From the perspective of logistics service providers, this is a prerequisite for adequately addressing customer needs. Logistics service providers are not only in horizontal competition with other logistics service providers but also with their shipper customers, who can weigh up between in-house and third-party production of logistics services. Thus, this competitive situation represents both a particular feature and a challenge for market segmentation (Hofmann & Wessely, 2009).

In principle, various criteria are available for segmenting logistics services (Mathauer & Hofmann, 2020). For example, the overall market can be delineated by the type of transport mode (truck, rail, ship, air). The type of goods (e.g., pharmaceuticals) or a delimitation by logistics objects (general cargo, CEP, FTL...) represent further segmentation criteria. The segmentation of Kille and Schwemmer

(2012) offers an orientation to the services available in the market and distinguishes 13 different logistics segments. All approaches to segmenting logistics and freight markets in the literature have in common their sole focus on physical logistics services.

Platforms aim with their service promises at the efficient networking of supply and demand to reduce the transaction costs of the market players through bundling effects—as is the case with classic logistics service providers. In contrast to these, however, market access often differs in understanding its core service. While logistics service providers view their core service in terms of (physical) logistics service provision and develop market segments on this basis, platforms are fixated on their technological solutions, which are used as a basis for developing market segments. The service spectra and market segments of logistics platforms cannot be entirely derived based on logistics market segmentation. Therefore, this paper aims at integrating the service spectra of platforms as well. This increases the number of possible segmentation criteria. Consequently, a focused selection of individual suitable segmentation criteria for developing a framework is to be identified to segment the market of digital logistics platforms and reflect it by logistical service categories. This should result in an overview of the market segments in which digital logistics platforms are active, where overlaps may occur, and in which areas a service offering may still be lacking.

3.2 Segmentation Criteria for Digital Logistics Platforms

From the perspective of platform users and operators, segmentation approaches focus on a specific platform market aspect. Users are confronted with the challenge that it is often unclear which platform is suitable for which purpose and which services a platform addresses market segment. The identification of segmentation criteria specifically tailored to the digital logistics market provides a basis for this.

Since individual providers' enumeration is neither structured nor actionable, the formation of superordinate categories of the relevant service features may help distinguish or group providers from one another systematically. In principle, there are various approaches to this. A cross-industry look at other markets opens up the possibility of identifying segmentation logic and patterns that can be transferred to the market for digital logistics platforms. One approach to segmenting digital platforms is provided by Evans and Gawer (2016), who distinguish between generic platform types. These can be divided into two overarching approaches, which differ in how platforms place their services on the market. Accordingly, the design can be transaction-centric or data-centric. In the case of transaction platforms, the focus is on the function as an intermediary between two market sides.

The platform enables the realization of transactions by bringing together various players in a digital marketplace. In contrast, data-centric digital platforms are primarily concerned with data-based networking, whereby a (digital) ecosystem is to be created by linking complementary products. According to Evans and Gawer (2016), most digital platforms fall into transactional platform forms, accounting for around 90%. In addition to the three categories described above, digital platforms can also be evaluated and classified according to their degree of openness (van Alstyne et al., 2016). The more open a digital platform and its underlying infrastructure is to producers and customers, the more influence and scope for action the respective actors have in their actions. In an open platform, the platform operator exerts less control, which favors user numbers' growth.

In contrast, a closed approach can positively influence the quality of the offering through the platform operator's control. A pronounced technology focus often drives the business models of startups. In digital platform business models, a so-called basic technology usually represents the fundamental foundation for the market's solution's functionality. Individual base technologies such as cloud computing or artificial intelligence are defined as categories into which individual platforms are classified according to their dominant base technology. Thus, the type of technology represents a different approach to differentiating digital logistics platforms' service offerings (Schwemmer et al., 2020). In practice, it can be observed that cloud and mobile computing often form the basis of many platform operators. Individual technologies can also be combined. In principle, any number of new "technology categories" can be formed from the many possible technological combinations.

To map the market segments served by logistics platforms and to be able to distinguish individual platform forms from one another, the service spectra of the platforms must be taken into account, in addition to the logistics service categories. For users, the first question is what scope of services a platform offers. This can be very specifically geared to a niche or can also represent a complete service that, in addition to the core service, may also include other services such as real-time-based shipment tracking or payment processing. These practical questions about the range of services offered by a platform will be taken into account in the development of a framework. This framework is based on an overview of relevant segmentation criteria that are important for digital logistics platforms (see Fig. 1).

Various perspectives are incorporated into the criteria to view logistical service categories and platforms' functional structure. As classic criteria from the segmentation of freight transport markets, the distinction between the mode of transport and logistics object is central to the physical provision of services. With general cargo, partial, and full loads, and the highly demanding logistics objects of

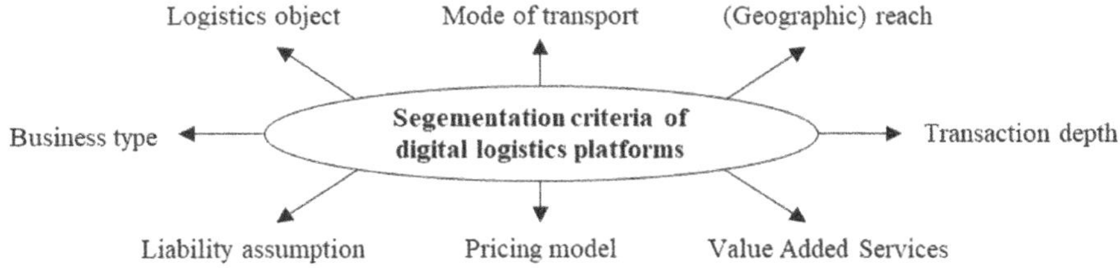

Fig. 1 Overview of relevant criteria for segmenting digital logistics platforms

dangerous goods and thermal freight on the one hand, and the various modes of transport, there are a wide variety of combination options to choose from. Concerning the reach of digital platforms, these can be differentiated according to their geographical scope. Since there is considerable scope for the functional design of a platform between supply and demand and positioning as a one-stop store, transactions via different platforms vary in terms of their transaction depth and the extent to which the platform provider assumes liability. The latter can be fully assumed, analogous to a traditional freight forwarder's performance, or completely excluded. This results not only in differences in the coverage of the type of business, which is geared to the spot or contract market, but also in the underlying pricing models for the user groups. The respective characteristics of the individual segmentation criteria are specified in Sect. 3.3 and summarized in a morphological box.

3.3 Framework for Market Segmentation of Digital Logistics Platforms

The segmentation of digital logistics platforms can be derived using a market-oriented framework, whereby individual market segments of digital logistics platforms can be identified and differentiated from one another. A morphological box is used as a methodological tool (Schawel & Billing, 2012). This creativity method is mainly used for the systematic analysis of complex problems. The core of the morphological box offers a multidimensional matrix. With the help of which the totality of a topic (in this case, the entire digital platform landscape in logistics) is broken down into partial aspects. This methodology is used to identify individual platforms' functional characteristics and then assign them to individual platform categories. Figure 2 shows the criteria with possible characteristics in each case.

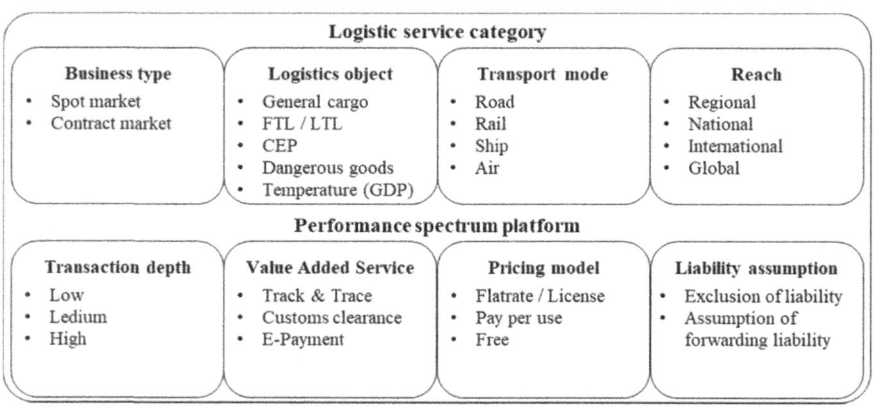

Fig. 2 Morphological box for market segmentation of digital logistics platforms

Using this predefined matrix structure, the specific configuration of any platform can be listed. Individual players can be clearly distinguished from one another. Patterns can be identified, from which, in turn, the market segments of digital logistics platforms can be derived. As an example, Fig. 3 shows the “matcher” and the “automator” with both terms chosen strikingly to highlight the respective platform pattern’s central function. Matchers are characterized by the fact that their core value to customers is networking with the other side of the market to optimize transportation resource utilization. Freight exchanges such as Timocom are typical representatives of this category. Digital freight forwarders, such as Instafreight and Sennder, mainly fall into the identified pattern of automation providers. Their range of services is geared to orders that are as standardized as possible in order to be able to automate the processing of orders as consistently as possible.

In contrast to matchers, digital freight forwarders appear on the market as liable freight forwarders and offer a distinctive range of services. They aim to be perceived by their customers as a one-stop store. They position themselves as an alternative to traditional forwarders in the spot market segments FTL and LTL, which tend to be standardized. Their pay-per-use pricing model is based on the classic order-based price offered by freight forwarders on the spot market. In contrast, matchers are characterized by a low transaction depth on the platform. Due to their ease of use and speed, the flat-rate pricing model fits well with the high frequency of use daily.

The schematic characterization of individual platforms based on the morphological box shows that digital platforms focus primarily on standardized logistics services that can be automated with algorithms’ support. Therefore, FTL/LTL and general cargo as logistics objects focus more on transaction-centric platforms than complex orders with customer-specific service adjustments. The more complex and customer-specific a service, the more likely platforms offer their added value in matching alone rather than in their function as a one-stop store. Gaps in the market segments served are revealed accordingly in the case of complete services on the contract market. At present, platforms do not act as automator here. So far, this market segment has been addressed primarily by process-supporting bidding

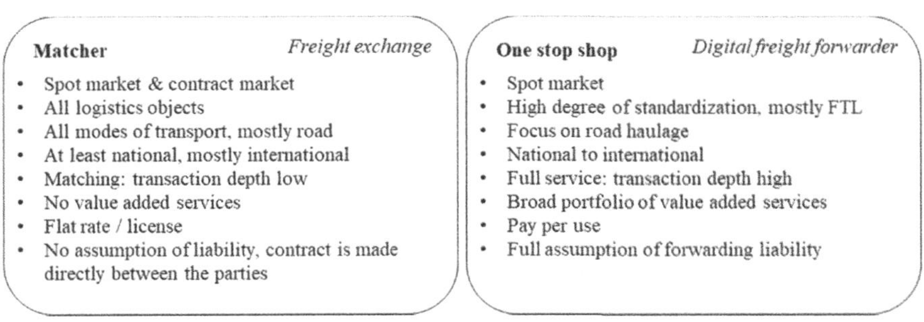

Fig. 3 Identified patterns in the segmentation of digital logistics platforms

platforms. The focus from the customer's point of view is less on matching and more on the efficient awarding of contracts to a selected group of providers. Nevertheless, the intensity of competition among providers is also pronounced here, as shown in Sect. 4. Here, we will first examine the individual market players and consider which transaction mechanisms are used to bring together supply and demand on platforms.

4 Transactions on Digital Logistics Platforms

4.1 Market Players and Transaction Mechanisms

The following concretization refers to the transport sector, where the demand side initially includes shippers who do not operate their fleet. Freight forwarders also buy transport capacity on the market when their fleet is at capacity. Also, it can make sense for fleet operators not to transport individual shipments themselves in order to prevent underutilized tours. The pronounced networking of players via digital platforms favors business models that rely on an asset-light approach, i.e., largely do without their own transport units. Digital freight forwarders mainly pursue this approach and schedule all loads via a network of freight carriers, who realize the physical handling of transports as cooperation partners. The market segment of one-stop stores is fed by demand from shippers. Primarily, it is shippers without their fleet directly addressed by the market segment of one-stop stores. On the other hand, it can be observed that forwarders and freight carriers use freight exchanges, in particular as matchers, for internal optimization. Thanks to better networking of the supply side with the demand side, these offer the added value of acting as a neutral intermediary, increasing route utilization, or avoiding underutilized routes.

Transaction mechanisms

The configuration patterns of individual platform types identified based on the morphological box show that platform-related transactions differ significantly in terms of scope of services and transaction depth. The matching of demanded and offered services is a core component of a platform. Marketplaces also generally offer few or no additional functions. Since they primarily offer users a platform for buying and selling freight capacity without directly negotiating contracts between shippers and carriers or directly providing freight capacity, the transaction depth on marketplaces is low. The primary value proposition of matchers is the generation of direct and indirect network effects, which is achieved by maximizing the number of users on both sides of the market, rather than competitive advantages, by optimizing internal activities (Becker et al., 2019). However, the concrete design of service offerings and how they come about is the users' responsibility.

In contrast to the one-stop store of digital freight forwarders, the matcher primarily offers an infrastructure. This includes the provision of a functioning digital marketplace where users can post and view offers. Users communicate bilaterally and not with the platform. Accordingly, the depth of transactions is low and, on the demand side, often limited solely to targeted searches.

The process-oriented support offered by tendering platforms to shippers and service providers in negotiating transport or contract logistics agreements makes it clear that the scope of services does not have to be limited to the physical provision of services. Within the given platform governance, users have flexibility in processing tenders and can configure services individually. By focusing on handling bidding processes, pure bidding platforms cover the specific aspect of contract award, which cannot be fully mapped digitally in view of the often high degree of individualization of value-added services. Tenders via platforms can only be processed via a defined standard if, as in FTL or LTL, standardized services and load carriers are involved. Suppose the focus is on high customer specificity and value-added services, on the other hand. In that case, a platform takes on a toolbox and communicative interface for the exchange of tender documents and offers.

In contrast, the one-stop store market segment in the area of transport services functions as a central contact point for shippers to handle all transport-related services. The demanders communicate exclusively with the platform itself and use the platform's standard process to book transport capacities. The contract is therefore concluded directly with the platform, which acts as the liable forwarder. Digital freight forwarders guarantee delivery fulfillment and act actively by purchasing offered capacities on the market. The process also involves little effort for the offering carriers, as they automatically receive calculated prices that they can accept or reject.

4.2 Attractiveness of Digital Logistics Platforms from the Perspective of Market Players

The attractiveness of digital logistics platforms can be derived from the challenges in individual market segments. What are these challenges, and what added value do platforms promise?

In the competitive transport market, productivity and quality improvements are seen as crucial levers for consolidating a company's own market position and meeting the requirements of new and existing customers in the future. In view of the substitutability of individual players for standardized services in the area of general cargo and freight transport and low barriers to market entry, the existing cost and margin pressure are intensifying further. These circumstances, combined with the minimal scope for upward price adjustments, are driving digitization in the industry. All market players are united by the goal of planning and managing logistics activities as efficiently and cost-effectively as possible.

On the supply side, freight forwarders and transport companies hope to increase their route utilization using matcher platforms. Analogous to the function of freight forwarding cooperatives, capacity utilization is increased by consolidating loads across companies. They can achieve this by searching for cargo or loading space on specific routes involving more players than just their network, thanks to an increased virtual reach. Shippers without their own fleet are partly targeting other value propositions. On the one hand, the handling of logistics services is in many cases associated with a high level of coordination effort because few processes run as quickly and automatically as booking a flight or an overnight stay on an electronic booking portal. Irrespective of the actual costs for the provision of logistics services, the reduction of process-related transaction costs during the commissioning process is, therefore, already a service promise of a platform desired by shippers. For example, in tender processes, the time-intensive handling on both sides of the market can be simplified if standards are clearly defined on platforms and templates are used. By eliminating or at least reducing bilateral coordination, business transactions can be processed more efficiently, thus reducing transaction costs.

In addition, platforms help to increase market transparency. In view of the largely homogeneous services in the transport market, individual providers' prices become comparable for shippers. In view of the previous lack of insight into price formation, price transparency allows shippers to compare their own logistics costs with market prices and consequently, to work toward a price reduction if necessary. However, platforms are not perceived as a threat on the supply side per se either. Many forwarders and carriers are proactively tapping into platforms and appreciate the flexibility to utilize free capacities as needed at the highest possible market price. Thanks to the sizeable virtual reach, digital platforms can also open up new customer segments.

In the long term, platforms offer the potential to connect all players centrally to their own platform, eliminating the need for customer-specific adaptations in the area of ICT systems, since the availability of data in the required format is guaranteed. The fact that digital logistics platforms, with their possible consequences—increased market transparency, cost, and transaction cost reductions—address a market need is demonstrated not only by their attractiveness from the point of view of the market players but also by the intense competition digital platform market.

4.3 Competition of Digital Logistics Platforms

The platform landscape's dynamic development in logistics points to pronounced competition in the industry taking place on two levels: First, between platforms and established logistics service providers, and second, among the platforms themselves, directly depending on the market segments served. If individual platforms cover different specific market segments, the various providers can coexist in a competitively neutral manner without addressing the same user groups. The situation is different when market segments overlap, and there is a high level of competition between providers, with individual platforms courting the same market participants. The intensity of competition is currently most significant in those market segments where logistics services are standardized. In fragmented road freight transport, this applies to full loads, which can be dispatched to carriers with little effort. In the last few years, numerous technology-driven providers have positioned themselves in this area with Instafreight and Sennder, which have set themselves the goal of fully automated order processing. Figure 4 illustrates the typical configuration pattern of digital freight forwarders for standardized service provision. Based on their comprehensive range of technological services, the focus is increasingly broadening: digital freight forwarders are also increasingly entering the market for partial loads. However, the greater complexity of route planning has so far been a hurdle for automated dispatching based on artificial intelligence. It can also be assumed that competition will remain intense in the market segment for standardized tendering processes, not only because new providers are continuing to enter the market but also because of strategic considerations on the part of shippers not dependent on a single platform. This also tends to point to a broad spectrum of providers in the long term.

The capacity utilization potential available for improving route utilization in road freight transport reflects the generally high intensity of competition in the road mode of transport. In particular, matcher platforms compete across all logistics objects, from general cargo to hazardous goods to full loads. Among these freight exchanges, there is the most significant overlap, as their central resource is the provision of infrastructure, which aims to link companies. Since the transaction depth of matchers is low, a wide variety of logistical service categories can be served with little additional effort in principle. Individual providers are likely to aim at permanently expanding their range of services and targeting new market segments.

With Timocom, for example, a dominant player has emerged, which means that the barriers to market entry for new competitors are now higher. It is, nevertheless, questionable whether the consolidation of providers observed in other sectors will be possible to the same extent in the logistics market. Customer requirements are less standardized overall, and the physical provision of services is much more

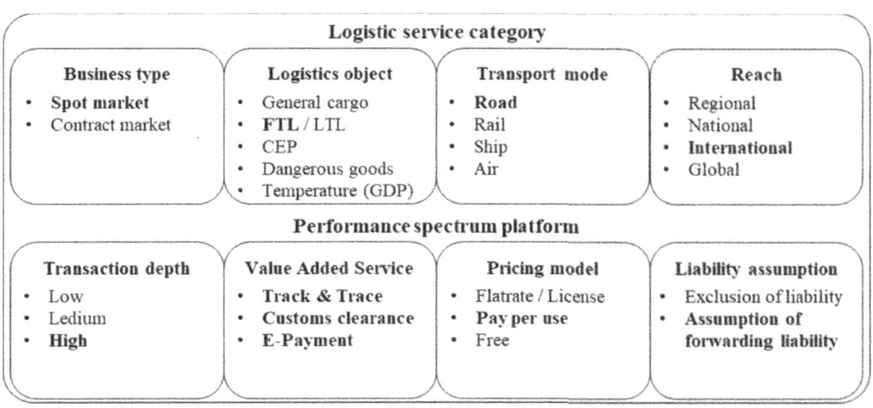

Fig. 4 Typical configuration pattern of a digital forwarder based on the morphological box

customer-specific. Because of the broad range of services on the digital platform market, the question arises as to which business models will prevail among logistics platforms in the long term.

5 Business Models of Digital Logistics Platforms—Quo Vadis?

Platforms create the necessary foundation for implementing digital business models and are characterized by the fact that they fundamentally offer the structure to realize significant scale economies. For digital logistics platforms to establish themselves successfully in their market segments in the long term, their activities must be based on a sustainable business model (Gassmann et al., 2017). Given the opportunities offered by digitization, it can be assumed across all industries that value creation will increasingly be generated via digital business models and will comprise physical and digital value creation components in an integrative manner. The right incentives must be set to link the customer groups with each other and thus trigger positive network effects.

The market segmentation patterns identified as examples show that digital logistics platforms serve an overall heterogeneous market. To do this, they draw on different business models, whereby the fundamental differences between individual market segments must be taken into account. While the spot market primarily facilitates transactions of standardized services and is primarily tailored to the freight forwarding market, the contract market focuses on establishing long-term business relationships. The transaction volumes here are much higher than on the spot market due to the long terms of several weeks to years. Accordingly, supplier quality assessment becomes even more critical for the customer before the contract is awarded. Particularly in the outsourcing of contract logistics services, the complexity of services connected with value-added services can be high, which is why the transaction depth in tenders via digital logistics platforms is significantly higher than on the spot market. For both shippers and logistics service providers, standardized platform structures open up a field of tension in which platforms must position themselves.

On the one hand, the high degree of standardization of a platform limits the possibility of creating individual offers, but on the other hand, services and prices become more comparable. In the case of less complex services without individual service adjustments, such as the shipment of a general cargo consignment, automated processing is desirable from the market players' point of view. Simultaneously, a higher degree of interaction is required for complex tenders, which can be supported by functions such as chats to resolve ambiguities. Since invitations to tender are often addressed to a selected group of recipients, filter functions should be provided to enable an invitation to tender to be issued to the public or closed. System-side connections to TMS or ERP via interfaces are of great benefit due to their use on a daily basis, especially in the spot market segment on marketplaces.

However, they are rarely the focus of decision-making criteria in tenders. Even if tenders are due every several months to several years, the tender contents are usually similar, so they use templates to reduce the workload.

When deciding for or against a specific platform, users also have to consider the associated costs to weigh the possible benefits against the costs. Freight exchanges usually generate their revenue through a license fee. Timocom, for example, charges a fixed monthly fee for the use of the platform and charges a fee per user. Another business model is being established by digital freight forwarders who position themselves to their customers as one-stop stores and, like traditional freight forwarders, offer logistics services as a core service while also acting as liable freight forwarders. Compared to traditional forwarders, they promise low transaction costs as added value. On the other hand, their high level of process automation based on the use of artificial intelligence should reduce the internal administrative effort so that digital freight forwarders can operate more cost-effectively on the market. Current business models are opening up a digital platform market in logistics, which is being actively developed by some new players targeting multiple market segments and expanding their range of services to gain market share (Wyman, 2020). Other players operate (initially) in the niche and successively expand their range of services. Even though the business models of digital logistics platforms, like all other business models, are subject to dynamic market conditions, two development strands can be identified in the platform landscape with cooperative and competitive platform forms from traditional logistics service providers' perspectives. The new platform companies founded in recent years are predominantly active in using artificial intelligence and Big Data to achieve a high level of process automation and forecast how the supply and demand markets will develop through predictive analyses. In this context, the question must be raised as to whether previous business models have not been driven too much by a resource-based approach? It is also an open question of how the new players will position themselves in the logistics market and the other market players in the long term. Future analysis and research on this topic should aim to identify a roadmap to show the digital platform landscape developments in the coming years.

References

Baron, R., Zintel, M., Zieries, M. & Mikulla, D. (2017). *Digital platforms in freight transportation: A true industry disruptor.* Frankfurt, Arthur D. Little.

Becker, W., Eierle, B., Fliaster, A., Ivens, B., Leischnig, A., Pflaum, A., et al. (2019). *Geschäftsmodelle in der digitalen Welt. Strategien, Prozesse und Praxiserfahrungen.* Wiesbaden, Springer Fachmedien.

BDI. (2017). Herausforderungen und Perspektiven für die Logistik, (2025). *Unter welchen Vorzeichen stehen die Veränderungen in der Industrie und in der Logistik in Deutschland?* Bundesverband der deutschen Industrie.

BMWi. (2016). *Grünbuch Digitale Plattformen.* Bundesministerium für Wirtschaft und Energie.

BVL. (2021). *Logistikumsatz und Beschäftigung—Bedeutung der Logistik für die deutsche Wirtschaft.* Retrieved from https://www.bvl.de/service/zahlen-daten-fakten/umsatz-und-beschaeftigung.

Evans, P. & Gawer, A. (2016). *The rise of the platform enterprise: A global survey*. Retrieved from https://www.thecge.net/app/uploads/2016/01/PDF-WEB-Platform-Survey_01_12.pdf.
Gassmann, O., Frankenberger, K., & Choudury, M. (2020). *The business model navigator: The strategies behind the most successful companies*. Pearson.
Haller, S., & Wissing, C. (2018). Normstrategien für das Service Business Development zur Berücksichtigung digitaler Plattformen in der Wertschöpfung. In M. Bruhn & K. Hadwich (Eds.), *Service business development* (pp. 167–188). Wiesbaden.
Haucap, J. (2020). Plattformökonomie: Neue Wettbewerbsregeln—Renaissance der Missbrauchsaufsicht. *Wirtschaftsdienst, 100*(13), 20–29.
Hofmann, E., & Wessely, P. (2009). Wie lassen sich Logistik- und Güterverkehrsmärkte segmentieren? *Internationales Verkehrswesen, 61*(11), 424–429.
Kersten, W., Seiter, M., von See, B., Hackius, N. & Maurer, T. (2017). *Trends and strategies in logistics and supply chain management: Digital transformation opportunities*. Hamburg, DVV Media Group.
Kille, C. & Schwemmer, M. (2012). *Challenges 2012—Prognosen, Hochrechnungen und Finanzkennzahlen zum Logistikmarkt*. Erlangen, Hamburg: Fraunhofer SCS, DVV Media Group.
Klötzer, C. & Pflaum, A. (2015). Cyber-physical systems as the technical foundation for problem solutions in manufacturing, logistics and supply chain management. In *5th International Conference on the Internet of Things*. Seoul, South Korea.
Kress, P. (2018). *The impact of digital technologies on the value creation of companies in the manufacturing industry*. Fraunhofer.
Mathauer, M., & Hofmann, E. (2020). *Dezentrale Technologien in der Supply Chain—Vertiefungsstudie Logistikmarkt Schweiz*. Universität St.
Obermaier, R. & Mosch, P. (2019). Digitale Plattformen—Klassifizierung, ökonomische Wirkungslogik und Anwendungsfälle in einer Industrie 4.0. In: R. Obermaier (Ed.). *Handbuch Industrie 4.0 und Digitale Transformation* (S. 379–417). Wiesbaden, Springer Gabler.
Rauen, H., Glatz, R., Schnittler, V., Peters, K., Schorak, M. H., Zollenkop, M., Lüers, M. & Becker, L. (2018). *Plattformökonomie im Maschinenbau: Herausforderungen—Chancen—Handlungsoptionen*. Frankfurt, VDMA.
Riedl, J., Jentzsch, A., Melcher, N. C., Gildemeister, J., Schellong, D., Höfer, C. & Wiedenhoff, P. (2018). *Why road freight needs to go digital—fast*. Retrieved from https://www.bcg.com/pl-pl/publications/2018/why-road-freight-needs-go-digital-fast.
Saglietto, L. (2013). Towards a classification of fourth party logistics (4PL). *Universal Journal of Industrial and Business Management, 1*(3), 104–116.
Schawel, C., & Billing, F. (2012). *Top 100 management tools*. Springer Gabler.
Schwemmer, M., Schmitt, M., Müller, M., & Schwinning, S. (2020). Einflussbereich Neue Geschäftsmodelle und Logistikansätze. In C. Kille & M. Meissner (Eds.), *Logistik 2020 Struktur- und Wertewandel als Herausforderung* (pp. 64–72). Hamburg.
Stölzle, W. & Burkhardt, J. (2016). Thesen zu Logistik 4.0. In: O. Gassmann & P. Sutter (Eds.). *Digitale Transformation im Unternehmen gestalten, Geschäftsmodelle—Erfolgsfaktoren—Fallstudien* (pp. 59–64). München, Hanser.
Strandhagen, J. O., Vallandingham, L. R., Fragapane, G., Strandhagen, J. W., Stangeland, A. B. H. & Sharma, N. (2017). Logistics 4.0 and emerging sustainable business models. *Advances in Manufacturing, 5*(4), 359–369.
Sucky, E., & Asdecker, B. (2019). Digitale Transformation der Logistik—Wie verändern neue Geschäftsmodelle die Branche? In W. Becker, B. Eierle, A. Fliaster, B. Ivens, A. Leischnig, A. Pflaum, & E. Sucky (Eds.), *Geschäftsmodelle in der digitalen Welt* (pp. 191–212). Wiesbaden.
van Alstyne, M. W., Parker, G. G., & Choudary, S. P. (2016). Plattform statt pipeline. Harvard business. *Manager, 6*, 23–33.
van Alstyne, M. W. & Schrage, M. (2016). The best platforms are more than matchmakers. *Harvard business review*, 94(7/8).

Wyman, O. (2020). *Digitale Logistik: Verdrängungskampf um Marktanteile*. Retrieved from https://www.oliverwyman.ch/ch-de/Pressemitteilungen/pressemitteilungen/digitale-logistik-verdraengungskampf-um-marktanteile.html.

Winkelhaus, S. & Grosse, E. H. (2020). Logistics 4.0: A systematic review towards a new logistics system. *International Journal of Production Research*, *58*(1), 18–43.

Industry 4.0 Digital Platforms: Collaborative Business Models for SMEs

Nikolai Kazantsev and Ingo Martens

Abstract

Digital platforms interconnect small and medium-sized enterprises (SMEs) to facilitate their demand-driven collaboration for tendering and manufacture, which calls for changes in their business models. We define what a collaborative business model is in the context of SME manufacturing, layout aviation, and automotive collaborative business models developed during the EU-funded project DIGICOR (2016–2019) and generalize the collaborative business model for the 'platform of platforms' to support the development of Industry 4.0 in the European Union. In particular, this model supports SMEs working in 'lot size of one' and circular economy manufacturing.

1 Introduction

Industry 4.0 is a revolutionary paradigm to improve the productivity of industrial SME clusters in terms of quality, time, cost, and flexibility, as well as human and machine interaction (Mittal et al., 2020). The implementation of the concept is promising to enable demand-driven collaborations between suppliers of various sizes to respond to fast-changing market needs, ever shorter product lifecycles, and 'lot size of one' manufacturing (Kazantsev et al., 2018). Although SME suppliers play an essential role in industrial value creation, they often lack the skills and

N. Kazantsev (✉)
Alliance Manchester Business School, The University of Manchester, Oxford Rd, Manchester M13 9PL, UK
e-mail: nikolai.kazantsev@postgrad.manchester.ac.uk

I. Martens
HANSE Aerospace, Gotenstraße 12, 20097 Hamburg, Germany

K.-I. Voigt and J. M. Müller (eds.), *Digital Business Models in Industrial Ecosystems*, Future of Business and Finance, https://doi.org/10.1007/978-3-030-82003-9_8

resources to enable digital tools and to use them by undertaking new manufacture orders (Horváth & Szabó, 2019; Moeuf et al., 2020). Currently, SMEs expect a lower impact through Industry 4.0 and perceiving the concept as more beneficial for larger enterprises (Müller & Voigt, 2018; Sahi et al., 2020).

The lack of organizational and managerial support drives the need for SMEs to work collaboratively and to develop business value together. By working collaboratively, SMEs may better utilize their capabilities and explore new opportunities to make profits (Moeuf et al., 2020; Sahi et al., 2020). At the same time, supra-national bodies such as European Union and Original Equipment Manufacturers (OEMs), such as Airbus, invest in digital platforms which automate the roles for inter-organizational facilitation, as usually taken by (Tier-1) system suppliers. These platforms enable interactions between two or more sides (de Oliveira & Cortimiglia, 2017; Hagiu & Wright, 2015). In manufacturing, multi-sided platforms interconnect suppliers and customers, which enables their network interaction (Müller, 2019). From the business perspective, a digital platform in manufacturing can be defined as

1. an open, participative infrastructure with governance conditions (Parker et al., 2016).
2. an environment provided by an intermediary to facilitate users' interactions with each other (Hagiu & Wright, 2015).
3. a business on the exchange between two or more interdependent groups, usually consumers and producers (Moazed, 2016; de Oliveira & Cortimiglia, 2017; Hagiu & Wright, 2015; Müller, 2019).

Digital platforms are expected to have a multitude of potential for SMEs (Müller, 2019; Müller et al., 2020a). Once established, these platforms force SME production process redesign by supporting the formation and execution of *collaborative business models* (Müller et al., 2018; Veile et al., 2020). These are characterized by the altered business partners cooperation, new organizational forms, and novel market environments, which imply the growth of the platform ecosystem (Schmidt et al., 2020). At the same time, the concept of a collaborative business model is still vague, and there is a lack of examples and no consensus regarding its definition (Al-Debei et al., 2008; Gassmann et al., 2013; Ibarra et al., 2018; Müller et al., 2016).

Figure 1 depicts the key in a digital platform ecosystem: producers, consumers, providers, and an owner.

The aim of this chapter is to define a collaborative business model for SME, to present the earlier collaborative business models in aviation and automotive manufacturing developed during the project DIGICOR (2016–2019), and to generalize a collaborative business model for Industry 4.0 Platform of Platforms in the European Union.

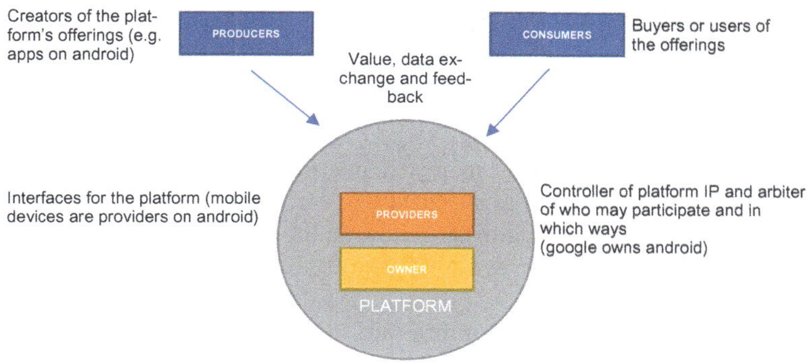

Fig. 1 The players in a platform ecosystem (adapted from (VanAlstyne et al., 2016))

2 Digital Manufacturing Platforms

Currently, many manufacturing firms have taken steps toward collaborative work and joined platforms (Constantinides et al., 2018; Huber et al., 2017). In contrast to traditional downstream contracting in a supply chain, in digital platforms firms are held together through formal contracting and/or mutual dependency to collaboratively deliver work by a technology-enabled environment (Gawer & Cusumano, 2014; Hein et al., 2020). Digital platforms may enable an ecosystem (Baines et al., 2007), where the value is co-created, but captured separately (Jacobides et al., 2018), but a broader digital ecosystem may also embrace multiple digital platforms (Adner, 2016).

Digital platforms provide an environment for information sharing and interconnection, which is seen as a central prerequisite to SME participation in Industry 4.0 (Kagermann et al., 2013; Müller et al., 2020b). For instance, collaborative condition monitoring (CCM)[1] enables network participants to increase the service life of machines, by pulling their transactional data on digital platforms and running correlation and AI data analysis. Such multilateral cooperation makes partners from competitors, grows the ecosystem, and enables collaborative business models, giving access to more jobs, mutual learning, and product mass personalization. Still, a majority of business models developed for collaborative, network-based work focus on a focal firm as a single actor (Palo & Tähtinen, 2013). Collaborative business models for SMEs should allow to better explore platform-driven markets, benefit from demand-driven collaborations (Doganova & Eyquem-Renault, 2009;

[1]Plattform Industrie 4.0—Collaborative data-driven business models (plattform-i40.de) (accessed 30.05.2021).

Kazantsev et al., 2018), and comprise together a coherent solution (Palo & Tähtinen, 2013). Therefore, a design for a collaborative business model is critical (Morris et al., 2005; Zott et al., 2011). In order to define a collaborative business model, we inherit from two definitions:

1. '[a business model is] a way to match internal resources of organizations to external opportunities (Zott et al., 2011).
2. '[a business model is] the rationale of how an organization creates, delivers, and captures value (Osterwalder & Pigneur, 2010, p. 14).

In digital manufacturing, resources are SME production capabilities and capacities. The external opportunities are large manufacturing orders often disseminated on the procurement portals of OEMs. The collaborative business model stems from composing capabilities and capacities of SMEs in demand-driven virtual organizations (Afsarmanesh & Camarinha-Matos, 2007), which could be quickly proposed on digital platforms due to automated order decomposition and matchmaking (Cisneros-Cabrera et al., 2021). Following the need to revise this definition in the platform-enabled context of digital manufacturing, we define a collaborative business model as follows:

A collaborative business model presents a rationale of how two or more organizations [SMEs] jointly create and deliver a Value [i.e. by composing their capabilities to match the manufacturing request from the OEM] and capture this Value, by diving it between the partners [e.g. according to its share in the service provided].

This paper continues with the description of an EU-funded project, which has enabled this definition and produced examples of collaborative business models (a) when a digital platform enables an ecosystem (Baines et al., 2007), and (b) where an ecosystem embraces multiple digital platforms (Adner, 2016).

3 EU-Funded Project DIGICOR

DIGICOR (Digital Agile Collaboration Across Supply Chains) provides a collaboration platform and tools for European companies to create and coordinate collaborative networks across the value chain.[2] The platform reduces the burden to set up production networks and collaboration between SMEs,[3] by shortening the time to jointly respond to business opportunities and to enter supply chains of OEMs. In DIGICOR, manufacturers create calls for tendering, disseminate over the platform, and expect collaborative supplier bids (Cisneros-Cabrera et al., 2021). The digital platform embraces several subscriptions based on costs for access, use of tools, duration of access, number of participations in tenders, access to standardized

[2]https://www.digicor-project.eu/ (accessed 1 April 2021).

[3]D1.3: Service Concept & Business Model, vf-OS Document Template (https://www.filesusr.com) (accessed 30 May 2021).

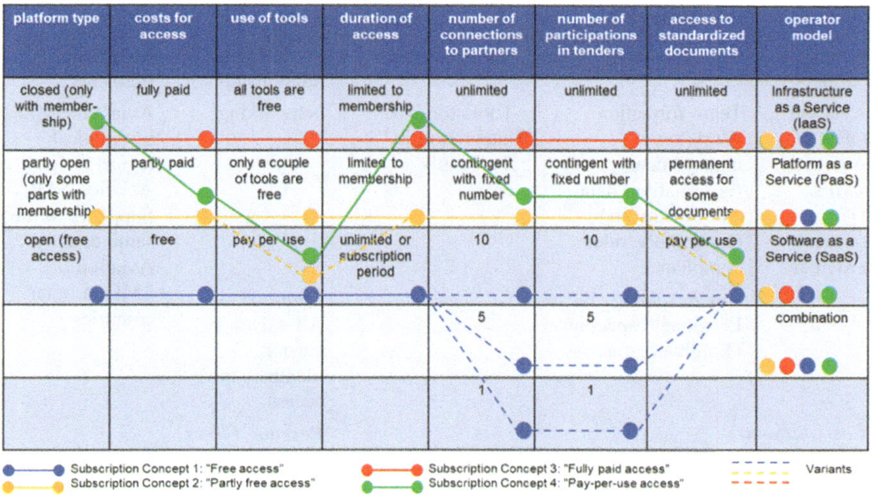

Fig. 2 Subscription concept scenarios

documents, and operator model. The main scenarios are (1) Free access; (2) Partly free access; (3) Fully paid access; (4) Pay-per-use access (Fig. 2), cf. Fig. 2.

4 Collaborative Business Models in DIGICOR

While a collaborative business model in aviation represents the sample of a digital platform enabling an ecosystem (Baines et al., 2007), the collaborative business model in the automotive industry is the case of a broader digital ecosystem that embraces multiple digital platforms (Adner, 2016). Following Osterwalder Canvas (Osterwalder, 2004; Osterwalder & Pigneur, 2010), we describe these collaborative business models using 9 areas: platform partners, activities, resources, value creation, cost structure, customer relationship, channels, customer segments, and revenue streams.

4.1 Aviation Business Model—Digital Platform Enabling an Ecosystem

Highly customized aircraft products require specific solutions provided by small but innovative SMEs. The customized aircraft must be designed and produced in a very short time, which typically requires a demand-driven supply network. To this end, the OEM, such as Airbus and their SMEs, needs digital platforms to simplify the setup and management of collaborative production, since extensive risk-sharing

Table 1 Collaborative business model in the aviation industry

Key partners	Key activities	Value creation	Customer relationship	Customer segments
Aviation OEM Aviation SMEs IT service providers	Team formation Workflow management (information, data and documents) Governance rules compliance	Tools for SME integration in the supply chains	Networking	Aviation SMEs in the local region Aviation SMEs Suppliers in the same country Aviation SMEsin other countries
	Key Resources Personnel capacities IT infrastructure		*Channels* All existing cluster members have access	
Costs Structure			*Revenue Flows*	
Platform hosting, maintenance and operation customer hotline support			Subscription model (a fixed or variable annual membership fee, which depends on the size of the company)	

requirements, complex procurement, and collaboration procedures, rules, and diversity of IT systems create strong barriers for SMEs to become a first-tier supplier of those companies (Table 1).

4.2 Automotive Business Model: Digital Ecosystem Embraces Multiple Digital Platforms

The regional automotive manufacturing ecosystem embraces many portals and forums, which are competing against each other to provide the right type of services. Companies in such a cluster are driven by maximizing Overall Equipment Effectiveness (facilities, time, and material) and increasing performance by data-driven analytics. A collaboration facilitator is making profits from the successful winning of tenders by members of the various forums, and the percentage payment would be negotiated from the outset of project engagement. A collaborative business model must enable services to be accessible for SMEs distributed across several platforms (supply side of an ecosystem) so that it increases chances for SMEs to match with business opportunities. Table 2 shows the business canvas to justify the use of services to enhance the product offering, where the focus is on providing shop-floor tools to manufacturing companies and ultimately offering services to the community.

Table 2 Collaborative business model in the automotive domain

Key partners	Key activities	Value creation	Customer relationship	Customer segments
OEMs Automotive SMEs IT service providers Exisitng digital platforms	Provision of cloud—based services	Manufacturing toolkit Collaboration facilitation Data-driven collaboration support	Networking	Launch: Automotive SMEs Thereafter: aviation, shipping and broader manufacturing
	Key Resources Algorithms to interpret/ find trends Domain knowledge, expertise		*Channels* Strategic partnership with machine providers Industry portals Web adds	
Costs Structure			*Revenue Flows*	
Data is not available			Initial trails for free, pay upon demonstrated success After initial customers, no free trialsAfter initial customers, no free trials	

5 Collaborative Business Model for Platform of Platforms

The European Factory Foundation[4] is an association that encourages the adoption of digital solutions from the owned digital platform[5] to promote interoperability across the digital systems and industrial platforms through a common, collaborative, and interoperable framework. The EFPF platform interlinks digital manufacturing platforms, smart factory tools, and Industry 4.0 concepts to realize and support a connected and federated smart factory ecosystem of the European Union. The platform is offered to users through a unified EFPF Portal with value-added features to hide the complexity of dealing with different platform and solution providers. At the moment, the business model for EFPF is being shaped by two additional cases of collaborative value creation.

Case 1: Lot Size One in Furniture Manufacturing:

The production of lot size of one products requires the transformation of conventional supply chains to enable partner search and task assignment for a specific project, monitoring and coordination of manufacturing, and real-time supply and delivery planning. New customer channels, such as hospitality industry, require an integral transparent service of furnishing and decoration. EFPF is expected to support this case in the collaborative business model.

[4]https://efactoryfoundation.org/ (accessed 09.05.2021).

[5]https://www.efpf.org (accessed 09.05.2021).

Table 3 Collaborative business model for the 'platform of platforms'

Key partners	Key activities	Value creation	Customer relationship	Customer segments
OEMs from all industries SMEs from all industries App providers Sustainability experts Organisation for Economic Co-operation and Development European Union	Provision of cloud manufacturing services *Key Resources* Data interoperability infrastructure Services for: Collaboration formation, IPR Compliance and fovernance rules enforcement	Full stack of cloud manufac-turing tools SME networking and collaboration tools	Networking *Channels* Industrial value chains Circular economy projects	Test: Use cases of EFPF in aerospace, automotive, furniture and circular economy Launch: EU-based SMEs from any industry Thereafter: industrial SMEs from any country
Costs Structure			*Revenue Flows*	
Data is not available			Data is not available	

Case 2: Agile Supply Networks in Circular Economy:

Waste tracking, tracing functionality, and zero lag in material transition phases are new requirements behind circular economy trends for EU-based SMEs. Therefore, companies require services for negotiating waste collection, management, and purchase-back of the processed/recycled material by the manufacturing companies. Multi-sided manufacturing marketplace could enable new business opportunities that enable SMEs to take part in closed-loop supply chain activities. EFPF is expected to support this case in the collaborative business model.

Table 3 visualizes the business canvas of the collaborative model of SMEs working on the platform of platforms.

6 Conclusion

This chapter presented business models for collaborative tendering and manufacture used in the EU-funded project DIGICOR. We defined a collaborative business model, presented collaborative business models in the aviation and automotive sectors, and generalized a collaborative business model for the platform of platforms which is currently built in the EU to support the expansion of Industry 4.0. Further work is needed to specialize the generalized model.

References

Adner, R. (2016). Ecosystem as structure: An actionable construct for strategy. *Journal of Management, 43*(1), 39–58.

Afsarmanesh, H., & Camarinha-Matos, L. M. (2007). Towards a semi-typology for Virtual Organization Breeding Environments. *IFAC Proceedings Volumes (IFAC-PapersOnline), 8*(1), 43–48.

Al-Debei, M. M., El-Haddadeh, R., & Avison, D. (2008). Defining the business model in the new world of digital business. In *14th Americas Conference on Information Systems*. Toronto.

Baines, T. S., Lightfoot, H. W., Evans, S., Neely, A., Greenough, R., Peppard, J., Roy, R., Shehab, E., Braganza, A., Tiwari, A., Alcock, J. R., Angus, J. P., Basti, M., Cousens, A., Irving, P., Johnson, M., Kingston, J., Lockett, H., Martinez, V., & Wilson, H. (2007). State-of-the-art in product-service systems. *Proceedings of the Institution of Mechanical Engineers, Part b: Journal of Engineering Manufacture, 221*(10), 1543–1552.

Cisneros-Cabrera, S., Pishchulov, G., Sampaio, P., Mehandjiev, N., Liu, Z., & Kununka, S. (2021). An approach and decision support tool for forming Industry 4.0 supply chain collaborations. *Computers in Industry, 125*, 103391.

Constantinides, P., Henfridsson, O., & Parker, G. G. (2018). Platforms and infrastructures in the digital age. *Information Systems Research, 29*(2), 381–400.

De Oliveira, D. T., & Cortimiglia, M. N. (2017). Value co-creation in web-based multisided platforms: A conceptual framework and implications for business model design. *Business Horizons, 60*(6), 747–758.

Doganova, L., & Eyquem-Renault, M. (2009). What do business models do? Innovation devices in technology entrepreneurship. *Research Policy, 38*(10), 1559–1570.

Gassmann, O., Frankenberger, K., & Csik, M. (2013). Revolutionizing the business model. *Management of the Fuzzy Front End of Innovation, 18*(3), 89–97.

Gawer, A., & Cusumano, M. A. (2014). Industry platforms and ecosystem innovation. *Journal of Product Innovation Management, 31*(3), 417–433.

Hagiu, A., & Wright, J. (2015). Multi-sided platforms. *International Journal of Industrial Organization, 43*, 162–174.

Hein, A., Schreieck, M., Riasanow, T., Setzke, D. S., Wiesche, M., Böhm, M., & Krcmar, H. (2020). Digital platform ecosystems. *Electronic Markets, 30*(1), 87–98.

Horváth, D., & Szabó, R. Z. (2019). Driving forces and barriers of industry 4.0: Do multinational and small and medium-sized companies have equal opportunities? *Technological Forecasting and Social Change, 146*, 119–132.

Huber, T. L., Kude, T., & Dibbern, J. (2017). Governance practices in platform ecosystems: Navigating tensions between cocreated value and governance costs. *Information Systems Research, 28*(3), 563–584.

Ibarra, D., Ganzarain, J., & Igartua, J. I. (2018). Business model innovation through industry 4.0: A review. *Procedia Manufacturing, 22*, 4–10.

Jacobides, M. G., Cennamo, C. & Gawer, A.(2018). Towards a theory of ecosystems. *Strategic Management Journal, 39*(8), 2255–2276.

Kagermann, H., Wahlster, W., & Helbig, J. (2013). Recommendations for implementing the strategic initiative Industrie 4.0. *Securing the future of German manufacturing industry*. Final report of the Industrie 4.0 Working Group, Munich: Acatech-National Academy of Science and Engineering and Forschungsunion.

Kazantsev, N., Pishchulov, G., Mehandjiev, N., & Sampaio, P. (2018). Exploring barriers in current inter-enterprise collaborations: A survey and thematic analysis. *Lecture Notes in Business Information Processing, 319*, 319–327.

Mittal, S., Khan, M. A., Purohit, J. K., Menon, K., Romero, D., & Wuest, T. (2020). A smart manufacturing adoption framework for SMEs. *International Journal of Production Research, 58*(5), 1555–1573.

Moazed A.(2016). *Platform Business Model—Definition | What is it? | Explanation*. Retrieved from https://www.applicoinc.com/blog/what-is-a-platform-business-model/.

Moeuf, A., Lamouri, S., Pellerin, R., Tamayo-Giraldo, S., Tobon-Valencia, E., & Eburdy, R. (2020). Identification of critical success factors, risks and opportunities of Industry 4.0 in SMEs. *International Journal of Production Research, 58*(5), 1384–1400.

Morris, M., Schindehutte, M., & Allen, J. (2005). The entrepreneur's business model: Toward a unified perspective. *Journal of Business Research, 58*(6), 726–735.

Müller, S. C., Böhm, M., Schröer, M., & Bakhirev, A. (2016). *Geschäftsmodelle in der digitalen Wirtschaft—Vollstudie*. Studien zum deutschen Innovationssystem No. 13–2016.

Müller, J. M., & Voigt, K. -I. (2018). Sustainable industrial value creation in SMEs: A comparison between industry 4.0 and made in China 2025. *International Journal of Precision Engineering and Manufacturing—Green Technology, 5*(5), 659–670.

Müller, J. M., Buliga, O., & Voigt, K. -I. (2018). Fortune favors the prepared: How SMEs approach business model innovations in industry 4.0. *Technological Forecasting and Social Change, 132*, 2–17.

Müller, J. M. (2019). Antecedents to digital platform usage in Industry 4.0 by established manufacturers. *Sustainability, 11*(4), 1121.

Müller, J. M., Buliga, O., & Voigt, K. -I. (2020a). The role of absorptive capacity and innovation strategy in the design of industry 4.0 business models-A comparison between SMEs and large enterprises. *European Management Journal*. (in press).

Müller, J. M., Veile, J. W., & Voigt, K. -I. (2020b). Prerequisites and incentives for digital information sharing in Industry 4.0—an international comparison across data types. *Computers and Industrial Engineering, 148*, 106733.

Osterwalder, A. (2004). *The Business Model Ontology a Proposition in a Design Science Approach* (Dissertation). University of Lausanne.

Osterwalder, A., & Pigneur, Y. (2010). *Business Model Generation*. Hoboken, John Wiley & Sons.

Palo, T., & Tähtinen, J. (2013). Networked business model development for emerging technology-based services. *Industrial Marketing Management, 42*(5), 773–782.

Parker, G. G., van Alstyne, M. W., & Choudary, S. P. (2016). *Platform revolution: How networked markets are transforming the economy and how to make them work for you*. New York, W. W. Norton & Company.

Sahi, G. K., Gupta, M. C., & Cheng, T. C. E. (2020). The effects of strategic orientation on operational ambidexterity: A study of indian SMEs in the industry 4.0 era. *International Journal of Production Economics, 220*, 107395.

Schmidt, M. C., Veile, J. W., Müller, J. M., & Voigt, K. -I. (2020). Ecosystems 4.0: Redesigning global value chains. *International Journal of Logistics Management*. (in press).

VanAlstyne, M. W., Parker, G. G., & Choudary, S. P. (2016). Pipelines, platforms, and the new rules of strategy: Scale now trumps differentiation. *Harvard Business Review, 94*(4), 54–62.

Veile, J. W., Schmidt, M. C., Müller, J. M., & Voigt, K. -I. (2020). Relationship follows technology! How industry 4.0 reshapes future buyer-supplier relationships. *Journal of Manufacturing Technology Management*. (in press).

Zott, C., Amit, R., & Massa, L. (2011). The business model: Recent developments and future research. *Journal of Management, 37*(4), 1019–1042.

Industrial Data-Driven Business Models

Industrial Data-Driven Business Models: Towards a Goods-Service-Data Continuum

Kai-Ingo Voigt, Fabian Brechtel, Marie-Christin Schmidt, and Johannes Veile

Abstract

Current developments and trends in the business environment, like digitalization or servitization, are transforming industrial value creation logic and especially business models. Therefore, this study analyzes the impact of data on industrial business models and how newly emerging industrial data-driven business models (IDDBMs) can be systematically clustered. Given the novelty of the research topic, we choose an exploratory study design that consists of two parts. Firstly, we analyze the body of literature on data-driven business models and discuss existing clustering approaches, including elemental classifications and archetype schemes. Using the insights from the analysis of our literature sample, we develop a preliminary conceptual-theoretical classification framework. In a second step, we match, adapt, and enrich this initial framework with empirical data from seven expert interviews, strengthening practical embeddedness and generalizability. The resulting IDDBM cluster framework consists of six clusters for IDDBMs that differ in the manner by which data is transferred to the customers. While business models in the first cluster extensively use data to improve their product portfolio, in the fifth cluster, data is only used to provide a service to the customers. Business models in the sixth cluster, in contrast, generate value with their data alone without any product or service in the process. Thereby, our model expands the well-established goods-to-service continuum towards a goods-service-data continuum. Against the backdrop of the currently proposed service-dominant logic, we propose a data-dominant logic to sensitize industrial companies for the disruption that is about to influence their

K.-I. Voigt (✉) · F. Brechtel · M.-C. Schmidt · J. Veile
Chair for Industrial Management, Friedrich-Alexander-University Erlangen-Nürnberg, Lange Gasse 20, 90403 Nürnberg, Germany
e-mail: kai-ingo.voigt@fau.de

K.-I. Voigt and J. M. Müller (eds.), *Digital Business Models in Industrial Ecosystems*, Future of Business and Finance, https://doi.org/10.1007/978-3-030-82003-9_9

business models. Therefore, several recommendations are given for corporate practice to adapt to this uprising new business environment. At the same time, our model is suited to function as a research agenda on IDDBMs by channeling and structuring future research efforts into a unified framework.

1 Introduction

Recent developments in markets, consumer behavior, and technology are re-shaping industrial value creation caused by differentiated, increasingly data-related forces from multiple sides (Hirsch-Kreinsen et al., 2018; Schwab, 2016).

From the industrial business perspective, the Industrial Internet of Things (IIoT) is emerging and maturing, while smart devices and applications are progressively diffusing and increasingly integrated into value creation. This challenges the current industrial value creation logic, which traditionally takes on a product-oriented focus, and only recently has begun to set out on its journey towards a "servitization" of its value proposal (Vargo & Lusch, 2008), while the value of data is still highly neglected. Following this logic, also industrial business models (BMs) are subject to severe transformation, eventually forcing industrial companies to react and to adapt to the newly emerging data-savvy environment. Herein, data-driven business models (DDBMs) pose a key response to these developments, constituting a lever for future developments and a chance for disruptive change in industrial settings (Bouwman et al., 2017).

In the business to consumer (B2C) domain, examples of disruption through DDBMs are well-documented: Companies like Amazon, Netflix, or Spotify show exemplarily, how brick and mortar businesses are disrupted by competitors that are employing data-driven approaches (Cozzolino et al., 2018). Meanwhile, the displayed inability to react properly to disruptive DDBMs is referred to as incumbent inertia (Gilbert, 2005). This behavioral phenomenon describes that traditionally successful companies fail to assess the newly emerging DDBMs correctly, underestimate their impact, and therefore adhere to their traditional BMs, eventually leading to failure.

In contrast to the well-documented disruptions of DDBMs in the B2C context, the industrial business to business (B2B) domain has been dragging behind with its adoption of DDBMs, scarcely exploiting their potentially disruptive impact on the market structure. However, the well-established value creation mechanisms in an industrial B2B context are not less affected by uprising societal shifts and trends like "digitalization" and "sustainability" that initially have triggered disruption in the B2C domain. Therefore, in a likewise manner, industrial companies must anticipate, understand, and proactively shape the transformation process towards a data-driven business environment by adapting their value creation logic and BMs to ensure future competitiveness (Chen et al., 2012; McAfee & Brynjolfsson, 2012).

Digital platforms and DDBMs play a prominent role in this context, due to the masses of still widely unused data that industrial businesses are able to generate and aggregate across value creation stages. This results in new possibilities for cross-referencing, analyzing, insight generation, and eventually value offering in

BMs. Industrial BMs that focus on extensively using this data and thereby provide value for their customers based on data are referred to as IDDBMs. These novel BMs have the potential to transform and reshape the mechanisms of industrial value creation and market structures (de Reuver et al., 2018).

Management research has issued fundamental scientific approaches to tackle the field of DDBMs (Brownlow et al., 2015) and basic attempts regarding IDDBMs (Endres et al., 2019; Laudien & Daxböck, 2016). However, research is still fragmented, since scientific approaches are unnuanced, and only limited niche classifications exist that do not provide a comprehensive guideline for managers to adhere to, when confronted with the disruptive potential of IDDBMs. Especially, a holistic, unified classification model for IDDBMs is still missing. This exhibits a clear lack of understanding concerning the IDDBM phenomenon in the B2B context. For scientific research, this issues an explicit mandate to develop a unified, comprehensive, and industry-spanning framework, based on theoretically established structures and the perspective of corporate practice at the same time.

The work at hand, therefore, tackles the research question of how IDDBMs can be classified, clustered, and comprehensively differentiated.

To answer this research question, we synthesize conceptual-theoretical findings with qualitative-empirical data to distil a systematic IDDBM clustering. Accounting for the inherent industrial value creation logic, in terms of creating goods and services, we integrate the "goods to service continuum" as discriminating factor into our methodical proceeding (Vargo & Lusch, 2008).

Proposing a holistic IDDBM framework, we actively support industrial corporate practice by shedding light on changes in the value creation logic and upcoming success determinants in the B2B context. We raise awareness and understanding for the wide-ranging implications of a data-driven business environment and digital disruption. This paves the ways for a smooth adaptation of companies to this emerging phenomenon. Furthermore, our research emphasizes the potential of IDDBMs and thereby stimulates the transformation of current BMs and the emergence of novel IDDBMs that generate new value to the customer.

2 Theoretical Background and State of Research

Research in BM innovation has only lately begun to focus on DDBMs. Given the novelty of the subject, IDDBM research is a fragmented field with several analyses located in diverse corners of management science. Against this backdrop, only some first integrative classification attempts of DDBMs can be observed (Hartmann et al., 2016).

Having a detailed look on DDBMs research, two general streams can be identified that cluster classification efforts. The first stream concentrates on the componential level of individual BM elements, whereas the second one sheds light on more holistic archetypical BM structures. Hence, we refer to the first stream as "DDBM elemental classifications" and to the second stream as "DDBM archetypes."

In order to ensure a comprehensive understanding and eventually to distil a holistic scheme, we analyze the most prominent classification attempts and research findings within each stream in the following section. The report detects there is no holistic, widely applicable, and industry-spanning classification scheme to cluster DDBMs leaving a specific research gap for our investigation.

2.1 DDBM Elemental Classifications

As far as the individual level of BM elements is concerned, the following research findings and classification schemes prevail in the context of DDBMs.

Firstly, examining service-based BMs, Kindström (2010) conducts a multiple case study and analyzes seven cases. The observed companies were all in the process of shifting from a product to a service-based BM. The developed classification describes BM elements that were identified to be crucial for companies during that shifting period.

Focusing on a specific industry sector, Remane et al. (2017) dedicate their research to digital BMs in the mobility sector. They employ a mixed method approach based on expert interviews and desk research uncovering 63 BMs for personal mobility. In five iterations, they deduce dimensions that are suitable to differentiate between these 63 BMs for each field of the well-known VISOR framework by El Sawy and Pereira (2013).

Schaefer et al. (2017) limit their research on DDBMs to Industry 4.0 BMs. Gathering data from a multiple case study of four cases, they identify important BM elements for each DDBM. After aggregating them, the conjoint elements are assigned to one of the nine fields, the Business Model Canvas by Osterwalder and Pigneur (2010) has to offer.

On a greater related level, Brownlow et al. (2015) have created their DDBM elemental classification to provide companies with a guideline to conceptualize and implement DDBMs. Their classification was developed examining 40 companies that were in the process of implementing or transitioning to a BM based on Big Data. The authors deduce key questions that need to be addressed by companies in similar situations. Those questions are then summarized and distilled into the distinctive DDBM elements.

Taking a holistic view on the different elemental classifications and their perspectives reveals, they differ in scope and width of research content, for instance, they regard varying industry sectors or they analyze different phenomena within the digital transformation. Nevertheless, all approaches share a common logic that is rooted in the general business model attributes they excerpted. These commonalities include some form of value proposition, elements that describe the value creation mechanism, and aspects that can be allocated to a revenue scheme. With regard to the specificities of IDDBMs, the models offer unique aspects contributing some further individual jigsaw pieces to the general picture, such as "Data Source" and "Inhibitors" (Brownlow et al., 2015) or "Interface" and "Service platforms" (Remane et al., 2017).

2.2 DDBM Archetypes

Taking a greater level of abstraction, the second stream of research deals with archetypes of DDBMs with the most prominent examples being discussed in the following.

Exclusively relying on theoretical data material, Endres et al. (2019) conduct a qualitative content analysis of 1.043 scientific publications. They focus on data about start-ups and incumbents that maintain BMs within the IIoT environment. Ultimately, they process their data into archetypes that distinguish four categories of BMs on a high aggregation level, of which DDBMs represent only a subset.

On a similar aggregation level, Laudien and Daxböck (2016) apply a multiple case study approach to identify archetypes of BMs that emerge due to the rise of the IIoT. Their case data stems from expert interviews conducted with representatives of 11 German companies in the manufacturing sector influenced by the IIoT. Their comprehensive cross-case analysis reveals three BM archetypes that rely on IIoT technologies. These archetypes differentiate three levels of impact that the IIoT has on the firms' BMs. On the first level, the main transformation occurs in the supply chain processes. The second archetype encompasses BMs, where the IIoT causes a redesign of the firm's value creation logic. On the third level, the entire BM is remodeled by the IIoT to accommodate for the creation and usage of data.

Hence, Endres et al. (2019) and Laudien and Daxböck (2016) contribute to the body of research by integrating DDBMs into a larger framework of BMs but do not actually provide a classification of DDBMs themselves. The following scientific contributions however, focus on DDBMs and derive archetypes within that domain.

Zolnowski et al. (2016) dedicate their work to analyze the innovation process that leads to DDBMs and deduce archetypes for the emerging transformation patterns. Following a multiple case study method, they gathered data from 20 international companies that have completed the transformation process to data-driven innovations. Applying a morphologic analysis to their case data, they develop two dimensions to classify the transformation patterns. Along the first dimension, the beneficiary party is distinguished. The innovation benefits either only the focal firm itself or also its partners along the value chain. The second dimension distinguishes the type of innovation, being either a productivity improvement or a value innovation. These two dimensions result in the four archetypes "Cooperative value innovation," "Customer-centric value innovation," "Cooperative productivity improvement," and "Company-centric productivity improvement."

Finally yet importantly, Hartmann et al. (2016) synthesize data from a literature review and freely accessible qualitative data of 100 start-ups. They apply a similar methodological approach as Zolnowski et al. (2016). However, Hartmann et al. (2016) do not focus on the transformation patterns towards DDBMs, but derive archetypes for data-driven business models themselves. The dimensions used to differentiate the DDBMs archetypes are "Key activity," ranging from data aggregation to data generation and "Key data source," ranging from freely available data to tracked data. From these axes, Hartmann et al. (2016) deduce the six archetypes, "Free data collector and aggregator," "Analytics-as-a-service," "Data generation and analysis," "Free data knowledge discovery," "Data-aggregation-as-a-service," and "Multi-source data mash-up and analysis."

The scientific works by Hodapp et al. (2019), Leminen et al. (2020), Remane et al. (2016), Weking et al. (2018), and Müller and Buliga (2019) also comprise models of archetypes. However, they only apply for very specific contexts, e.g., machine-to-machine communication providers (Leminen et al., 2020), Internet of Things platforms (Hodapp et al., 2019), US mobility sector tech start-ups (Remane et al., 2016), or the Industry 4.0 domain (Müller & Buliga, 2019; Weking et al., 2018).

2.3 Synthesis of Perspectives and Research Gap

The overview of current scientific literature on the subject of DDBMs unveils that scientific research has generated componential and archetypical classifications. Within this range, the classifications' focuses include industry sectors, company types, and other contexts. The following Fig. 1 summarizes the state of research based on the componential and archetypical DDBM classifications.

Having a detailed look at the state of research reveals that there is no holistic, context spanning, and widely applicable classification scheme to cluster DDBMs and especially IDDBMs, leaving a specific research gap. Dissecting complex phenomena such as DDBMs into smaller tranches and examining those individually is a relevant first step in generating insights. Building on existing literature that examines these smaller tranches, however, a following step is to deduce a framework that aggregates the insights into an all-embracing picture. In order to account for this, we distil a holistic model with a broad validity across contexts.

Abstraction level / Contentual focus	Componential DDBM classifications	Archetypical DDBM classifications	Holistic DDBM classifications
Industry sectors	Remane et al., 2017	Laudien et al., 2016	
Company types	Kindström, 2010	Endres et al., 2019; Hartmann et al., 2016; Hodapp et al., 2019	Adressed research gap
Specific contexts	Brownlow et al., 2015 Schaefer et al., 2017	Zolnowski et al., 2016	

Fig. 1 State of research of DDBM classifications and research gap

3 Method

To develop a conceptual framework on how to structure and classify IDDBMs from a research and practice perspective, the study's methodology is based on two columns – a conceptual-theoretical part synthesized with a qualitative-empirical part.

3.1 Conceptual-Theoretical Part

Initially, scientific literature from the field of Business Management was identified in several databases ensuring all relevant publications were sighted and the entire research status quo was uncovered. The author team then extensively studied, compared, contrasted, and critically analyzed the literature as well as the underlying frameworks. In a next step, we critically discussed the identified literature in team, to qualitatively analyze existing research gaps, grasp the research status quo, and synthesize it in several iterative sessions. In the course of the analysis, several gaps were identified which current frameworks have left. Based on the existing frameworks and given literature, the author team then distilled an original concept addressing the unveiled research and conceptual gaps. We extensively discussed and evaluated our initial concept against the backdrop of the research status quo and research question, and accordingly adapted the framework iteratively.

3.2 Qualitative-Empirical Part

Forming the second part of this study, a qualitative-empirical analysis was conducted to add empirical insights, validation, and content to our theory-derived concept based on qualitative data from corporate practice. This procedure founds and embeds our IDDBM concept empirically.

Thereby, our exploratory qualitative-empirical study design allowed an open research approach to cover the entire complexity of IDDBMs, to shed light on their complex environments, and to grasp individual nuanced differences (Edmondson & McManus, 2007; Eisenhardt, 1989; Eisenhardt & Graebner, 2007; Yin, 2014). This approach ensures that relevant knowledge and insights for our conceptual framework could be generated and has proved to be a valuable source for further knowledge.

The study relies on seven interviews that were conducted between June and September 2019 with experts from German companies of different sizes and industry sectors (Eisenhardt & Graebner, 2007; Yin, 2014). All companies successfully run their own IDDBM and all experts possess extensive knowledge in the field. The interview duration varies from 22 to 79 min (average: 46 min). The companies' sales volume varies from less than one to approximately one hundred billion Euro in 2019 (average: 26 billion Euro), and the number of employees

Table 1 Characteristics data sample

Interview	Position	Industry sector	Employees [2019; in thsnd.]	Sales [2019; in bil. Euro]	Duration [min:sec]
A	Middle	IT and software	(200–400]	(50–100]	22:36
B	Lower	Automotive	(50–100]	(10–50]	34:03
C	Top	Mechanical engineering	(10–50]	(0–10]	49:00
D	Top	Raw materials	(100–200]	(10–50]	45:44
E	Top	IT and software	(0–10]	(0–10]	67:27
F	Lower	IT and software	(0–10]	(0–10]	23:02
G	Middle	Infrastructure	(200–400]	(10–50]	79:06

reaches from 50 to more than 300.000 (average: 126.000 employees). Industry sectors include automotive, IT and software, mechanical engineering, infrastructure, and raw materials. Table 1 summarizes the sample characteristics. All interviews follow a structured guideline, they were audio-recorded, and hereafter transcribed forming the study's database.

In a next step, the author team analyzed the qualitative-empirical data against the backdrop of the research question to generate new insights. The stepwise content analysis and coding procedure followed the approach of Gioia et al. (2013) to meet quality requirements in qualitative-empirical research studies.

Merging the findings from the theory-driven and qualitative-empirical analyses, we match our theory-based IDDBM cluster with the empirical findings. Therein, the author team initially conducted the synthetization individually, whereupon the individual results were discussed and improved in team. This process entailed several iteration loops, which resulted in a rigorous synthesis of theory and empirical practice constituted in our unified IDDBM cluster, aligning with the well-known concept of the goods-to-service continuum. The cluster is presented in the following results section.

4 Presentation and Interpretation of Results

Our conceptual model of IDDBM clustering was created to classify and further understand IDDBMs in the industrial sector. Herein, among other benefits, one main advantage is its inherent scale of measurement rooted in the alignment with the goods-to-service-continuum (Vargo & Lusch, 2008). Our theory- and empirically- based framework covers the great variety of current as well as prospective IDDBMs and clusters them into six dimensions. Thereby, it also accounts for possible further developments and forms of IDDBMs.

Generally, the conceptual model differentiates IDDBMs according to the way they transfer data to the customers, i.e., data combined with a product, data integrated into a service offering, or directly provided in its pure form. The associated six clusters are presented in the following.

4.1 Product Only IDDBM

As a first group of IDDBMs, we propose a cluster of BMs in which the value delivery mechanism is solely built upon selling a product, whereas the data is generated on this product. As a differentiation from further groups, the product-only cluster does not intend to provide any additional value to the customers through services or data interpretations. For a product-based IDDBM, data plays a crucial role, especially for creating innovative products or for continuously improving existing products. This can be achieved by utilizing data on the products' usage, returned by the products themselves or by aggregating metadata on the customers and their experience with the product.

From an empirical lens, support is given by the statements of expert D, whose company employs a product-based IDDBM approach:

> We mainly provide turnkey facilities at a fixed price. Digitization will not have a huge impact on this specific business model. Simply because our customers do not request it. I personally call our products digitally enhanced, as they are ready for retrospectively implementing data-based services. (Expert D)

4.2 Product with Additional Service IDDBM

In contrast, there are IDDBMs that do not only sell the product and generate data but also offer additional services, forming the second cluster. Companies within the second cluster utilize data for the design of additional, complementing services to the products that capture value for customers. Whereas the product still represents the main source of value, data and additional services play an ever more increasing crucial role. Among others, these BMs can frequently be observed in the automation, the plant engineering, and construction sector. Aggregating and analyzing data collected from installed or sold products allows rendering additional services, such as condition monitoring or predictive maintenance.

Expert B explains that they offer a data-based service in addition to their traditional product business. Therefore, this BM belongs to the cluster product with additional service:

> It usually starts by selling hardware in the first place, following the old-fashioned model. On top, there is a monthly fee for additional services like condition monitoring that generate a constant cash flow as long as the service is rendered. (Expert B)

4.3 Hybrid Product IDDBM

The third cluster is characterized by an equilibrium of product and service relevance in the IDDBM. Companies with BMs belonging to this cluster do not only create and capture value by selling products and services alike, but products and services are equally important value generators in terms of data. Herein, both are fundamental for improvements in the value proposition. Against this backdrop, data gathered by the products may be used for the continuous improvement of existing services and for the creation of new offers. Data and data interpretations pave the way for the expansion and improvement of the product and service portfolio.

Expert E hints that within their BM, the two dimensions, product and service coexist in a symbiosis:

> The hardware price is calculated to fit a lower level than usual for industrial products. This in turn fosters the license fees charged for the associated rendered services. (Expert E)

4.4 Service with Additional Product IDDBM

Furthermore, IDDBMs exist that predominantly comprise data-related services but additionally enrich their portfolio with products. In contrast to the hybrid cluster, products play a minor determining role when compared to the provided services. Accordingly, the products' raison d'être only bases on their complementary effect but they also serve as sources for data generation within the offered services. Subsequently, products may contribute to the improvement of existing services and the creation of new services offerings.

One expert has described the role of service enhancing products as a part of the company's service-oriented IDDBM as follows:

> For our service, there are three different quality levels on offer. The annual fee for the service depends on the functional range. We additionally offer physical communication modules on our online shop. Customers can mount them on different machines and then use more functionalities within their service subscription. (Expert C)

4.5 Service Only IDDBM

In contrast, companies could also set up IDDBMs that do not include a physical product, but generate the entire revenue and all data solely based on services.

The empirical data indicates three different IDDBMs that fall into that cluster. Firstly, infrastructure-as-a-service can be identified. In this type, the focal company's BM focuses on providing and managing infrastructure (and relating data analyses) for a time- or usage-based subscription fee. Infrastructure may take two forms: Either physical infrastructure similar to an operator model or virtual IT infrastructure. Secondly, platform-as-a-service models can be observed. Thereby, a platform provider bridges supply and demand, and in so doing, manages the exchange of data, goods, and services between all actors. Thirdly, software-as-a-service-models are identified as an IDDBM. In such a BM, service providers offer their software to users for a license fee instead of a fixed price and sell corresponding data analyses and data management.

In corporate practice, hybrid forms between the everything-as-a-service IDDBMs occur:

> We manage a platform where users can interact with each other. Our revenue stems from the subscription fee that we charge our users. In a limited scope, our parental company uses the platform to offer their own software-as-a–service to the user community. (Expert A)

4.6 Data Only DDBM

Finally, yet importantly, IDDBMs exist that rely neither on products nor on services, but data per se represents the sole purpose of value creation: Collecting, aggregating, clustering, analyzing, and selling both raw data and insights based on interpretations represents the core of these BMs.

There are three conceivable ways to gain access to external data: Buying them, generating them, or compiling them, each requiring a different approach.

Firstly, buying data is the most straightforward way to acquire data. Hereby, a key task is to identify promising data in order to capture value from data that exceeds the initial invest undertaken for the data acquisition.

Secondly, generating data within a data only IDDBM, a company could offer products and services free of any charge but retain the data ownership. In this context, Expert A describes a BM relying on sensors and retrieved data:

> Usually for business models, companies are quite conservative. So far, no one is brave enough to hand out sensors for free and profit off the data and learnings collected this way. (Expert A)

This procedure also applies to services, e.g., by providing customers with free infrastructure or a free platform for data exchange. This enables companies to access a superior user base that paves the way for comprehensive data usage, to analyze the data, and work with it. However, this approach poses a similar challenge like buying data: Costs occur either for the data acquisition or for freely providing the customers with products and services. Therefore, insights from the data and the profit generated with the data is required to exceed prior investment and organizational efforts to obtain a sustainable competitive BM.

Thirdly, the last option of data compilation differs from the other approaches in the significance of the initial invest. Offline and online sources could provide a large quantity of freely accessible data. Especially, online sources offer the possibility to compile large datasets using automated programs like web crawlers. In turn, however, the advantage of lower initial invest comes at the price of a lower data quality and a challenging process to generate valuable insights.

Nevertheless, IDDBMs that offer value only in processing and transferring data are in their infancy in industrial contexts. When it comes to this cluster of BMs, Expert G accurately summarizes:

> I can clearly see a trend pointing towards a purely data-driven value offering. However, there are so many obstacle to overcome that I cannot see us doing this at the moment without jeopardizing our competitive edge. (Expert G)

4.7 The Conceptual IDDBM Framework as Synthesis of Clusters

The above-discussed six individual clusters of IDDBMs can be subsumed in a holistic IDDBM framework. Herein, they follow a conceptual vertical axis along a continuum from goods towards services, increasingly enriched with data. On a horizontal axis, a bidirectional data flow illustrates that data does not only flow from a value provider towards the recipient but also backwards, paving the way for advanced data usage and applications.

From a meta-level of observation, the six clusters can be subdivided into three subgroups: In subgroup I (clusters 1 and 2), the product plays the most prominent role in value creation, whereas data and services only play a secondary role. In subgroup II (clusters 3 and 4), in contrast, the product still represents an integrative part of value offering, being a main provider of data. Therefore, product, services, and data are of similar value. Subgroup III (clusters 5 and 6) solely focuses on an implicit dimension with data and services standing to the fore, the product business widely loses importance in the value offer.

In such a framework, a wide field of current and prospective data applications and BMs can be accommodated. Figure 2 depicts the proposed framework.

According to several experts, the current distribution of BMs clearly brings subgroup I to the fore, with the majority of current IDDBMs functioning on a product-based value logic. At the same time, subgroup II is rising in importance, since in an industrial context, mixed forms of BMs basing on products, services, and associated data are emerging, following the trend of servitization and the service-dominant logic. Thereafter, subgroup III-clustered IDDBMs are still dragging behind, with data-dominant BMs only playing a minor role in industrial value creation. Therefore, we propose that current IDDBMs and industrial value logic as of today follows a 60/30/10 rationale, with 60% of IDDBMs falling in subgroup I, 30% in subgroup II, and only 10% in subgroup III. This illustrates a major potential for data-dominant IDDBMs to be implemented.

However, according to our experts, in this logic an upward trend on the goods-service-data continuum can be observed. This indicates that IDDBMs increasingly evolve towards subgroup III and especially the "data only" cluster, and could therefore in the future gradually reverse the current 60/30/10 rationale.

Following this line of argumentation, prospective industrial BMs increasingly focus on a data-dimension rather than on a purely product-focused approach. Even

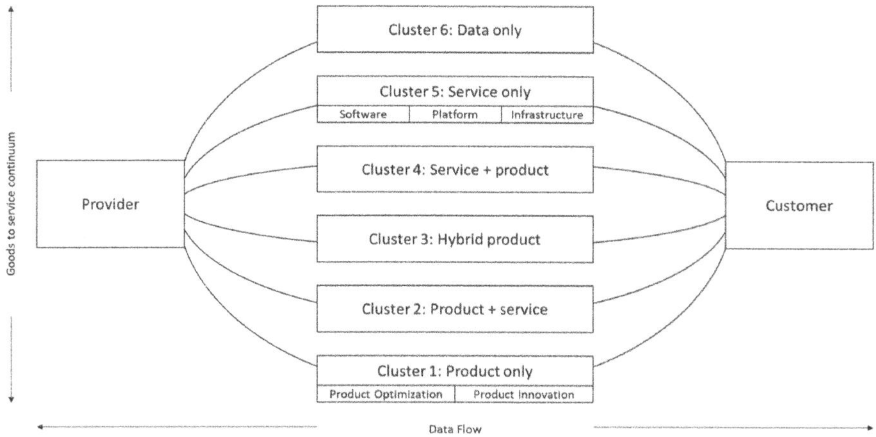

Fig. 2 The IDDBM cluster framework

pure data-broker BMs are plausible, in which industrial companies turn their back on their traditional product or service business, to compete in a data-driven business environment. Herein, these companies could neither offer a product, nor a service *based on* data, but instead only provide a service *with that* data. This turnaround could force industrial companies to evolve increasingly into technology firms. These developments, however, raise severe basic question for the future of industrial value creation. We therefore propose the "data-dominant logic" in industrial value creation as an amendment to the current state of research, adding a new perspective to the diverse existing concepts discussed in this paper.

5 Concluding Remarks and Implications

5.1 Managerial Implications

From the conceptual and theoretical work in this article, manifold implications for managerial practice can be retrieved that are presented and discussed in the following.

Firstly, the article emphasizes the potentials data has for companies and their value proposition. The findings alongside the conceptual framework could sensitize managers for the relevance of data in value creation accordingly.

Secondly, this article proposes a transition towards a "data-dominant logic" in the digital era extending the contemporary "service-dominant logic" perspective, which has been widely discussed in scientific literature and applied in corporate practice. The "data-dominant logic" implies that data becomes a value proposition itself and represents a key lever, whereas products and services begin taking a backseat role dependent on the intensity of data-driven level (as proposed in the framework). In turn, managers could rethink their value propositions and the opportunities a transition brings for their companies' differentiation on their respective markets. Against this backdrop, data could represent a further stream of revenue that is highly profitable especially at a large scale given its low variable cost. Eventually, this has the potential to severely reshape the industrial value creation logic.

Thirdly, from a holistic BM-perspective, data and thereupon-based DDBMs represent key levers to create and maintain a competitive advantage in industrial contexts. Those companies will succeed and have a competitive advantage that are able to best manage and interpret the data and that are capable of determining the correct course of action in the context of IDDBMs. Companies could therefore search for opportunities to reshape their BMs and evaluate strategic options accordingly. Perceived from the opposite side, IDDBMs may disrupt traditional BMs, and keeping that in mind, the awareness of managers could be increased for the dangerous potential a competitor's IDDBM brings for their own BMs. Therefore, managers must take adequate and sufficient countermeasures to maintain their company's competitiveness in the digital era.

Fourthly, the conceptual work indicates different forms of data-driven levels that form a maturity process from predominantly product-centered to exclusively data-centered businesses. The continuum of possible characteristics provides managers with a portfolio of conceivable strategic actions that they can evaluate against the backdrop of their own situations and environment, discuss the best options, and start the comprehensive transition process.

Fifthly, the results point out that the transformation towards IDDBMs requires vast efforts and investments. Among other things, sufficient personnel is required just like capacity to undertake the transition to ensure a sustainable success. In addition, companies need to establish a "data-culture" that paves the breeding ground for data-driven developments including an entire new way of thinking value creation and processes.

It is hoped that these insights lead managers to join in sharing our passion for IDDBMs and encourage them to push and advance IDDBMs so that the implications could in turn contribute to the ongoing developments in corporate practice.

5.2 Limitations and Research Implications

In the course of the analysis, several white spots become evident asking for further research attention. The article at hand only represents an initial effort to grasp and structure the complex topic of IDDBMs creating a conceptual framework based on theoretical insights and some first empirical evidence.

It is without saying that research is ought to gather further and more comprehensive qualitative-empirical data. In this context, questions of relevance include but are not limited to the following aspects: Do the propositions and the conceptual structure of the "goods-service-data continuum" as well as the "data-dominant logic" withstand a larger empirical analysis or are there any adaptions required? To what extent does the conceptual structure really serve to cover all existing forms of IDDBMs in practice? What does the actual distribution among the BM categories look like in corporate practice? Learning on these aspects would further help to understand IDDBMs in their entirety. Analyzing a heterogeneous sample of IDDBM cases from different countries thereby widens the focus and increases generalizability. Relying on such a heterogeneous sample would then allow conducting differentiated analyses, for example, differentiated according to countries and industry sectors. Insights on cultural or industry-specific differences and corresponding implications would allow considering these aspects in the IDDBM creation.

In addition, further research could conduct longitudinal studies and, in so doing, shed light on developments over the course of time. For instance, analyses could explore the initiation process of IDDBMs, how IDDBMs then evolve over time, and whether transformations from product-centered to data-centered can be observed, as suggested by our results. Against this backdrop, it remains to be analyzed what the actual drivers and motivators for creating IDDBMs are and which antecedents for initiating subsequent transformations can be identified.

By including further aspects, research can extend our concept and embed it in its wider context to improve practical applicability. Firstly, representing the key determinant of IDDBMs, special attention should be given to data itself. Research could analyze data forms predominantly used in IDDBMs, for instance, internal sensor data from machines and externally crawled online data. In this context, it is of interest how to best gather, aggregate, analyze, manage, and use the data, and how to set up IDDBMs accordingly. Secondly, IDDBMs could rely on different forms of value propositions that vary in customer benefit. Future research can shed light on this aspect, discuss the interlinkage for creating competitive advantages, and emphasize the relevance. Thirdly, the creation of IDDBMs and wide-ranging transformations include manifold challenges for companies. Further studies could bridge our findings with insights on challenges alongside lessons learned on how to cope with them in order to develop a IDDBM success model.

Finally yet importantly, a clear definition of IDDBMs is still lacking, and in turn, in some cases a clear differentiation to digital BMs and platform BMs remains difficult. Hence, research should take the opportunity to clarify the terminology paving the way for a common and consistent understanding of DDBMs.

In spite of its limitations, the authors hope the article at hand provides valuable, thought-provoking insights into the new and relevant topic of DDBMs, and, based on the given research implications, would stimulate further research in this field.

References

Bouwman, H., de Reuver, M. & Nikou, S. (2017). The impact of digitalization on business models: How IT artefacts, social media, and big data force firms to innovate their business model. In *14th International Telecommunications Society (ITS) Asia-Pacific Regional Conference*, Kyoto.

Brownlow, J., Zaki, M., Neely, A., & Urmetzer, F. (2015). Data and analytics-data-driven business models: A Blueprint for Innovation. *Cambridge Service Alliance, 7*, 1–17.

Chen, H., Chiang, R. H. L., & Storey, V. C. (2012). Business intelligence and analytics: From big data to big impact. *MIS Quarterly, 36*(4), 1165–2118.

Cozzolino, A., Verona, G., & Rothaermel, F. T. (2018). Unpacking the disruption process: New technology, business models, and incumbent adaptation. *Journal of Management Studies, 55* (7), 1166–1202.

de Reuver, M., Sørensen, C., & Basole, R. C. (2018). The digital platform: A research agenda. *Journal of Information Technology, 33*(2), 124–135.

Edmondson, A. C., & McManus, S. E. (2007). Methodological fit in management field research. *Academy of Management Review, 32*(4), 1246–1264.

Eisenhardt, K. M. (1989). Building theories from case study research. *Academy of Management Review, 14*(4), 532–550.

Eisenhardt, K. M., & Graebner, M. E. (2007). Theory building from cases: Opportunities and challenges. *Academy of Management Journal, 50*(1), 25–32.

El Sawy, O. A. & Pereira, F. (2013). VISOR: A unified framework for business modeling in the evolving digital space. In O. A. El Sawy & F. Pereira (Eds.), *Business modelling in the dynamic digital space* (pp. 21–35). Berlin, Heidelberg: Springer.

Endres, H., Indulska, M., Ghosh, A., Baiyere, A. & Broser, S. (2019). Industrial internet of things (IIoT) business model classification. In *Proceedings of the 40th International Conference on Information Systems (ICIS)*, Munich.

Gilbert, C. G. (2005). Unbundling the structure of inertia: Resource versus routine rigidity. *Academy of Management Journal, 48*(5), 741–763.

Gioia, D. A., Corley, K. G., & Hamilton, A. L. (2013). Seeking qualitative rigor in inductive research: Notes on the Gioia methodology. *Organizational Research Methods, 16*(1), 15–31.

Hartmann, P. M., Zaki, M., Feldmann, N., & Neely, A. (2016). Capturing value from big data—A taxonomy of data-driven business models used by start-up firms. *International Journal of Operations & Production Management, 36*(10), 1382–1406.

Hirsch-Kreinsen, H., Ittermann, P. & Niehaus, J. (2018). Fazit: Konturen eines Leitbildes digitaler Industriearbeit. In H. Hirsch-Kreinsen, P. Ittermann & J. Niehaus (Eds.), *Digitalisierung industrieller Arbeit* (pp. 383–396). Baden-Baden, Nomos.

Hodapp, D., Remane, G., Hanelt, A. & Kolbe, L. M. (2019). Business models for internet of things platforms: Empirical development of a taxonomy and archetypes. In *14th International Conference on Wirtschaftsinformatik*, Siegen.

Kindström, D. (2010). Towards a service-based business model—Key aspects for future competitive advantage. *European Management Journal, 28*(6), 479–490.

Laudien, S. M., & Daxböck, B. (2016). The influence of the industrial internet of things on business model design: A qualitative-empirical analysis. *International Journal of Innovation Management, 20*(8), 1640014.

Leminen, S., Rajahonka, M., Wendelin, R., & Westerlund, M. (2020). Industrial internet of things business models in the machine-to-machine context. *Industrial Marketing Management, 84*, 298–311.

McAfee, A., & Brynjolfsson, E. (2012). Big data: The management revolution. *Harvard Business Review, 90*(10), 60–68.

Müller, J. & Buliga, O. (2019). Archetypes for data-driven business models for manufacturing companies in industry 4.0. In *International Conference on Information Systems 2019 Special Interest Group on Big Data Proceedings*, Munich.

Osterwalder, A. & Pigneur, Y. (2010). *Business model generation: a handbook for visionaries, game changers, and challengers*. Hoboken, Wiley.
Remane, G., Hildebrandt, B., Hanelt, A. & Kolbe, L. M. (2016). Discovering new digital business model types—A study of technology startups from the mobility sector. In *Proceedings of 20th Pacific Asia Conference on Information Systems (PACIS)*, Chiayi, Taiwan.
Remane, G., Hanelt, A., Nickerson, R. C., & Kolbe, L. M. (2017). Discovering digital business models in traditional industries. *Journal of Business Strategy, 38*(2), 41–51.
Schaefer, D., Walker, J. & Flynn, J. (2017). A data-driven business model framework for value capture in industry 4.0. *Advances in Transdisciplinary Engineering*, *6*(2017), 245–250.
Schwab, K. (2016). *Die Vierte Industrielle Revolution*. Munich, Pantheon.
Vargo, S. L., & Lusch, R. F. (2008). Service-dominant logic: Continuing the evolution. *Journal of the Academy of Marketing Science, 36*(1), 1–10.
Weking, J., Stöcker, M., Kowalkiewicz, M., Böhm, M. & Krcmar, H. (2018). Archetypes for industry 4.0 business model innovations. In *Proceedings of the 24th Americas Conference on Information Systems (AMCIS)*, New Orleans.
Yin, R. K. (2014). *Case study research: Design and methods, applied social research* (5th ed.). Sage.
Zolnowski, A., Christiansen, T. & Gudat, J. (2016). Business model transformation patterns of data-driven innovations. In *Twenty-Fourth European Conference on Information Systems*, Istanbul.

Realizing New Data-Driven Business Models by Launching Containers into the Cloud

Mathias Zink, Victor Naumann, Andreas Harth, and Alexander Pflaum

Abstract

Data-driven business models are modern ways for innovation in traditional environments. The vision of the Internet of Things (IoT), by making products smart and leveraging the data into services, is a modern paradigm of value creation. A representative case study evolved business models for industrial containers in the automotive industry into a cloud-based data-driven business model. This publication outlines the background for industrial containers and provides insights into the relevant technological architectures. Additionally, the data-driven business model and the expansion of the ecosystem are outlined. Thereby this publication enhances the necessary interdisciplinary understanding of business model research and information science.

M. Zink · V. Naumann (✉)
Fraunhofer Institute for Integrated Circuits, Nordostpark 84, 90411 Nuremberg, Germany
e-mail: victor.naumann@iis.fraunhofer.de

A. Harth
Chair of Technical Information Systems, Friedrich-Alexander-University Erlangen-Nürnberg, Lange Gasse 20, 90403 Nuremberg, Germany
e-mail: andreas.harth@fau.de

A. Pflaum
Chair for Supply Chain Management, Otto-Friedrich-Universität Bamberg, Feldkirchenstraße 21, 96047 Bamberg, Germany
e-mail: alexander.pflaum@uni-bamberg.de

K.-I. Voigt and J. M. Müller (eds.), *Digital Business Models in Industrial Ecosystems*, Future of Business and Finance, https://doi.org/10.1007/978-3-030-82003-9_10

1 Data Enabling Industrial Business Models

The Internet of Things (IoT), big data and data-driven services are changing the business landscape everywhere. The implementation of IoT technologies in products and the resulting availability of data allow for new data-driven business models along the lifecycle of industrial products (Porter & Heppelmann, 2014; Prockl & Pflaum, 2015). Additionally, significant process improvements in the supply chain based on the systematic evaluation of product and process data can be achieved (Klötzer & Pflaum, 2015).

Smart product-service systems (Smart PSS) are such data-driven business models. They can be understood as the purposeful bundling of smart products and smart services to jointly fulfil customers needs by using data (Valencia et al., 2015). The objective to generate value from data raises questions at the edge of business model innovation and IoT solution design:

- Which problem can be addressed by a value proposition?
- How can the necessary data be generated? Which technologies are suited for this purpose?
- How can data be semantically transformed and how can it be processed to generate value?

Questions like these are often overlooked in theoretical business model development. However, finding answers is essential for realizing new business models by launching industrial products into the cloud.

The case study of iSLT.NET (BMWi, 01MA17006F) served as an empirical field to derive exemplary answers to the outlined questions. It provided the environment to realize data-driven business models for a network of smart modular containers in the German automotive industry. The IoT value chain, from innovative sensor nodes to new business models, was prototypically implemented. To realize the paradigm of data-driven business models, the previous industrial ecosystem of three stakeholders—an OEM car manufacturer, a supplier of the OEM and a manufacturer of special load carriers-was expanded by new actors. The design and manufacturing of special load carriers is a complex process, as they have to be revised every time a new model/derivate of a car is started. Due to their specialization to specific omponents and even car series, they are rather expensive and have little to no reusability. Both the container and the actual good transported in it are rather valuable, which is decisive for the business calculations later on. Therefore, the business model development focussed on the bundling of smart products and services for such special load carriers.

2 Industrial Scenario for New Business Models

Industrial containers, which exist in various forms (Rosenthal, 2016), can be seen as central objects in supply chains. Containers are used to transport and protect materials to ensure the production processes (Raab et al., 2011). Container management can be seen as a task of supply chain management (Hofmann & Bachmann, 2006).

Containers can be used in generally three different kinds of circuits: internal closed-loop, cross-company closed-loop and cross-company open-loop systems. In intra-company closed-loop systems, the system consists of a closed loop in which containers ensure internal flows of materials and components as in the stocking of own material supermarkets. In a cross-company closed-loop system, the containers are used to enable the external supply of material or partly and fully finished products. Containers therefore regularly leave the company's boundaries to customers or suppliers. They are often moved along defined paths. Examples are special containers for products from suppliers, which are filled again by the supplier. The third kind of container circuit is a cross-company open-loop system. There are no restrictions on the flow direction of the containers and the source and sink vary for the standardized containers. A practical example being the Euro pallet system (Hofmann & Bachmann, 2006).

A representative setting for the intra-company closed-loop circuits is intense just-in-sequence material supplies in the automotive industry. Per car, 50–60 large components are supplied in such intense processes, using special load carriers. Such special load carriers are unique for each car series and generation and their lifecycle is limited to the period between start and end of production (Naumann, 2019). The following figure shows the schematic process and identified problems:

There are potential and cost-intensive risks associated with the container supply chain process. These risk factors will be explained in more detail using this cross-company closed loop as an example. The loop involves three different companies. The Container Manufacturer, shown in Fig. 1, is indirectly involved in the loop. The Manufacturer produces the containers according to customer requirements. With the transfer to the Supplier, at the top of Fig. 1, the container is then fed into the recurring part of the cycle. At the Supplier, goods are loaded into the empty containers and shipped to the OEM. The process involves various operational supply risks. One example is the insufficient availability of containers due to a lack of transparency and information for planning. If there are too few, the supplier has to search ad hoc for alternative packaging options for the shipment that comes with additional costs. If there are too many, problems can arise with storage capacity for containers and the high costs increase the capital employed. Therefore, the right number of containers at the right time is a decisive criterion. Further, the transport of the filled containers may also cause problems. Delays or even damage to the transported goods and containers are possible, impacting the just-in-sequence production and leading to costly repairs. At the OEM's site, all load carriers must be booked to register the supplied goods. If the manual process of registration is not carried out correctly, incomplete inventory will occur, leading to chain reactions of incorrect activities.

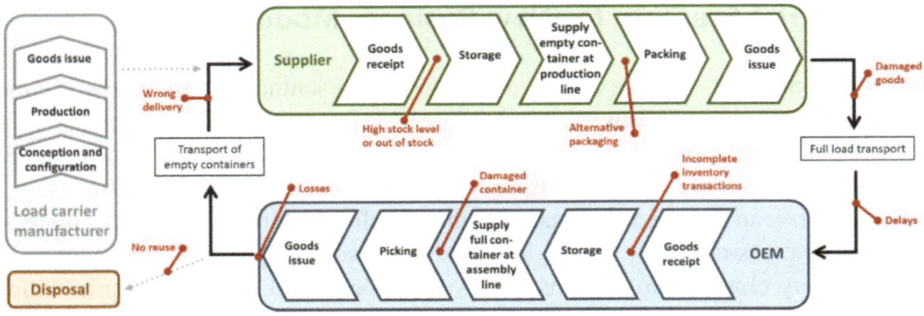

Fig. 1 Potential problems (red) are shown in the container circuit between OEM and supplier (and load carrier manufacturer) (Romer et al., 2018)

After the material is taken out, the containers are returned directly to the Supplier. A possible hazard can be a transport to the wrong supplier or the wrong location. In summary, the biggest risk factor in the loop remains the lack of transparency regarding container movement and inventory.

The recurring part of the cycle lasts as long as the specific product is manufactured, at best a few years. As soon as the good reaches its end of production, the container is no longer needed and becomes a waste. To act in a cost-effective and environmentally friendly manner, most parts of the containers should be reused instead.

Upgrading containers to smart products by integrating IoT technologies enables data collection and its utilization can make container processes transparent, flexible and more robust (Goldmann et al., 2019). Furthermore, data provides the potential to help to automate manual activities and thus to minimize the sources of potential errors.

3 Pillars of Future Container Networks

The container supply chain process can be viewed as a formation with four essential units (Fig. 2). The three application pillars, the modular, physical container, the IoT devices and infrastructure and the cloud-based platform are the foundation for data-driven business models. Each of these pillars holds its own potential for more flexibility overall in the container supply chain.

Modular Physical Product

The main focus of the modular container design approach is flexibility. The container is thus split into a standardized set of components: the base frame, stand, bracket, bracing and base (Fig. 3). Additionally, special modules can be included for the interior, if necessary.

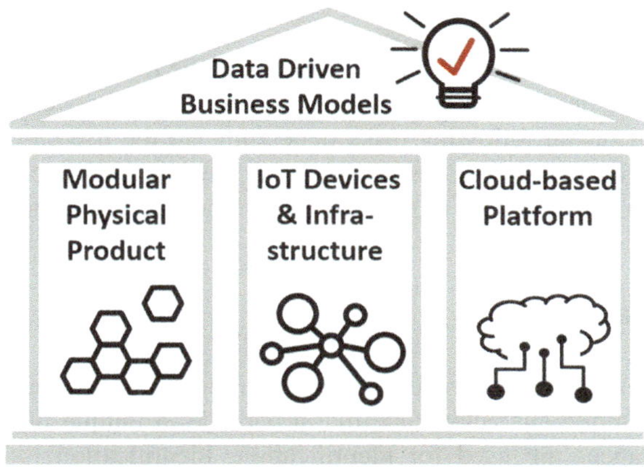

Fig. 2 Pillars of container networks supporting data-driven business models

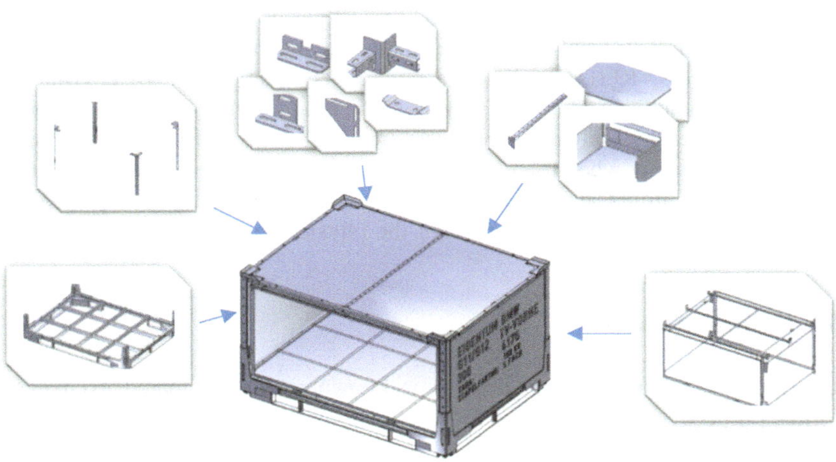

Fig. 3 Modular concept for a special load carrier presented in the iSLT.NET project (Graßl et al., 2021)

Containers can be assembled according to the mix and match principle. This modular feature brings great advantages, as the tailored container can be built faster for the individual needs of customers and specific load types. This results in a considerable amount of timesaving in development. Besides, it is possible to repair the containers faster and cheaper and to reuse parts after the container lifecycle.

The modularity enables the container manufacturer to offer different business models and to adjust prices, for example based on the percentage of reusable parts, a specific customer returns after the lifecycle.

IoT Devices and Infrastructure

The central pillar of the digital container network is the IoT hardware infrastructure, specifically an IoT device, which is attached to the containers. The IoT device has to fulfil a subset of the following tasks depending on the use case: identification, communication, localization and environmental sensing and, since the devices are mostly battery powered, all of this with as little energy consumption as possible.

3.1 Identification

Identification describes the process of unambiguous recognition of an already known entity. Unique characteristics, like a barcode, a unique number or various external appearances are used for identification. Identification is needed so that other participants of a task know whom or what they are dealing with, for example, which load carrier was just unloaded.

In the project, a barcode was used for identification, as smart containers had to be integrated into the daily business of the project partners, where manual scanning of barcodes is already used to validate incoming and outgoing cargo. In a more automated process, RFID (Radio-Frequency IDentification) or BLE (Bluetooth Low Energy) could be used instead. The barcode is additionally used to link the IoT Devices with the physical containers they are attached to and therefore the actual goods in the container when referencing the order data. Whenever either a container or a device is identified, the respective other perspective and the transported good can be inferred, creating a digital twin of the physical container (Table 1).

3.2 Communication

Radio communication between devices is known as an automated exchange of information between devices or with a central control centre using different access networks (Boswarthick et al., 2012).

Many different radio communication technologies with different characteristics exist (Fig. 4). However, there is no single "optimal" technology that has it all: high data rates, low latency, long-range reception and low energy use. In addition, there are restrictions regarding energy consumption for data transmission and frequency to comply with in Germany. Thus, one or two suitable technologies should be selected per use case to approximate the requirements. Each increases the cost, complexity and energy consumption of the device (Table 2).

Table 1 Deployed identification techniques in the project

Identification
Barcode
LoRa

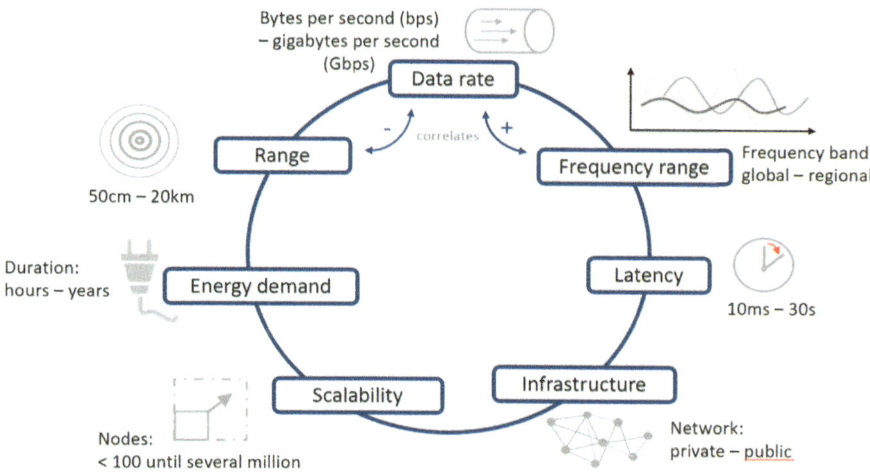

Fig. 4 Criteria for selection of IoT solution in smart product-service systems

Different technologies vary regarding all those parameters making it inevitable to prioritize or combine different approaches to fulfil all requirements (Table 3).

For iSLT.NET, reception range and power consumption were prioritized over data rates and latency, as the considered container cycle process is not as time critical. For this reason, the LPWAN (Low Power Wide Area Network) technology LoRa using their low power LoRaWAN protocol was selected. The group of LPWAN technologies is able to send very small data packages over long ranges with very little power consumption.

LoRa was chosen over comparable options as the technology had bigger market visibility at the time of selection, and therefore also a bigger variety of device manufacturers available. It also is mainly available in a private network structure, which was another prioritized requirement, due to the high data protection regulations of the partners. In the end, the partners installed their own antennas/gateways and the servers were hosted internally.

One of the limitations of LoRa is its scalability once we reach 1000+ devices (Haxhibeqiri et al., 2017), but this was not an issue in this ~160 container use case.

3.3 Localization

Knowing the position of an object along the supply chain, where it currently is, where it came from and especially where it was at the time of a specific event, i.e. a sensor reading, occurred, creates a lot of valuable information. Due to its importance, humankind has already found a variety of approaches to locate objects in a defined space. Most of them rely on geometric calculations starting from another,

Table 2 Key questions to select suitable IoT technologies for any use case

Requirement	Key questions	Typical results
Range	What is the average and maximum distance data has to be transmitted in the application context?	Average and maximum distances in metres
Data rate	How much data has to be sent out and in which interval?	Average size and interval of a data package in byte
Frequency	Are there frequency bands, which are banned due to country or company policies (e.g. because they are already occupied by more critical applications)?	Exclusion of specific frequency bands and therefore technologies using this frequency band
Latency	How much time is justifiable between the occurrence of an event and the arrival of the message at the server?	Time in seconds
Infrastructure/network type	Is it needed to control the complete data flow by setting up a own (=private) network or is it possible to use the public network of a local provider? How many access points are needed for my private network, where can they be installed to cover the full premise and how much will this cost approximately?	Cost estimation for both private and public network usage
Scalability	How many smart objects need to be connected in the business model? How many smart objects are sending data to the same access point?	Number of smart products overall and maximum number of objects in the area of a single access point
Energy demand	How long will the device last in the field without a battery change? Is it possible to reduce this to a few months?	Timeline for a recharge or replacement process. Exclusion of many communication technologies if the needed operating time surpasses a few months

already known location and measuring distances, using for example the travel time of a radio signal. The most renowned location technique is GPS (Global Positioning System), which uses satellites (and static base stations on earth) and multilateration to globally locate GPS-receivers with an accuracy of only a few metres. The idea of multilateration can also be used with static access points, like private gateways or cell towers. As radio signals travel with speeds close to the speed of light, the time differences for transmissions are in the magnitude of nanoseconds. This is why GPS is more accurate, as those extremely complex and similar expensive satellites can

Table 3 Specification of the used communication technology LoRa (Bouguera et al., 2018; Haxhibeqiri et al., 2017)

Communication via LoRaWAN	
Frequency	868 MHz (Europe)
Range	Urban: 2–5 km Rural: 15 km
Data rate	up to 250 kbps
Latency	1–2 s
Standard	LoRaWAN R1.0
Power consumption	<1 mJ per transmission
Scalability	<1000 per gateway

Table 4 Deployed localization techniques in the project iSLT.NET

Localization
GPS
Gateway affiliation

differentiate those gaps much better than an average private gateway. The associated problem with GPS is its rather high energy demand while trying to pick up and interpret the signals of multiple satellites.

Another and much simpler approach can be used to localize smart devices locally and needs just one gateway in reach. By knowing the location of a gateway and the range in which it can receive messages, the position of the object can be easily derived from the circle with radius = range around the gateway (Table 4).

In the project, a combination of the approaches to localize the load carriers was applied. All devices came with an integrated GPS module, which determines the global position of the load carriers in fixed time intervals between 10 and 120 min. The GPS function was deactivated in a handful of devices to have a reference for battery runtime and to check how much value this global localization adds.

The gateway affiliation approach was used when the containers reached the actual production sites of the OEM or the supplier. Gateways with limited ranges of 200–500 m allowed us to infer events like "goods receipt" (see Fig. 1) once the devices were in the range of the gateway in the receiving area of the production facility. The accuracy of this approach depends solely on the gateway range, meaning it's 200–500 m. This approach is only applicable for a correspondingly large production area and is prone to errors if the overall process, for example where to store the containers after they arrived, is not adhered to.

Table 5 Deployed sensors in the project iSLT.NET

Sensors
Temperature
Humidity
Inclination/orientation
Acceleration

3.4 Sensors

Sensors detect and collect chemical or physical properties and convert them into electrical signals. This creates usable information for further processing. While not in range of a Gateway, data can also locally be stored on the device until the next message is sent out or a daily/weekly/monthly update is scheduled.

In iSLT.NET sensors for temperature, humidity, inclination (or orientation) and acceleration were agreed upon (Table 5).

3.5 Energy Consumption

All of the mentioned tasks of identification, communication, localization and sensing the environment need energy. While a smartphone, which can also fulfil those tasks needs to recharge almost daily, optimized IoT devices should be able to function over months, maybe even years, depending on their application. The most important feature of such devices is their ability to power down to a minimum level whenever they are not actively assigned to fulfil a task. In this state of "deep sleep", the devices only supply their core functions, so they can retain saved data and wake up when needed.

The energy consumption for identification and communication depends mainly on the chosen technology, which sends or receives specific data. The longer such a transmission/receive window is, for example because a lot of data has to be sent out at once, the more energy is needed. Low power communication protocols like BLE or the LPWAN technologies were specifically designed to reduce the amount of data for each transmission.

The power demand of localization again depends on the used method. Stand-alone solutions like GPS need a lot of energy, as the GPS module is rather powerful and needs to be powered on until signals received from at least four satellites. Other methods use the already integrated communication technology to infer the location. This not only reduces the complexity of the device, but also reduces the accuracy of the localization significantly. There are also approaches to reduce the amount of scheduled GPS fixes, by linking the GPS activation to specific events, rather than a timer interval. This means that a GPS fix is only scheduled when the container moves again after some storage time (acceleration sensor) or when something unexpected, like a big shock, happens.

The energy consumption of the sensors is kind of negligible compared to the demands of communication and localization, but can still be optimized by powering down when not needed and using less complex sensors.

Over the course of the project, the GPS functionality reduced the lifetime of the devices significantly from around two years to a few months (depending on the time interval of GPS fixes). The increased cost for manually accessing and changing the batteries in shorter interval has to be taken into account when analysing the advantages of a more accurate position.

3.6 Cloud-Based Software

A cloud-based platform analyses and visualizes the data, which is collected by the IoT Device, allowing for services like condition monitoring, tracking and tracing or damage reporting. It acts as a data hub, an interface between data and user, and in addition is used to couple the physical and virtual objects. Making the platform cloud based allows for easy accessibility and enables the use of handy features provided by renowned IoT cloud service providers, like Microsoft Azure or Amazon Web Services (AWS).

The functioning of the three technical pillars (see Fig. 2) can be demonstrated by looking at a special "shock warning" use case.

The sensors on the IoT Device record the inclination and acceleration of the containers continuously and send them to the backend in fixed time intervals (time-based) or depending on other conditions (event-based). When using communication technologies with limited reach, it might also be necessary to store the data on the device itself for some time, until a gateway is in reach again. Once the server receives the data, it is compared to given thresholds from legal or contractual guidelines. When exceeding these, alerts are sent out to given recipients, for example a service employee. He can then check the exact values and the position of the container on the platform and prepare for its arrival, by ordering an inspection or informing the repair team. This reduces the manual work for inspections of every delivery drastically and allows for much faster and more efficient repairs. It also gives the involved parties assurance about liability issues, as intensity and location can easily be reproduced. Liability is an often overlooked aspect, as the parties normally have to share the cost for repairs and reintegration of the damaged containers, while all think the damage was the other guy's fault, leading to potentially damaged business relations.

All in all having condition and location data of containers available on a platform increases the transparency of the container flow a lot. The "live" data of condition and location of containers can be used to improve the container process in real time. The historical tracing data can additionally be used to clarify liability issues and will be used to train machine learning algorithms in the future.

4 Data-Driven Business Models

The roofs of future container networks (see Fig. 2) are data-driven business models that create value through data from the pillars. Following the established field of PSS research, especially smart product-oriented and smart use-oriented PSS are realized using such data. Additionally, from a business model perspective, the ecosystem expands by new actors.

4.1 Smart Product-Oriented Product-Service Systems

Product-oriented PSS encompass the traditional selling of a physical product and the offering of services related to the lifecycle of the product (Tukker, 2004, 2015). In the described research project, there were some non-digital services developed. These encompass the repair and maintenance of physical modular containers, which aspire to extend the lifecycle of the product. Additionally, cleaning and reconfiguration of modular containers to new specifications and recycling of components were services designed. Emphasizing the potential of data in an IoT environment, in smart product-oriented PSS, the underlying products are smart and the data generated by these products is the key resource for services related to the product. Therefore, the smart services based on the IoT data will be described in more detail.

The first service is tracking. It combines identification and localization functions and ensures transparency along the container circuits during the lifecycle. The ability to localize allows the tracking of interorganizational container movements. Another smart service is tracing. This service aggregates tracking data of the past and thereby enables traceability of containers, which can be especially helpful to comprehend container movements, usage rates, shortages and the overall capacity design in the circuits. The next service, condition monitoring, aggregates all IoT sensor data in a cloud layer, thereby making information on temperature, humidity or shocks available. Combined with the tracking service, full transparency for incidents can be provided. Additionally, users can define critical tolerances for sensor values. If these tolerances are crossed, the service condition monitoring automatically transmits an even-based warning message to relevant stakeholders with all the available information. This can help to identify critical stages in the container circuity and to eliminate processual root causes for incidents. Other smart services are automatic bookings of container movements and the crossing of certain processual stages for incoming and outgoing containers from production sites. A software application analyses the tracking data for containers and documents the material flows. In case of differences between, i.e. number of ordered materials, wrong containers or similar events, the service creates warnings. As containers are continuously listed in accounts for suppliers and OEMs, the time-consuming comparison of the container account balances can be automatized. Geofencing, an application for the analysis of localization data in the context of geographic areas, can enhance the bookings by even providing more detailed analyses for certain areas of production sites. The service lifecycle captures and visualizes all data of an individual container along the lifecycle, by combining the data from the different IoT functions and the other services in a reporting. This can be a closing loop source for future container developments of detailed sustainability reportings as CO_2 footprints of containers. The most extensive and complicated service is circuit planning. Additionally to the data captured by the lifecycle service, it analyses the over-capacity and shortages of containers in the whole value-creation process by comparing container movements with production planning information. This service facilitates the holistic optimization of container circuits.

4.2 Smart Use-Oriented Product-Service Systems

Based on the product-oriented services, especially the information made available by such services, smart use-oriented PSS can be realized. In such smart use-oriented PSS, the ownership remains with the provider. Customers of such business models benefit from flexible usage through traditional models as leasing, rent or pooling models. (Tukker, 2004, 2015) While product-oriented propositions are based on the outlined IoT functions, use-oriented models are based on all four pillars.

As outlined in Sect. 2, the open-loop circuits need a standardized product, which traditional special load carriers are not. Through the modularization of the special load carriers, these traditionally individual products can be reconfigured for different customers. The standardization on the level of load carrier components allows the flexible adaption and provision of load carriers for different customers. The multi-usability of the components also enables to reuse components multiple times, thereby shifting the lifecycle perspective of the load carrier towards the modular components. In such a setting, being able to provide load carriers to customers is a proposition with different benefits. The traditional owner saves the initial investment costs for the acquisition of load carrier capacities. Instead, the carriers are consumed through more flexible business models.

The IoT solution provides data along the lifecycle of the load carrier. Such data, as outlined in Sect. 3 is enabling the tracking of carriers across the closed-loop circuits in the just-in-sequence automotive environment. The tracking is the basis for pricing models, as pay per use, which are flexible ways of renting industrial goods for use. The OEM and the supplier only pay for the real usage time. Overall the systemic impact of such smart use-oriented PSS encloses the reduction of load carriers needed in the automotive industrial system.

4.3 IoT Ecosystem

The importance of business ecosystems has been researched for a long time and they can exemplarily be defined as “an economic community supported by a foundation of interacting organizations and individuals—the organisms of the business world” (Moore, 2006). Moore (2006) describes customers, lead producers, competitors and other stakeholders as key actors in a business ecosystem. For smart PSS, the business ecosystem must be expanden grow. By following Paper (2017) in the development of an ecosystem model for the realization of the IoT services, an ecosystem was defined for smart containers (see Fig. 5). The ecosystem consists of all actors needed to realize the business model. The actors can be separated into four sub-ecosystems: the central sub-ecosystem, the smart product ecosystem, the application sub-ecosystem and a product-based sub-ecosystem, which are interrelated around the customers.

The central subsystem encloses all actors to conceptualize and organize the business model. These actors cannot be exchanged as solution providers and a solution integrator develops, offers and implements the smart PSS. Consultancies,

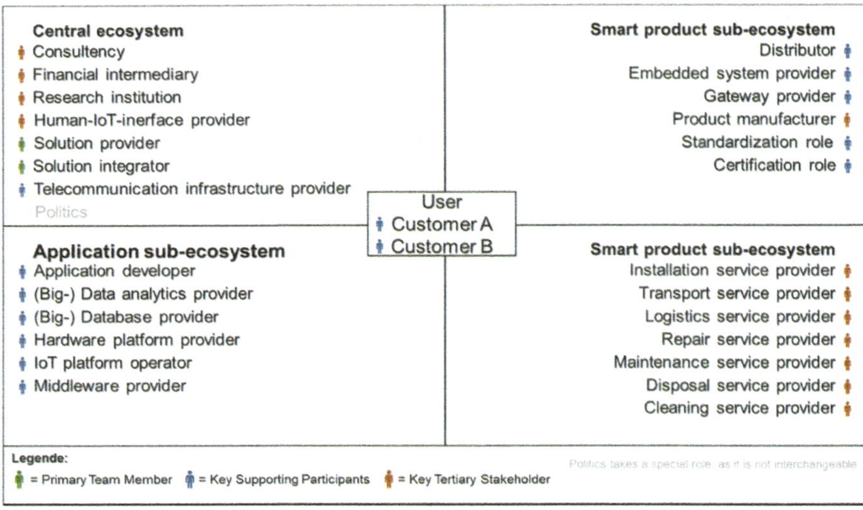

Fig. 5 IoT ecosystem for smart PSS business models

Financial intermediaries, research institutions and human IoT Interface providers contribute to the design, support, financing and user acceptance of the smart PSS.

In the application sub-ecosystem, all the technological tasks—as outlined in pillar three—are managed. IoT Platform provider provides the technical platform and manages the data. The application developer delivers the necessary software applications and works closely together with data analytics experts, which generate the necessary analytics algorithms. Database providers ensure the security and perform saving of data. Hardware-platform providers deliver, i.e. servers, for the application sub-ecosystem. Middle-ware providers contribute by developing solutions to integrate the smart containers into existing information systems as well as their management.

The smart product ecosystem covers all actors, necessary to enhance products to smart products as the foundation of smart PSS. The distributor ensures the supply of hardware, as IoT devices to the solution provider and integrator. The producer of the products provides the physical product, here the containers. Important groups of actors are the certification role and the standardization role, which have to issue the required standards and certifications for the use of the smart product in PSS. Embedded-system providers develop micro-electronical components that can be integrated by the distributor or the solution integrator. Manufacturers of gateways contribute the necessary technology to supply the interfaces needed between the technology layers for continuous data exchange.

While the product-based ecosystem encompasses the actors that had to be involved in traditional business models for containers, the number of actors in the other ecosystems shows the increasing complexity of ecosystems for smart PSS. Another very important group of actors is the telecommunication provider that ensures the IoT data transmission.

5 Conclusion

This publication contributes to the business model, smart PSS and IoT research by outlining the importance of aligning the different disciplines activities. The importance of applying an interdisciplinary perspective of the coordination of IoT solution, service and physical product becomes obvious. The research disciplines must converge their doing in order to leverage the potential of data as enabling resource for business models. The case study in the automotive industry outlines the orchestration of business needs, technological capabilities and value creation. It becomes obvious that the benefits of new business models can only be realized when an IoT solution is used and the business ecosystem is expanded.

Realizing data-driven business models is a major step towards platform and data economies and thereby the transformation of traditional value creation. Less than the physical load carrier, its availability at the right location at the right point of time becomes data-based value for customers. Traditional manufacturing companies shift their business model from a product seller towards a solution provider. Entrepreneurial initiatives following this trend will be seen in the Automotive Industry and the idea is ready to be transferred to other industries, such as food or pharma. The technological development of IoT solutions can be described as dynamic leading to new approaches to gather, transfer, structure and save data. This will enhance the value propositions of data-driven business models. They can reduce the number of necessary containers in the systems, reduce the lifecycle costs and allow optimization of processes. Additional new services fees can benefit the provider. However, the cost for the three pillars has to be carefully managed.

References

Boswarthick, D., Elloumi, O. & Hersent, O. (2012). *M2M communications: A systems approach*. Chichester: Wiley.

Bouguera, T., Diouris, J. F., Chaillout, J. J., Jaouadi, R., & Andrieux, G. (2018). Energy consumption model for sensor nodes based on LoRa and LoRaWAN. *Sensors, 18*(7), 2104.

Goldmann, E., Graßy, M. & Neumann, H. (2019). Entwicklung datenbasierter Dienstleistungen zur Umsetzung eines unternehmensübergreifenden C-Teile-Managements. In V. Stich, J. H. Schumann, D. Beverungen, G. Gudergan & P. Jussen (Eds.), *Digitale Dienstleistungsinnovationen* (pp. 209–223). Berlin, Heidelberg: Springer.

Graßl, M., Falter, L., Harth, A., Zink, M., Fottner, J., Zeiler, J., Meißner, S., Romer, M., Schlittenbauer, S., Seitz, R., Voigt, G. und Naumann, V. (2021). Schlussbericht iSLT.NET: Netzwerk für intelligente, modulare Sonderladungsträger. in press.

Haxhibeqiri, J., van den Abeele, F., Moerman, I., & Hoebeke, J. (2017). Lora scalability: A simulation model based on interference measurements. *Sensors, 17*(6), 1193.

Hofmann, E., & Bachmann, H. (2006). *Behälter-management in der praxis: State-of-the-art und Entwicklungstendenzen bei der Steuerung von Ladungsträgerkreisläufen*. Deutscher Verkehrs-Verlag.

Klötzer, C. & Pflaum, A. (2015). Cyber-physical systems as the technical foundation for problem solutions in manufacturing, logistics and supply chain management. In *5th International Conference on the Internet of Things*, Seoul, South Korea.

Moore, J. F. (2006). Business ecosystems and the view from the firm. *The Antitrust Bulletin, 51*(1), 31–75.

Naumann, V. (2019). *Geschäftsmodelle in der digitalen Welt am Beispiel eines intelligenten Sonderladungsträgers*. Fraunhofer IPA.

Paper, M. (2017). Entwicklung eines Ökosystemmodells für das Internet der Dinge. In A. Pflaum (Ed.), *Schriftenreihe Logistik und Informationstechnologien* (Vol. 4.). Stuttgart, Fraunhofer.

Porter, M. E., & Heppelmann, J. E. (2014). How smart, connected products are transforming competition. *Harvard Business Review, 92*(11), 64–88.

Prockel, G. & Pflaum, A. (2015). A business model framework for supply chain visibility: value, architecture and development of loT technologies. In *The 27th NOFOMA Conference 2015: Towards Sustainable Logistics and Supply Chain Management*, Molde, Norway.

Raab, V., Petersen, B., & Kreyenschmidt, J. (2011). Temperature monitoring in meat supply chains. *British Food Journal, 113*(10), 1267–1289.

Romer, M., Zeiler, J., Meißner, S. & Fottner, J. (2018). The internet of load carriers. design of a cloud-based service-system for smart and connected load carriers. In *Proceedings of the 15th International Joint Conference on e-Business and Telecommunications* (ICETE 2018), Porto, Portugal.

Rosenthal, A. (2016). *Ganzheitliche Bewertung modularer Ladungsträgerkonzepte*. Springer Fachmedien.

Tukker, A. (2004). Eight types of product-service system: Eight ways to sustainability? Experiences from SusProNet. *Business Strategy and the Environment, 13*(4), 246–260.

Tukker, A. (2015). Product services for a resource-efficient and circular economy—A review. *Journal of Cleaner Production, 97*, 76–91.

Valencia, A., Mugge, R., Schoormans, J.P.L., Schifferstein, H.N.J. (2015). The design of smart product-service systems (PSSs): An exploration of design characteristics. *International Journal of Design*, 9, 13–28.

Wölker, M. (2004). *Automatische Identifikation und Datenerfassung*. Retrieved from http://www.identifikation.info/.

AI and Blockchain in Production and Supply Chain Management

If You Go for AI, Be Aware of the Psychological Hurdles Around It —Practical and Theoretical Insights on the Industrial Application of Artificial Intelligence

Quirin Demlehner, Daniel Schoemer, and Sven Laumer

Abstract

Artificial intelligence (AI) is often seen as one of the main enabling technologies behind Industry 4.0, especially within the next decade. In this chapter, we reflect on a frequently neglected type of adoption hurdles, founded in the psychology of the individuals purchasing, developing, and working with those types of systems. Within this work, we integrate both insights from the latest scientific releases on the industrial application of AI as well as our practical experience from that field to a handy six-point list of psychological key success factors. That list is supposed to help both managers and practitioners in the field to ensure the effective deployment of AI within their organizations in the future.

1 Introduction

Along with the introduction of the vision of Industry 4.0 ten years ago, artificial intelligence (AI) has been postulated as one of the major enabling technologies behind it (Kagermann, Wahlster, & Helbig, 2013; Müller et al., 2018). And since

Q. Demlehner (✉) · D. Schoemer
Siemens AG, Gleiwitzer Straße 555, 90475 Nürnberg, Germany
e-mail: quirin.demlehner@fau.de

D. Schoemer
e-mail: daniel.schoemer@fau.de

Q. Demlehner · D. Schoemer · S. Laumer
Schöller Endowed Chair for Information Systems, Digitalization in Business and Society, Friedrich-Alexander-University Erlangen-Nürnberg, Lange Gasse 20, 90403 Nürnberg, Germany
e-mail: sven.laumer@fau.de

K.-I. Voigt and J. M. Müller (eds.), *Digital Business Models in Industrial Ecosystems*,
Future of Business and Finance, https://doi.org/10.1007/978-3-030-82003-9_11

then, it has taken a similar curve regarding its appreciation within both research and practice (Demlehner & Laumer, 2019; Demlehner & Laumer, 2020b). After experiencing almost unlimited euphoria in the beginning, in the following years more and more articles and experience reports featuring rather pessimistic overall assessments were aired (Mertens et al., 2017).

In 2021, the overall picture has started to become more balanced. Regarding the potential, research and practice are still unanimous in their assessment that AI is most likely one of the key technologies for the upcoming decade in order to further improve manufacturing operations as well as to solve industrial problems that have been unsolvable until now (Dwivedi et al., 2019). However, they also acknowledge that the threshold for unlocking that potential is not as low as many people might have thought in the beginning. Since then, a number of very valuable lessons regarding what it takes to leverage AI advantageously within an industrial setting have been learned and also published (Demlehner, 2021; Demlehner & Laumer, 2020a; Webb, 2018; Winkler et al., 2019).

Consequently, most corporations are now aware of the fact that they need vast amounts of high-quality data to be able to build useful AI models based on that—and they also know how much time and effort it can take to get to that point (Tubaro & Casilli, 2019). They are conscient that leveraging AI at scale requires a clear AI strategy including top-level management support to overcome both functional silos and individual reservations toward giving up on one's exclusive access to potentially pivotal data (Webb, 2018). They know that they have to have constant access to experienced AI experts not only during the implementation process but also for the maintenance of the models created (Demlehner & Laumer, 2020a). And they are aware that the initial expectations regarding the comprehensiveness and the return on investment for many industrial AI use cases might indeed have been a little bit too optimistic in the past (Cam et al., 2019).

But what most companies are still unaware of is that, even if they align with all the aforementioned points, in many cases human psychology still prevents AI from being successfully scaled (Demlehner, 2021). Prejudices, mistrust, and personal reservations are repeatedly reported as being major barriers for the adoption of AI within the industrial environment (Birkel et al., 2019). According to two recent large-scale surveys, only 16 % of the interviewed employees trust AI-generated results (Webb, 2018) and 45 % fear impending personal privacy infractions due to the use of AI at their workplace (Cam et al., 2019). In consequence, in many industries, AI is currently stuck at a one-digit diffusion rate and facing an increasing number of companies that consciously refrain from using it for the moment (Winkler et al., 2019).

Therefore, managers associated with the industrial application of AI need to be aware of the psychologically induced issues and adoption hurdles around that technology class, especially if they want to foster its diffusion within their organizations in the coming years. On the following pages, we share a number of insights on that complex topic. They stem from a collection of different studies and surveys on that topic as well as the experience gained throughout our practical work in the field of industrial AI within the last years.

2 AI for AI's Sake

Especially in large and historically very successful companies, one is often confronted with a situation in which the management decision to deploy AI is or was not based on the capability of the technology itself or a specific problem that needs to be solved but rather on the fact that AI is or was in vogue at that very moment. When competitors' marketing departments start boasting with their first (burnished) successes around the application of AI, resulting in (allegedly) spectacular savings for the customers, and even politicians announce huge public funding programs for AI, many executives see themselves forced to stick with the development out there in the market in order to avoid being possibly accredited with a crucial oversight a few years later (Demlehner & Laumer, 2020a).

While such a behavior might be understandable from that individual's perspective, it leaves the organization with a high chance of developing costly technology for which there is no native application domain. In consequence, the AI model or system developed is not used to solve a year-long nagging problem for which everyone is happy as soon as it is gone. Instead, it is pushed into environments where it then cannibalizes the incumbent systems that have painstakingly been developed and optimized over many years. And in many cases, the initial performance then even lacks behind the previous system's, as it is usual for almost any new system.

The underlying psychological phenomenon behind such a managerial behavior is called "regret avoidance" within the scientific literature and marks a common mistake or bias in human decision-making (Lee & Joshi, 2017; Samuelson & Zeckhauser, 1988). For the affected employees, such hardly comprehensible decisions together with, in many cases, low and error-prone initial performances from the newly introduced AI-based systems can lead to massive resistance behavior and mistrust (Laumer & Eckhardt, 2012; Webb, 2018). Further, they often perceive their past efforts (e. g., for the optimization of the previous system) as losses after the change, a pattern to which literature usually refers as "perceived sunk costs" (Lee & Joshi, 2017; Samuelson & Zeckhauser, 1988).

For managers in industry, it is important to be aware of those quite common but all the more dangerous psychological patterns. They also need to keep in mind that implementing a change (here in the form of a new technology) without having created a sense of necessity and urgency among the affected employees first has barely proven successful in the past (Kotter, 1996; Laumer et al., 2016a). Or to put it with Cassie Kozyrkov, Chief Decisions Scientist at Google: "Don't waste time on AI for AI's sake. Be motivated by what it will do for you, not by how sci-fi it sounds."

If managers anyway intend to deploy AI for strategic reasons, they should browse for problems within their organization that are well-suited for that technology class. For starters, within the industrial environment, AI is especially qualified to solve problems for which the decision patterns are either too many or too complex to be deterministically modeled but the desired outcome itself is

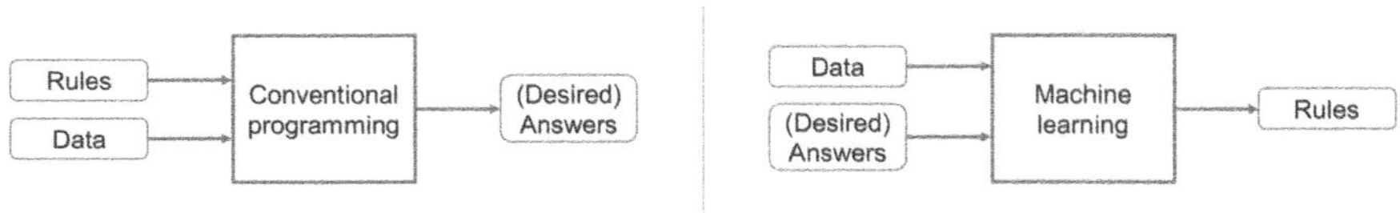

Fig. 1 Conventional programming compared to machine learning (Chollet, 2018)

clearly definable (Luckow et al., 2018). In 2021, that almost inevitably leads to AI applications from the area of machine learning (Brynjolfsson & Mitchell, 2017; Chollet, 2018). Within the same, the resulting algorithms are trained instead of explicitly programmed, leaving the system with the task of coming up with the rules itself but also with the need of being fed enormous amounts of data to learn from (Fig. 1).

A good example therefore is, for instance, the quality inspection for finished parts or products through pictures made by high-resolution cameras (Demlehner et al., 2021). In that case, the programmers do not have to come up with a set of deterministic rules to model the binary outcome on whether a product is ok or not. Instead, the model learns and trains the rules to itself in a probabilistic approach by relying on historic data which has been enriched manually with the respective judgment on whether that particular product or part in the picture does meet the necessary quality requirements or not. Another good example is the application of AI to predict upcoming service needs, usually referred to as predictive maintenance. In that case, an AI algorithm is able to detect patterns, correlations, and dependencies within millions of different historic data points (enriched by the information on when within that time series the system was running smoothly and when an unplanned downtime took place) and to predict analog incidences up to 36 h in advance based on the way the machine data is evolving over time during running operations (Siemens, 2020a).

Additional to their obvious business value, both these example use cases carry a fair share of value also for the employees. They either free them from looking at always the same parts for hours in favor of more value-adding and satisfying tasks, thereby increasing the overall quality due to the elimination of risks like fatigue, or significantly reduce stressful phases of unplanned machine downtime. And as they further tackle problems that quite obviously for everyone deserve solving, creating a sense of necessity for the change among the affected workers should not be much of a challenge. Consequently, resistance behavior is minimized (Laumer et al., 2016b).

3 Bias in Data

Data makes up the core of all AI-based systems, models, and applications (Russell & Norvig, 2016). Hence, irregularities within the data used to create a particular model usually also corrupt the model itself (Zou & Schiebinger, 2018).

A recent example therefore, which also created a lot of attention within the media, is the sexist AI recruiting algorithm from Amazon. It was ceased after the company found out that the model had taught itself that male candidates were preferable and thus discriminated against female candidates for their gender. It penalized resumes that included the word "women's" (e.g., in women's soccer team captain) and devaluated graduates from all-women colleges (Maedche et al., 2019; Schmalenbach & Laumer, 2020). The reason for that was the fact that historic hiring data had been used to train that model and hence the algorithm had learned the sexist bias reflected in that data without anyone noticing for quite some time (Crawford & Calo, 2016).

The not-noticing part thereby is a quite AI-specific problem. It is attributable to the fact that the vast majority of AI algorithms function as a black boxes for humans (Ochmann et al., 2021), at least in terms of what decision metrics they teach to themselves (to the next section for details on that problem). That this problem is hardly solvable with the currently available technological means, even if a company has plenty of AI knowledge and vast financial resources, is emphasized by the fact that Amazon is usually referred to as one of the world's leading tech and AI companies of today.

But the underlying problem of bias in data is of course not limited to recruiting and resume screening algorithms and systems. Also within the industrial context, contortions within the training data can corrupt the resulting models, and those flaws might even be harder to recognize due to the higher abstractness of industrial measurement data. To stick with the two aforementioned example systems, a typical mistake is to train AI-based visual quality control applications within a laboratory setting instead of directly on the shop floor. This happens because people do not want or are not allowed to constantly disturb the running operations as well as their colleagues within the factory. However, if the data created in that laboratory setting is then used for training, it typically leads to a misfit between the trained model and what input that model is then facing in practice because of things like a different camera position, different lighting, or other unplanned confounders like vibration (Luckow et al., 2018). That type of filthiness is usually referred to as measurement bias (Li et al., 2020; Mehrabi et al., 2019).

Another typical issue is the association or representation bias in which the learned model multiplies an uneven distribution within the data (Lloyd, 2018; Mehrabi et al., 2019). While that sort of bias could arguably also be the reason for the Amazon algorithm being sexist (i.e., not because the developers were sexist but Amazon hired mainly male employees during the phase that the training data covered due to the general dominance of male graduates in tech degrees in that time), it can also occur in industrial settings. If the training data only consists of data from machine type A in location A and machine type B in location B, the model will most likely not work for machines from type A operating in location B because for the trained model that situation simply does not exist. While these two biases are about half technologically induced and half psychologically induced, a third typical AI-related bias in data is almost purely psychologically induced.

When the developers and researchers involved subconsciously project their expectations and subjective opinions on the data or its interpretation, that usually results in what is called an observer bias within the same (Mehrabi et al., 2019). In the industrial context, this can for instance happen if they choose to collect data only from the machines that are working properly or easily accessible in their eyes and leave out the other ones or vice versa. Also, this is a common mistake during manual data labeling, especially when that work is done by little-qualified micro-workers or casual employees (Tubaro & Casilli, 2019).

Again, awareness for those kinds of things is the first step to avoiding them. Hence, managers as well as other employees involved in AI-related projects should keep their eyes open for those kinds of psychologically induced hurdles and ensure that the risk for their occurrence is minimized within their projects.

4 Black Box Nature of AI

Recent AI-based systems, especially within the subfield of machine learning, achieve tremendous (predictive) quality standards (Luckow et al., 2018). At the same time, the underlying models increasingly gain in complexity and size. Unfortunately, they do not learn in the same way as humans do but through iteratively adjusting numerical weights (Russell & Norvig, 2016). In consequence, it is difficult for individuals to understand the underlying reasoning for certain decisions or recommendations. This phenomenon is usually subsumed under the term "black box problem". Black boxes miss providing further information on how decisions are generated as they cover multiple levels of abstraction that are barely interpretable in a way that is aligned with human thinking and decision-making mechanisms (Ochmann et al., 2021; Ochmann et al., 2020b).

Prior research has shown that a lack of comprehensibility is detrimental to the acceptance of AI-based decisions and recommendations by the respective employees (Demlehner, 2021). The survey by Cam et al. (2019) ranks lacking explainability fourth within their list of major AI-related issues with 39 % of the respondents mentioning it (Fig. 2).

This effect is even enforced by the incapacity of most machine learning algorithms to indicate insecurity in such a way as most humans would expect it. If a traditional visual recognition system is confronted with an item that has not been part of the training data, it usually decides for that element within the training data that comes closest to the unknown item (by the model's abstract parameters, of course) instead of displaying an error message or at least indicating a high level of insecurity. Within the consumer world, e. g., when Amazon's Alexa mistakes your

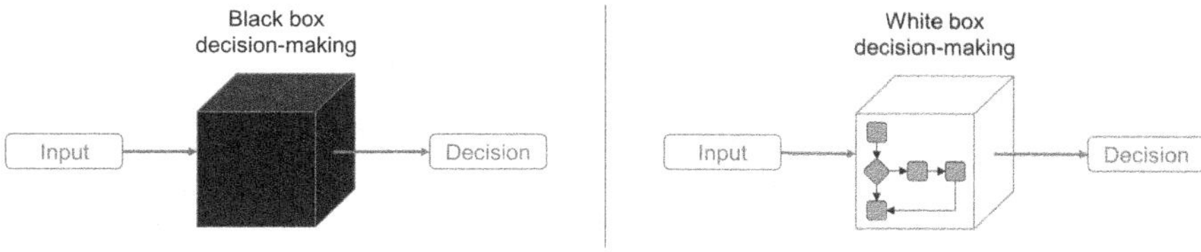

Fig. 2 Black box decision-making compared to white box decision-making

command for its exact opposite, such behavior may indeed be annoying (although in some cases perhaps even funny) but it is not dangerous. However, within an industrial environment, such habits can result in severe quality issues or even impose threats to the affected employees' safety. Therefore, there are currently methodologies being developed for the industrial context to avoid such dangerous (hidden) misjudgments. One relatively advanced example therefore is Siemens' strive to deliver their AI-based applications at an "industrial-grade level", meaning with audited algorithms that ensure a maximum of robustness, explainability, and security (Siemens, 2020b).

But regardless of such endeavors and the fact that many regulatory authorities and other initiatives have lately started to focus on the transparency of algorithms and to promote the concept of explainable AI (XAI) on a transcontextual and global basis (Adadi & Berrada, 2018), at the current point in time, it can not be expected that those things will become a common standard in the foreseeable future. Therefore, to overcome that psychological hurdle, which in most cases results in reduced acceptance and higher resistance rates on the employee side, it is important for firms to introduce the respective workers into the basic underlying mechanisms behind the new AI-based system. This leaves AI-related projects with high demands in terms of preparation and change management measures that should be planned and crafted before starting those projects.

5 Greater Trust in Human Judgment

Another factor that undermines the acceptance of AI-based systems by the employees is the widespread belief that human judgment is preferable compared to a machine-made one (Venkatesh, 2021). Whereas this bias is rather irrelevant for conventional industrial systems and machinery, the particular shift with AI-based systems is mostly powered by an evolvement from decision support to actual decision-making. With many AI-based systems, the human decision-maker, i.e., the employee, is relegated to playing a secondary role in terms of judgment and expected to follow the machine-made decision (Venkatesh, 2021).

That this is not a matter of course for a significant number of employees is shown by the fact that 19 % of the respondents within the survey from Webb (2018) report that many times "personal judgment overrides AI-based decision-making" and hence the expensive system is left unexploited. A similar phenomenon has been proven many times for different non-industrial contexts under the label of (human) algorithm aversion (Castelo et al., 2019; Ochmann et al., 2020a; Venkatesh, 2021). Unfortunately, the underlying psychological mechanism is completely under-researched as far as the industrial context is concerned.

To deal with that problem within the industrial practice, we have made the experience that it is of tremendous value to systematically analyze and document the performance resulting from the (manual or conventionally automated) status quo at the shop floor before the implementation of the respective AI-based system. Otherwise, the employees will inevitably compare the new system to a fictive 100 % performance. Also, it allows managers to argue based on objective facts and figures rather than on authority and their subjective opinion. In most cases, all involved parties will then clearly see, and hence most likely accept, that an AI decision/prediction accuracy of, for instance, 95 % falls indeed somewhat short of the aspired 100 % but is still better than the previous manual performance, especially when compared to the performance at the end of each shift.

6 Improper Expectations

Inflated performance expectations are not the only improper or unrealistic expectations that AI has to deal with today, especially when it enters the industrial shop floor. A media analysis from Fast and Horvitz (2016) has shown that the public awareness and discussion around AI has increased sharply since 2009. However, they also acknowledge that this discussion is of a rather polarized nature, ranging from high hopes, especially in the non-industrial fields of healthcare and education, to a stigmatization of AI as being borderline uncontrollable or a job killer.

With little prior hands-on experience with AI existing until now in most industrial firms (Webb, 2018; Winkler et al., 2019), the expectations of many employees today are mostly based on what experiences and impressions they have made with AI in their private lives. That can be the picture that the aforementioned public discussion and media have created of AI, but also previous experiences with consumer products (e.g., AI-based smartphone camera functions, conversational agents like Amazon's Alexa or Apple's Sir, Netflix, or chatbots). Within a previous study of ours, in which we interviewed 24 automotive blue-collar workers, one worker stated that his fear of an AI-based system getting out of control on the shop floor stems from the image that a Hollywood movie from 1984, namely, "The Terminator", draws of AI (Demlehner, 2021). This spillover effect of experiences and opinions from the employees' private lives to their professional ones is further enforced by the rather liberal use of the label AI in consumer marketing in recent years just as well as the term's rather blurry and undefined nature. The resulting improper and unrealistic expectations toward AI repeatedly lead to serious adoption and acceptance problems (Cam et al., 2019; Webb, 2018).

One particularly common mistake is the lacking differentiation between what "intelligence" means in connection with machines compared to humans. AI-based systems are usually extremely good at one particular and specific task, e.g., the aforementioned "looking" at always the same parts for hours to control for quality issues. Within the same, they tend to surpass human capabilities far and away and further feature the absence of things like fatigue and form fluctuations. However, they completely lack what humans call common sense. To stay with the visual quality control example, data scientists usually have to train the algorithm with mirror-inverted versions of the actual training images as well as alternating backgrounds in order to avoid that the algorithm focuses on in reality irrelevant parts of the pictures during the learning process—a thing that would simply not happen if the algorithm would have common sense.

Closely connected to that is the widespread expectation that AI-based systems should feature a far higher degree of autonomy than conventional ones and thus reduce workers' workload and their jobs' difficulty (Demlehner, 2021). Given the difference between what AI is currently able to do within an industrial setting (Demlehner et al., 2021) and what the popular media suggests it can (Fast & Horvitz, 2016), expectation management among the affected employees is hence key before launching any new system. And of course, the same also accounts for management expectations regarding things like return-on-invest and ramp-up time.

Additionally, our aforementioned study revealed another quite remarkable anomaly regarding the employees' adoption patterns toward AI-based systems, namely, an unusually high number of inhibitors, i.e., factors that solely discourage use if present (Demlehner, 2021). According to theory, technology acceptance through individuals is on the one hand influenced by the so-called enablers. That term refers to "those external beliefs regarding the design and functionality of a system that either encourage or discourage usage, dependent on valence. For example, systems that are perceived to be reliable are used; unreliable ones are not." (Cenfetelli 2004, p. 475). On the other hand, there are also usage inhibiting factors or the so-called inhibitors, i.e., perceptions about a system's attributes with exclusively negative effects if existing. The perhaps most prevalent inhibitor in the case of AI is the perception as a job killer. It solely discourages its use. For AI overall, recent scientific studies, including ours, suggest a remarkably high relevance of those so-called inhibitors within the adoption process (Reis et al., 2020; Venkatesh, 2021).

In our automotive case study, eight out of seventeen overall factors incorporated inhibitors, i.e., solely discouraging elements (Demlehner, 2021). Figure 3 presents an overview of the enablers (on the left side) and inhibitors (on the right side) identified within this study. As of today, to the best of our knowledge, it is the first and only peer-reviewed work that exhibits the employees' acceptance of AI-based industrial systems directly at the shop floor (Fig. 3).

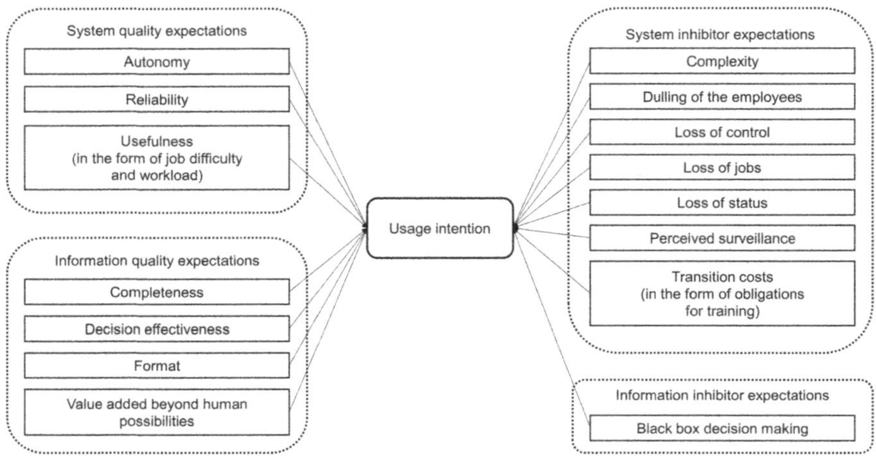

Fig. 3 Enablers and inhibitors for AI usage intentions of automotive blue-collar workers identified by Demlehner (2021)

After all, it is pivotal for a successful AI implementation to know what drives the many stakeholders involved and thereby especially the ones who are supposed to use that system on an everyday basis. For that, both the (still scarce) scientific literature on AI adoption and resistance as well as (the few existing) experienced experts and corporations familiar with the industrial application of AI can be of substantial value for the success of the overall project.

7 Psychological Key Success Factors for an Effective Industrial Implementation of AI

When integrating all those aforementioned psychological hurdles for a successful adoption of AI within an industrial environment, one remains with six major lessons, for which we are convinced that they in essence represent the psychological key success factors for an effective implementation of AI within an industrial environment.

We integrated them into a handy six-point guidance list for both managers and practitioners out there in the field who want to ensure that their industrial AI projects do not fail on the threshold of human technology acceptance. It combines both empirically validated results and insights from a number of different scientific studies as well as the vast amount of experience gained throughout our practical work in the field of industrial AI within recent years.

1. "Don't waste time on AI for AI's sake. Be motivated by what it will do for you, not by how sci-fi it sounds." (Cassie Kozyrkov, Chief Decisions Scientist at Google).
2. Get your and your employees' expectations straight. AI can be valuable, but it can neither save the world, nor a lousy process.
3. Bad data, worse predictions. As far as AI is concerned, data is key—make sure it is not biased.
4. Aim for explainability. If not through the algorithm itself, then by involving all affected employees.
5. Measure your improvements. That includes both measuring decision quality before and after implementing the new system.
6. Know your employees' fears—and address them openly!

References

Adadi, A., & Berrada, M. (2018). Peeking inside the black-box: A survey on explainable artificial intelligence (XAI). *IEEE Access, 6*, 52138–52160.

Birkel, H., Veile, J., Müller, J., Hartmann, E. & Voigt, K.-I. (2019). Development of a risk framework for industry 4.0 in the context of sustainability for established manufacturers. *Sustainability, 11*(2), 384.

Brynjolfsson, E. & Mitchell, T. (2017). What can machine learning do? Workforce implications. *Science, 358*(6370), 1530–1534.

Cam, A., Chui, M. & Hall, B. (2019). *Global AI Survey: AI proves its worth, but few scale impact.* Retrieved from https://www.mckinsey.com/featured-insights/artificial-intelligence/global-ai-survey-ai-proves-its-worth-but-few-scale-impact.

Castelo, N., Bos, M. W., & Lehmann, D. R. (2019). Task-dependent algorithm aversion. *Journal of Marketing Research, 56*(5), 809–825.

Cenfetelli, R. (2004). Inhibitors and enablers as dual factor concepts in technology usage. *Journal of the Association for Information Systems, 5*(11), 472–492.

Chollet, F. (2018). *Deep learning with python. Safari Tech books online.* Shelter Island, Manning.

Crawford, K., & Calo, R. (2016). There is a blind spot in AI research. *Nature, 538*(7625), 311–313.

Demlehner, Q. (2021). Designing AI-based systems to last: Identifying the enablers and inhibitors for the AI usage intentions of automotive blue-collar workers. In *Proceedings of the 29th European Conference on Information Systems (ECIS) 2021,* Marrackech, Morocco.

Demlehner, Q. & Laumer, S. (2019). Setting the hook—The digital transformation from a manufacturing point of view and what it really means. In *Proceedings of the 25th Americas Conference on Information Systems (AMCIS) 2019,* Cancun, Mexico.

Demlehner, Q. & Laumer, S. (2020a). Shall we use it or not? Explaining the adoption of artificial intelligence for car manufacturing purposes. In *Proceedings of the 28th European Conference on Information Systems (ECIS) 2020,* Marrakech, Morocco.

Demlehner, Q., & Laumer, S. (2020). Why context matters: Explaining the digital transformation of the manufacturing industry and the role of the industry's characteristics in it. *Pacific Asia Journal of the Association for Information Systems, 12*(3), 57–81.

Demlehner, Q., Schoemer, D. & Laumer, S. (2021). How can artificial intelligence enhance car manufacturing? A Delphi study-based identification and assessment of general use cases. *International Journal of Information Management, 58*, 102317.

Dwivedi, Y. K., Hughes, L., Ismagilova, E., Aarts, G., Coombs, C., Crick, T., Duan, Y., Dwivedi, R., Edwards, J., Eirug, A., Galanos, V., Ilavarasan, P. V., Janssen, M., Jones, P., Kumar Kar,

A., Kizgin, H., Kronemann, B., Lalf, B., Lucini, B., Medaglia, R., Le Meunier-FitzHugh, K., Le Meunier-FitzHugh, L. C., Misra, S., Mogaji, E., Kumar Sharma, S., Bahadur Singh, J., Raghavan, V., Raman, R., Rana, N. P., Samothrakis, S., Spencer, J., Tamilmani, K., Tubadji, A., Walton, P., Williams, M. D. (2019). Artificial intelligence (AI): Multidisciplinary perspectives on emerging challenges, opportunities, and agenda for research, practice and policy. *International Journal of Information Management*, *57*(4), 101994.

Fast, E. & Horvitz, E. (2016). *Long-term trends in the public perception of artificial intelligence.* Retrieved from http://arxiv.org/pdf/1609.04904v2.

Kagermann, H., Wahlster, W. & Helbig, J. (2013). *Recommendations for implementing the strategic initiative Industrie 4.0. Securing the future of German manufacturing industry.* Final report of the Industrie 4.0 Working Group, Munich: Acatech-National Academy of Science and Engineering and Forschungsunion.

Kotter, J. P. (1996). *Leading change.* Harvard Business School.

Laumer, S. & Eckhardt, A. (2012). Why do people reject technologies: A review of user resistance theories. In Y. K. Dwivedi, M. R. Wade & S. L. Schneberger (Eds.), *Integrated series in information systems. information systems theory* (pp. 63–86). New York: Springer.

Laumer, S., Maier, C., Eckhardt, A., & Weitzel, T. (2016a). User personality and resistance to mandatory information systems in organizations: A theoretical model and empirical test of dispositional resistance to change. *Journal of Information Technology, 31*(1), 67–82.

Laumer, S., Maier, C., Eckhardt, A., & Weitzel, T. (2016b). Work routines as an object of resistance during information systems implementations: Theoretical foundation and empirical evidence. *European Journal of Information Systems, 25*(4), 317–343.

Lee, K., & Joshi, K. (2017). Examining the use of status quo bias perspective in IS research: Need for re-conceptualizing and incorporating biases. *Information Systems Journal, 27*(6), 733–752.

Li, D., Cai, Z., Qin, B., & Deng, L. (2020). Signal frequency domain analysis and sensor fault diagnosis based on artificial intelligence. *Computer Communications, 160*, 71–80.

Lloyd, K. (2018). Bias amplification in artificial intelligence systems. In *Proceedings of the Conference for Artificial Intelligence in Government and Public Sector (AAAI FSS-18),* Arlington, VA.

Luckow, A., Kennedy, K., Ziolkowski, M., Djerekarov, E., Cook, M., Duffy, E., Schleiss, M., Vorster, B., Weill, E., Kulshrestha, A. & Smith, M. C. (2018). Artificial intelligence and deep learning applications for automotive manufacturing. In *2018 IEEE International Conference on Big Data*, Seattle, WA.

Maedche, A., Legner, C., Benlian, A., Berger, B., Gimpel, H., Hess, T., Hinz, O., Morana, S., & Söllner, M. (2019). AI-based digital assistants. *Business & Information Systems Engineering, 61*(4), 535–544.

Mehrabi, N., Morstatter, F., Saxena, N., Lerman, K. & Galstyan, A. (2019). *A Survey on Bias and fairness in machine learning.* Retrieved from http://arxiv.org/pdf/1908.09635v2.

Mertens, P., Barbian, D. & Baier, S. (2017). *Digitalisierung und Industrie 4.0—eine Relativierung.* Wiesbaden, Springer Fachmedien.

Müller, J., Buliga, O., & Voigt, K.-I. (2018). Fortune favors the prepared: How SMEs approach business model innovations in industry 4.0. *Technological Forecasting and Social Change, 132*, 2–17.

Ochmann, J., Michels, L., Zilker, S., Tiefenbeck, V. & Laumer, S. (2020a). The influence of algorithm aversion and anthropomorphic agent design on the acceptance of AI-based job recommendations. In *Proceedings of the 41st International Conference on Information Systems (ICIS) 2020.*

Ochmann, J., Zilker, S. & Laumer, S. (2020b). Job seekers' artificial intelligence-related black box concerns. In *Proceedings of the 2020 on Computers and People Research Conference,* Nuremberg.

Ochmann, J., Zilker, S. & Laumer, S. (2021). The evaluation of the black box problem for AI-based recommendations: An interview-based study. In *Proceedings of the 16. Internationale Tagung Wirtschaftsinformatik (WI) 2021, Duisburg, Essen.*

Reis, L., Maier, C., Mattke, J., Creutzenberg, M., & Weitzel, T. (2020). Addressing user resistance would have prevented a healthcare AI Project failure. *MIS Quarterly Executive, 19*(4), 279–296.

Russell, S. J., & Norvig, P. (2016). *Artificial intelligence: A modern approach* (3rd ed.). Pearson.

Samuelson, W., & Zeckhauser, R. (1988). Status quo bias in decision making. *Journal of Risk and Uncertainty, 1*(1), 7–59.

Schmalenbach, K. & Laumer, S. (2020). Does data-driven recruitment lead to less discrimination? —A technical perspective. In *Proceedings of the 15. Internationale Tagung Wirtschaftsinformatik (WI) 2020,* Potsdam.

Siemens, A. G. (2020a). *Digital transformation: Leading by example.* Retrieved from https://new.siemens.com/global/en/company/stories/industry/electronics-digitalenterprise-futuretechnologies.html.

Siemens AG (2020b). *Responsible AI—Transparency, Bias, and responsibility in the age of trustworthy artificial intelligence.* Retrieved from https://ingenuity.siemens.com/2020/11/responsible-ai-transparency-bias-and-responsibility-in-the-age-of-trustworthy-artificial-intelligence/.

Tubaro, P., & Casilli, A. A. (2019). Micro-work, artificial intelligence and the automotive industry. *Journal of Industrial and Business Economics, 46*(3), 333–345.

Venkatesh, V. (2021). Adoption and use of AI tools: A research agenda grounded in UTAUT. *Annals of Operations Research,* 1–12.

Webb, N. (2018). *AI adoption advances, but foundational barriers remain*. Retrieved from https://www.mckinsey.com/featured-insights/artificial-intelligence/ai-adoption-advances-but-foundational-barriers-remain.

Winkler, M., Tolido, R., Thieullent, A.-L., Finck, I., Buvat, J., Kadikar, A. & Hiral, S. (2019). *Accelerating automotive's AI transformation: How driving AI enterprise-wide can turbo-charge organizational value.* Retrieved from https://www.capgemini.com/us-en/accelerating-automotives-ai-transformation/.

Zou, J., & Schiebinger, L. (2018). AI can be sexist and racist—it's time to make it fair. *Nature, 559*(7714), 324–326.

Blockchain for Supply Chain Traceability: Case Examples for Luxury Goods

Christoph G. Schmidt, Maximilian Klöckner, and Stephan M. Wagner

Abstract

Blockchain presents multiple use cases for supply chain management. As supply chains are increasingly complex and global inter-organizational networks, trust and transparency are key success factors. Blockchain provides a promising solution to address supply chain transparency by enabling product tracing along the supply chain, potentially ensuring product authenticity and provenance as well as ethical production. This chapter focuses on supply chain traceability for luxury goods, where counterfeits present a special challenge. Three case examples in luxury goods illustrate the potential benefits of blockchain.

1 Introduction

Over the past few years, blockchain has received tremendous attention from academia, businesses, and media. Initially, the technology was often referred to as a "game changer" across all industries and its story was compared to that of the Internet (Iansiti & Lakhani, 2017; Johnson, 2018). In a 2017 Gartner survey, two thirds of the respondents believed that blockchain was a major business disruption (Burton & Barnes, 2017). Early adopters of the technology, such as Maersk and Walmart, made headlines around the globe and fostered an interest in the technology (Moise & Chopping, 2018; Nash, 2018).

C. G. Schmidt · M. Klöckner · S. M. Wagner (✉)
Department of Management, Technology, and Economics, Swiss Federal Institute of Technology Zurich (ETH Zurich), Weinbergstrasse 56/58, 8092 Zurich, Switzerland
e-mail: stwagner@ethz.ch

K.-I. Voigt and J. M. Müller (eds.), *Digital Business Models in Industrial Ecosystems*, Future of Business and Finance, https://doi.org/10.1007/978-3-030-82003-9_12

Since then, expectations have become more realistic. Technological uncertainty, scalability issues, and development costs dampen the ascribed potential. According to an industry report by the China Academy of Information and Communications Technology, about 92% of blockchain projects have failed since the inception of blockchain, with an average lifespan of only a little over a year (Disparte, 2019). Blockchain projects that make it past the initial pilot stage and transition to an operational and productive environment are still rare (Babich & Hilary, 2020; Furlonger & Uzureau, 2019). However, after going full circle from inflated expectations to disillusionment, blockchain is now slowly entering a transition period, where operational use cases and application areas are flushed out. In 2020, investments in blockchain solutions were estimated at $4.1 billion worldwide, marking an increase of more than 50% compared to 2019, and are expected to reach a total of nearly $17.9 billion in 2024 (Soohoo & Shirer, 2020). This surge is led by finance and manufacturing applications, including supply chain use cases.

The rise of blockchain applications in industrial supply chain settings is not surprising, given the unique characteristics of the field. Supply chains are increasingly complex and global inter-organizational settings, where trust and transparency are key success factors (Hastig & Sodhi, 2020). Tracing products along the supply chain, or even during their entire life cycle, facilitates transparency and has become a major objective for firms in the realm of Industry 4.0 (Park et al., 2018). In this context, blockchain provides a viable solution to enhance supply chain risk management and adhere to rising standards and expectations regarding product authenticity and provenance as well as ethical production (Schmidt & Wagner, 2019; Sodhi & Tang, 2019; Sunny et al., 2020). Blockchain is understood as a digital, distributed database of connected and verified transactional records (Babich & Hilary, 2020; Gaur & Gaiha, 2020). Blockchain's tamper-evident and decentralized nature allows for advanced data validation and data access management, making blockchain a prime technology candidate to address supply chain transparency by enabling product tracing (Iansiti & Lakhani, 2017; Kurpjuweit et al., 2021).

In practice, multiple firm consortia and startups explore blockchain's potential to facilitate supply chain traceability. As one of the first, the TradeLens project, initiated by the shipping company Maersk and IBM, uses blockchain-based cloud services to trace cargo and simplify customs processes. Other firms, including Walmart or Nestlé, started tracing food products from production to retail (IBM, 2019). Luxury goods are a specific case for supply chain tracing, as products are rare and of high individual value. Using blockchain to assure product authenticity and provenance could combat the biggest challenge for luxury goods—counterfeits. For example, the luxury goods conglomerate LVMH, in cooperation with Microsoft and blockchain software company ConsenSys,[1] launched the AURA platform (Dalugdug, 2019). Initially, the platform was used to ensure the authenticity of Louis Vuitton handbags and Christian Dior perfumes.

[1] https://www.consensys.net/.

This chapter provides an overview of blockchain and its use cases for supply chain traceability. The conceptual review is illustrated using three case examples in luxury goods supply chains, providing anecdotal evidence for the benefits of blockchain.

2 Blockchain and Supply Chain Traceability

2.1 Blockchain Technology

Firms have understood the need for digitalization, which is understood as a bundle of disruptive technologies, including big data analytics, machine learning, 3D printing, robotics, and drones, which are expected to radically transform the business landscape (Vendrell-Herrero et al., 2017). In the context of firm digitalization and corresponding Industry 4.0 initiatives, investments in supply chain technologies have reached a record high in 2020, at $52 billion, superseding 2018 ($34 billion) and 2019 ($32 billion) (Fuller, 2020). Blockchain, as one of the most prominently discussed technologies in this trend, is "a database architecture which enables the keeping and sharing of transaction records in a distributed and decentralized way, while ensuring its integrity through the use of consensus-based validation protocols and cryptographic signatures" (Benos et al., 2017, p. 1).

Transactional data stored on a blockchain is considered immutable. All transactions are timestamped, aggregated in coherent blocks, and cryptographically linked, creating a chain of blocks (Babich & Hilary, 2020). New transactions are verified using a consensus algorithm and then added to the chain. In the case of a data manipulation attempt, the cryptographic links between the blocks would "break", making manipulation easy to detect. Overall, these mechanisms establish the key features of blockchain: immutability, non-repudiation, distribution, and consensus validation (Klöckner et al., 2020). Potential application areas for supply chain management include inventory management and multi-party data sharing (Babich & Hilary, 2020), but especially transparency (Gaur & Gaiha, 2020; Sodhi & Tang, 2019) and counterfeit detection (Pun et al., 2021).

2.2 Supply Chain Traceability

Modern supply chains are complex and global transaction networks (Park et al., 2018). Supply chain transparency is understood as strategically sharing supply chain and sourcing information with stakeholders, including business partners, as well as investors. Supply chain transparency is a key factor to both create trust in complex supply networks, and improve efficiencies (Sodhi & Tang, 2019; Sunny et al., 2020). In addition, transparency is foundational to assuring compliance with new regulations and standards, for example, regarding sustainability. Thus, firms across multiple industries are under increasing pressure to create transparency on their multi-tier supply chains. Specifically, supply chain traceability, defined as the process of tracking the provenance and journey of a product and its inputs, from the very start of the supply chain through to end-use (Norton & Conlon, 2019), has become an important driver of transparency.

In some industries, including food and pharmaceuticals, where safety is critical, supply chain traceability is needed to ensure high standards for product quality. In general, regulatory requirements have tightened and customers are increasingly interested in the provenance of the products that they consume (Schleper et al., 2017; Schmidt & Wagner, 2019). Tracing goods along production and delivery using blockchain could also enable automated compliance to freight and trade regulations. Supply chain traceability further provides opportunities to find supply chain efficiencies, or even prevent potential disruptions (Sodhi & Tang, 2019). As information and communication technologies have always played an important role in supply chain innovation (Ateş et al., 2018; Wagner & Bode, 2014), firms are exploring new technologies to address the need for supply chain transparency and traceability. Blockchain's tamper-evident and decentralized nature allows for advanced data validation and data access management.

3 Blockchain and Luxury Goods

3.1 Challenges in the Luxury Goods Supply Chain

Luxury goods present a special case for blockchain-based supply chain traceability. The overall luxury market size was about €1.2 trillion in 2019, marking a 4% growth over two years (McKinsey & Company, 2019). The growing market has undergone structural changes over the past decade. In today's globalized markets, luxury goods supply chains exhibit a higher degree of complexity, as they extend globally and involve a diverse range of manufacturers, including a multitude of small-scale, highly specialized suppliers (Brun et al., 2008; Phau et al., 2014). The complex structure and diverse participants make luxury goods inherently hard to trace (Fontana et al., 2019). Reduced product tracing, and thus lower transparency, create vulnerabilities to outside manipulation and fraud, fostering the biggest challenge for luxury goods—*counterfeits*.

The Global Brand Counterfeiting Report has recently estimated losses of nearly $100 billion, demonstrating the growing extent of counterfeiting in luxury goods, especially in fashion, watches, and arts. While fake products have always been around, they have become more sophisticated over the years, making it harder for customers to spot "the real thing" (Fontana et al., 2019). One of the major challenges for luxury goods manufacturers is to assure customers that they are buying a genuine product. In addition, customers in the luxury goods sector have become increasingly aware of ethical and environmental issues. Labor compensation and conditions, ethical sourcing, animal testing, non-conflict materials, as well as clean production, including CO_2 emissions, waste management, and recycling efforts, have become increasingly important to customers of luxury goods.

Blockchain, in combination with other supplementary technologies, provides new opportunities for supply chain tracing in the luxury goods industry. Monitoring the entire life cycle of a product and collecting reliable information enables companies to create transparency in their sourcing and manufacturing processes. As each product would be registered on a blockchain, the authenticity and the rightful owner of a product could always be verified. In the following, three case examples (Table 1) illustrate the potential of blockchain in different luxury goods industries.

3.2 Case 1: Wine

In 2018, wine consumption worldwide was estimated at about 244 million hectoliters, with the United States, France, and Italy being the largest regional markets (Conway, 2020). Even with stagnating or decreasing demand in Europe and an ongoing shift towards the Asian wine market, the market for rare luxurious wines is prospering worldwide (Goncharuk, 2017; Yen & Huang, 2020). Rare wines are often sold at over $100,000 per bottle at exclusive auction houses. The global luxury wines and spirits market size was valued at $970 billion in 2019, and is anticipated to reach $1411 billion by 2027 (Kale & Deshmukh, 2020). It is not surprising that these luxury wines have also become a target for counterfeiters (Yen & Huang, 2020). The global fake wine market was estimated at about $15 billion in 2017 (Smith, 2019).

Consequently, a major challenge for all stakeholders in the luxury wine supply chain, including wineries, brokers, auction houses, collectors, and consumers, is to assure the authenticity and provenance of the wine and its ingredients (Danese et al., 2021). Wineries initially tried to prevent counterfeits by applying seals or etching laser trademarks into the bottles (Yen & Huang, 2020). However, counterfeiting has become more sophisticated and these measures became obsolete. Multiple wineries and startups have since developed blockchain-based platforms, as a potential solution (Goncharuk, 2017).

The startup Blockchain Wine Ltd. has collaborated with the EY OpsChain blockchain platform to create the TATTOO Wine marketplace[2] for consumers across the Asia Pacific region. Consumers can buy luxury wines directly on the blockchain-based platform in the form of digital tokens that identify the wines purchased (Burgess, 2019). The token provides information on vineyards, fertilizers, grapes, ingredients, and transportation, to ensure the provenance, quality, and authenticity of the wines (Yen & Huang, 2020). For identification, each bottle has its unique QR code “tattooed”. In addition, VeChain[3] also offers a blockchain-based solution to trace wine along the supply chain. For rare wines, they plan to include a breakable NFC seal within the wine stopper. Once the bottle is opened, the chip is

[2]https://www.tattoowine.com/.
[3]https://www.vechain.org/.

Table 1 Overview of the luxury goods case examples

	Case 1	Case 2	Case 3
Product	Wine	Diamonds	Watches
Major challenges	• Counterfeits • Low quality ingredients	• Counterfeits • Ethical production	• Counterfeits
Blockchain application	• Identification of product • Information on ingredients • Assurance of grape and wine quality	• Sourcing information • Assurance of ethical production • Information on product quality and characteristics	• Identification of product • Enable safe trading and secondary markets • Digital certificates
Blockchain firm	Blockchain Wine Ltd	Everledger	Adresta
Ext. IT service provider	EY OpsChain	IBM	–
Firm age	2 years (founded 2018)	5 years (founded April 2015)	1 year (founded December 2019)
Country	Singapore	United Kingdom	Switzerland

damaged and information on that bottle cannot be read or written anymore, providing an extra layer of protection against counterfeiters (PR Newswire, 2019).

3.3 Case 2: Diamonds

Diamonds are a traditional luxury good across the world. The global diamond industry is a low volume, high revenue business, with a market value of $79 billion in 2019 (Garside, 2020). While demand is stagnating, the industry is facing two major challenges: (1) counterfeits and (2) ethical issues (Thakker et al., 2021). While the counterfeit issues are similar to other luxury goods industries, the focus on mining and production conditions is more specific to diamonds. Diamond mines are often located in unstable geopolitical locations with civil wars and high poverty rates (Chan et al., 2020). Many diamond mines and cutting facilities are still subject to severe human rights abuses, especially worker exploitation and child labor (Chan et al., 2020; Thakker et al., 2021; Wexler, 2019). Miners work in highly unsafe conditions, often without training, safety equipment, or proper tools. In addition, diamond mining is also severely damaging land and water in the area. Soil erosion and uncoordinated deforestation can cause long-term environmental disasters. To combat these massive issues, shareholders, regulators, and customers demand greater transparency along the supply chain (Wexler, 2019).

To eliminate conflict stones, for instance "blood diamonds", and improve working conditions, the Kimberley Process Certification Scheme (KPCS) was established in 2003 (Rhode, 2014; Spiegel, 2014). However, the certification process is lengthy and there is a history of fraud and missing paperwork (Rhode, 2014). Blockchain enables a more secure tracing of diamonds. For example, Everledger,[4] in cooperation with IBM Blockchain, uses a bundle of technologies, including blockchain, AI, IoT, and nanotechnology, to create a digital twin of every diamond. To improve transparency, all diamond events across the full life cycle are immutably recorded on the blockchain (McKay, 2018). The digital record includes information on origin, cutting process, general characteristics and measurements, and ownership for each diamond (Roberts, 2018). The platform can also aid firms with creating and sharing compliance documentation and customs form, overall improving process efficiency. The system is a major step towards diamond provenance and verifiable ethical sourcing.

3.4 Case 3: Watches

The global watch market is worth about $17 billion, with the luxury segment being valued at $9.3 billion (Sabanoglu, 2020). The industry is plagued by counterfeits, as there is almost twice the number of fake watches than real ones sold around the world (Jaberg, 2020). According to the Federation of the Swiss watch industry, counterfeit watches already account for 9% of customs confiscations, placing watches second only to textiles as the most counterfeited product. Especially with the rise of so-called "super-fakes"—sophisticated counterfeits of high quality and not easily detected by experts—the need for authenticity and product provenance is increasing in the industry (Barber, 2020). However, the authentication of watches is a long and cumbersome process, relying on traditional warranty cards and paper certificates issued by manufacturers (Dillet, 2020; Jaberg, 2020). These are relatively easy to duplicate and provide little protection against modern counterfeit operations. Blockchain may offer a solution to ensure failsafe authentication and accountability in the luxury watch industry, as multiple startups are exploring the possibilities of creating an immutable digital identity for high-end watches.

Adresta,[5] for example, is a Swiss startup that creates digital certificates for luxury watches. They use blockchain to securely store these certificates, which also include information on the entire lifecycle of the watch, from manufacturer to service and repair. All subsequent sales and owners are also registered on the blockchain. Adresta's watch platform provides a tamper-proof blockchain-based solution that makes the history of every watch visible. The watch owners get secure and immutable documentation, increasing trust and transparency along the luxury watch's supply chain. Manufacturers are eager to explore and adopt these novel approaches. In October 2020, Breitling, for example, announced that it was going to

[4]https://www.everledger.io/.
[5]https://www.adresta.ch/.

issue an encrypted passport for each of its new watches, making the paper-based certificate of authenticity obsolete (Dillet, 2020). Hublot is also adding its watch warranties to the aforementioned LVMH AURA blockchain network (PR Newswire, 2020). Others are likely to follow.

4 Summary and Future Outlook

The case examples illustrate the high potential of blockchain to improve supply chain traceability. Specifically for luxury goods, tracing physical objects over their lifecycle along the product's supply chain creates transparency and facilitates trust across all stakeholders, especially customers, in the authenticity and provenance of a product.

Looking ahead, however, there is arguably one major challenge that needs to be solved to maximize the value that blockchain can generate for the tracing of physical assets, such as wine, diamonds, or watches. While data is comparatively secure, once it is recorded on the blockchain, entering the correct data in the digital blockchain ledger is the weak point for blockchain-based tracing solutions (Babich & Hilary, 2020; Tucker & Catalini, 2018). Data entry is oftentimes done manually, creating a systemic vulnerability that undermines the immutability potential of blockchain (Tucker & Catalini, 2018). In a case where the input data is corrupted or fraudulent, the system is compromised. While firms actively explore technical solutions utilizing IoT sensors, NFC or RFID chips, human intervention can still lead to manipulation and fraud along the supply chain (Babich & Hilary, 2020). Developing a reliable solution to bridge the physical and digital world, and to create truly tamper-proof digital twins, is a crucial next step.

Overall, blockchain exhibits enormous potential to improve supply chain management in the future. Specifically, the technology's ability to enable more efficient and reliable product tracing along the supply chain, ultimately enhancing supply chain transparency, benefits businesses, customers, and society.

References

Ateş, M. A., van Raaij, E. M., & Wynstra, F. (2018). The impact of purchasing strategy-structure (mis)fit on purchasing cost and innovation performance. *Journal of Purchasing and Supply Management, 24*(1), 68–82.

Babich, V., & Hilary, G. (2020). OM Forum—Distributed ledgers and operations: What operations management researchers should know about blockchain technology. *Manufacturing & Service Operations Management, 22*(2), 223–240.

Barber, T. (2020). *Blockchain could soon make it impossible to sell a stolen Rolex. Wired.* Retrieved from https://www.wired.co.uk/article/stolen-rolex-blockchain

Benos, E., Garratt, R., & Gurrola-Perez, P. (2017). *The economics of distributed ledger technology for securities settlement. SSRN.* Retrieved from https://ssrn.com/abstract=3023779

Brun, A., Caniato, F., Caridi, M., Castelli, C., Miragliotta, G., Ronchi, S., Sianesi, A., & Spina, G. (2008). Logistics and supply chain management in luxury fashion retail: Empirical investigation of Italian firms. *International Journal of Production Economics, 114*(2), 554–570.

Burgess, B. (2019). *EY blockchain platform supports Blockchain Wine Pte. Ltd. to launch TATTOO Wine marketplace across Asia Pacific. EY Press Releases*. Retrieved from https://www.ey.com/en_gl/news/2019/11/ey-blockchain-platform-supports-blockchain-wine-pte-ltd-to-launch-tattoo-wine-marketplace-across-asia-pacific

Burton, B., & Barnes, H. (2017). Hype cycles highlight enterprise and ecosystem digital disruptions: A Gartner trend insight. Stamford, Connecticut: Gartner Group.

Chan, D., Berger, R., & Man, T. W. Y. (2020). The impact of managerial characteristics on business strategies under the environmental change: An investigation of the Israeli diamond industry. *Journal of Small Business & Entrepreneurship, 32*(2), 123–148.

Conway, J. (2020). *Wine consumption worldwide from 2000 to 2019. Statista*. Retrieved from https://www.statista.com/statistics/232937/volume-of-global-wine-consumption

Dalugdug, A. J. (2019). *LVMH nearing launch of 1st global luxury blockchain. S&P Global*. Retrieved from https://www.spglobal.com/marketintelligence/en/news-insights/trending/Gx0509KVvHQl1uVgESBlkQ2

Danese, P., Mocellin, R., & Romano, P. (2021). Designing blockchain systems to prevent counterfeiting in wine supply chains: A multiple-case study. *International Journal of Operations & Production Management, 41*(2), 1–33.

Dillet, R. (2020). *Luxury watch maker Breitling issues digital certificates on the Ethereum blockchain. TechCrunch*. Retrieved from https://techcrunch.com/2020/10/15/luxury-watch-maker-breitling-issues-digital-certificates-on-the-ethereum-blockchain

Disparte, D. A. (2019). *Why enterprise blockchain projects fail. Forbes Magazine*. Retrieved from https://www.forbes.com/sites/dantedisparte/2019/05/20/why-enterprise-blockchain-projects-fail

Fontana, R., Girod, S. J., & Králik, M. (2019). *How luxury brands can beat counterfeiters. Harvard Business Review*. Retrieved from https://hbr.org/2019/05/how-luxury-brands-can-beat-counterfeiters

Fuller, C. (2020). *Supply chain tech investing is on fire: This is just the start. Freightwaves*. Retrieved from https://www.freightwaves.com/news/supply-chain-and-freight-tech-are-on-fire-this-is-just-the-start

Furlonger, D., & Uzureau, C. (2019). *The real business of blockchain: How leaders can create value in a new digital age*. Boston, Massachusetts: Harvard Business Review Press.

Garside, M. (2020). *Diamond jewelry market value worldwide from 2009 to 2019. Statista*. Retrieved from https://www.statista.com/statistics/585267/diamond-jewelry-market-value-worldwide

Gaur, V., & Gaiha, A. (2020). Building a transparent supply chain. *Harvard Business Review, 98*(3), 94–103.

Goncharuk, A. G. (2017). Wine value chains: Challenges and prospects. *Journal of Applied Management and Investments, 6*(1), 11–27.

Hastig, G. M., & Sodhi, M. S. (2020). Blockchain for supply chain traceability: Business requirements and critical success factors. *Production and Operations Management, 29*(4), 935–954.

Iansiti, M., & Lakhani, K. R. (2017). The truth about blockchain. *Harvard Business Review, 95*(1), 118–127.

IBM. (2019). *Carrefour and Nestlé partner with IBM to extend use of blockchain to new food categories. IBM Press Release*. Retrieved from https://www.ibm.com/blogs/think/2019/04/tracing-your-mashed-potatoes-on-ibm-blockchain

Jaberg, S. (2020). *French blockchain firms offer tracing for Swiss watches. SwissInfo News*. Retrieved from https://www.swissinfo.ch/eng/french-blockchain-firms-offer-tracing-for-swiss-watches/46179810

Johnson, S. (2018). *Beyond the Bitcoin bubble. New York Times*. Retrieved from https://www.nytimes.com/2018/01/16/magazine/beyond-the-bitcoin-bubble.html

Kale, R., & Deshmukh, R. (2020). *Luxury wines and spirits market by type and distribution channel: Global opportunity analysis and industry forecast, 2020-2027. Allied Market Research.* Retrieved from https://www.alliedmarketresearch.com/luxury-wines-and-spirits-market

Klöckner, M., Kurpjuweit, S., Velu, C., & Wagner, S. M. (2020). Does blockchain for 3D printing offer opportunities for business model innovation? *Research-Technology Management, 63*(4), 18–27.

Kurpjuweit, S., Schmidt, C. G., Klöckner, M., & Wagner, S. M. (2021). Blockchain in additive manufacturing and its impact on supply chains. *Journal of Business Logistics, 42*(1), 46–70.

McKay, R. (2018). *How blockchain tracks diamonds from mine to manufacturer. IBM Reports.* Retrieved from https://www.ibm.com/blogs/industries/how-blockchain-tracks-diamonds-from-mine-to-manufacturer

McKinsey & Company. (2019). *China luxury report 2019: How young Chinese consumers are reshaping global luxury. McKinsey & Company Reports.* Retrieved from https://www.mckinsey.com/featured-insights/china/how-young-chinese-consumers-are-reshaping-global-luxury

Moise, I., & Chopping, D. (2018). *Maersk and IBM partner on blockchain for global trade. The Wall Street Journal.* Retrieved from https://www.wsj.com/articles/maersk-and-ibm-partner-on-blockchain-for-global-trade

Nash, K. (2018). *Walmart-led blockchain effort seeks farm-to-grocery aisle view of food supply chain. The Wall Street Journal.* Retrieved from https://www.wsj.com/articles/walmart-led-blockchain-effort-seeks-farm-to-grocery-aisle-view-of-food-supply-chain-1529946347

Norton, T., & Conlon, C. (2019). *Supply chain visibility: Traceability, transparency, and mapping explained. BSR Reports.* Retrieved from https://www.bsr.org/en/our-insights/blog-view/supply-chain-visibility-traceability-transparency-and-mapping

Park, H., Bellamy, M. A., & Basole, R. C. (2018). Structural anatomy and evolution of supply chain alliance networks: A multi-method approach. *Journal of Operations Management, 63*, 79–96.

Phau, I., Teah, M., Brun, A., & Moretto, A. (2014). Organisation and supply chain for quality control in luxury companies. *Journal of Fashion Marketing and Management, 18*(2), 206–230.

PR Newswire. (2019). *The wine traceability platform co-developed by VeChain and D.I.G. kickstarted its second phase with the introduction of Penfolds Bin 407. PR Newswire.* Retrieved from https://www.prnewswire.com/news-releases/the-wine-traceability-platform-co-developed-by-vechain-and-dig-kickstarted-its-second-phase-with-the-introduction-of-penfolds-bin-407-300896782.html

PR Newswire. (2020). *HUBLOT e-warranty: The digitisation of the warranty card or how each watch becomes its own certificate. PR Newswire.* Retrieved from https://www.prnewswire.com/news-releases/hublot-e-warranty-the-digitisation-of-the-warranty-card-or-how-each-watch-becomes-its-own-certificate-301177428.html

Pun, H., Swaminathan, J. M., & Hou, P. (2021). Blockchain adoption for combating deceptive counterfeits. *Production and Operations Management*, 30(4), 864-882.

Rhode, D. (2014). *The Kimberley process is a perfect cover story for blood diamonds. The Guardian.* Retrieved from https://www.theguardian.com/sustainable-business/diamonds-blood-kimberley-process-mines-ethical

Roberts, J. J. (2018). *IBM Blockchain is tracking diamond rings across the globe. Fortune Magazine.* Retrieved from https://fortune.com/2018/04/26/ibm-blockchain-diamonds-helzberg

Sabanoglu, T. (2020). *Luxury watch market value worldwide from 2018 to 2025. Statista.* Retrieved from https://www.statista.com/statistics/940452/luxury-watch-market-value-worldwide

Schleper, M. C., Blome, C., & Wuttke, D. A. (2017). The dark side of buyer power: Supplier exploitation and the role of ethical climates. *Journal of Business Ethics, 140*(1), 97–114.

Schmidt, C. G., & Wagner, S. M. (2019). Blockchain and supply chain relations: A transaction cost theory perspective. *Journal of Purchasing and Supply Management, 25*(4), 100552.

Smith, R. (2019). *No one is safe from counterfeit wine. VinePair.* Retrieved from https://vinepair.com/articles/counterfeit-wine-protection

Sodhi, M. S., & Tang, C. S. (2019). Research opportunities in supply chain transparency. *Production and Operations Management, 28*(12), 2946–2959.

Soohoo, S., & Shirer, M. (2020). *Blockchain solutions will continue to see robust investments, led by banking and manufacturing, according to new IDC spending guide. IDC.* Retrieved from https://www.idc.com/getdoc.jsp?containerId=prUS46850820

Spiegel, S. J. (2014). Contested diamond certification: Reconfiguring global and national interests in Zimbabwe's Marange fields. In: R. Grynberg & L. Mbayi (Eds.), *The global diamond industry: Economics and Development,* 2, 153–180. New York, New York: Palgrave Macmillan.

Sunny, J., Undralla, N., & Pillai, V. M. (2020). Supply chain transparency through blockchain-based traceability: An overview with demonstration. *Computers & Industrial Engineering, 120*, 1–13.

Thakker, U., Patel, R., Tanwar, S., Kumar, N., & Song, H. (2021). Blockchain for diamond industry: Opportunities and challenges. *IEEE Internet of Things Journal, 8*(11), 8747–8773.

Tucker, C., & Catalini, C. (2018). *What blockchain can't do. Harvard Business Review.* Retrieved from https://hbr.org/2018/06/what-blockchain-cant-do.

Vendrell-Herrero, F., Bustinza, O. F., Parry, G., & Georgantzis, N. (2017). Servitization, digitization and supply chain interdependency. *Industrial Marketing Management, 60*, 69–81.

Wagner, S. M., & Bode, C. (2014). Supplier relationship-specific investments and the role of safeguards for supplier innovation sharing. *Journal of Operations Management, 32*(3), 65–78.

Wexler, A. (2019). *De Beers diamonds reflect a changing market. The Wall Street Journal.* Retrieved from https://www.wsj.com/articles/de-beers-diamonds-reflect-a-changing-market-11575109800

Yen, B., & Huang, M. (2020). *Can blockchain help Château Lafite fight counterfeits. HBR Case Study.* Retrieved from https://store.hbr.org/product/can-blockchain-help-chateau-lafite-fight-counterfeits

Lessons Learned from European Ecosystems

The Interrelationship Between Industry 4.0 and Servitization in Manufacturing SMEs: The Case of the Basque Country

Eduardo Sisti, Miren Estensoro, and Miren Larrea

Abstract

The implementation of Industry 4.0 brings about potential gains for firms in terms of efficiency, productivity, and the generation of new sources of income. A process that offers considerable opportunities for revenue generation is what is known as servitization. Both features (Industry 4.0 and servitization) are complementary and have critical implications for territories as regards technological upgrading and the diversification of their economy. Here, the extent to which the managerial conditions for transitioning towards Industry 4.0 and, specifically, for adopting digital technologies can influence small manufacturers' attitudes towards servitization is examined. The empirical study is carried out using both a quantitative approach based on an ordered logit model and a qualitative analysis of 174 manufacturing SMEs in the province of Gipuzkoa (Basque Country, Spain). Preliminary results show that firms' awareness of external and internal conditions for Industry 4.0 can be used as a lever of servitization. Furthermore, firms with a higher level of digitalization and involved in activities with a medium to a high level of technology intensity were found to have a more favourable attitude towards servitization.

1 Introduction

Industrial digitalization processes, sometimes considered a synonym of Industry 4.0, have been described as a fundamental strategic and operational challenge for manufacturing firms. The expected effects of adopting new technologies are related

E. Sisti (✉) · M. Estensoro · M. Larrea
University of Deusto, Mundaiz, 50, 20012 San Sebastián, Spain
e-mail: eduardo.sisti@orkestra.deusto.es

K.-I. Voigt and J. M. Müller (eds.), *Digital Business Models in Industrial Ecosystems*, Future of Business and Finance, https://doi.org/10.1007/978-3-030-82003-9_13

to potential gains in productivity as well as new sources of income generation. One of those main opportunities is the provision of new services associated with their manufacturing offer. This is what is known as servitization: a change in the business model from a product system to a product-service system (Kowalkowski et al., 2017; Neely, 2008; Vandermerwe & Rada, 1988). The topic of servitization began attracting considerable academic interest at the end of the 1980s (Baines et al., 2017; Bowen et al., 1989; Cohen & Whang, 1997; Rabetino et al., 2018; Vandermerwe & Rada, 1988); its implications for territorial growth and welfare also having been analysed (Lafuente et al., 2017).

The literature has demonstrated that there is indeed a link between the transition to Industry 4.0, or industrial digitalization, and servitization (Baines et al., 2017; Coreynen et al., 2017, 2020; Frank et al., 2019; Rabetino et al., 2018; Raddats et al., 2016, 2019; Vendrell-Herrero et al., 2017; Visnjic et al., 2018). This relationship is intricate, and perspectives of convergence, directionality (digitalization is an enabler for servitization), and the influence of demand-pull and technology-push forces have been raised (Coreynen et al., 2020; Frank et al., 2019). Thus, given the complexity of this phenomenon, one must consider a number of factors such as firms' heterogeneity (size, sector, etc.) as well as the broad spectrum of technologies applied that foster digitalization. These technologies include cyber-physical systems, cloud computing and the Internet of Things, and advanced manufacturing technologies (Kagermann et al., 2013; Liao et al., 2017). This huge variety of technological possibilities gives us an idea of the complexity and diversity of options that can be applied, depending on the firm's activity, products, or position in the value chain, among other aspects. Consequently, not all firms face the same challenges or start from the same baseline when opting for servitization (Crozet & Milet, 2017).

The main argument in this chapter is that due to resource constraints (e.g., skills, financial, strategic, etc.), smaller companies face different challenges when pursuing servitization. By answering the research question *Do the conditions for transitioning to Industry 4.0 foster servitization in manufacturing SMEs?*, it is taken a closer look at the conditions for transitioning to Industry 4.0 and firms' digitalization levels, and how these two factors are related to the firms' attitude towards servitization. The case analysis is framed in Gipuzkoa, a highly industrialized province in the Basque Country (Spain). The data is collected through a survey conducted with 174 manufacturing SMEs.

The remainder of the chapter is structured as follows: Section 2 briefly reviews the literature and develops the conceptual framework that helps formulate the hypotheses. Next, the data and methods used are described in Sects. 3, and 4 goes on to present the results. Finally, Sect. 5 focuses on discussing the findings and summarizing the conclusions.

2 Industry 4.0 and Servitization: Hypotheses Development

For manufacturing firms, their transition to Industry 4.0 means integrating new digital technologies and strategic capabilities into their business model (Kagermann et al., 2013; Liao et al., 2017; Müller, 2019; Schumacher et al., 2016). Such a process may lead to more efficient, less costly and flexible production systems as well as to firms opening up to the provision of services and developing new business models (Benesova & Tupa, 2017; Kagermann et al., 2013; Müller et al., 2020). In this regard, certain limitations and challenges could severely affect the expected results at both the firm and the territorial level. For example, a firm's requirements, choice, and application of new technologies and the corresponding changes in its business model could cause internal frictions which would call for a clear strategic vision and leadership (Birkel et al., 2019; Müller et al., 2018a). SMEs' limitations in terms of budget constraints and their diversity at the sectoral level show that further research is needed for a better understanding of the drivers of the 4.0 transition in SMEs (e.g. Ghobakhloo, 2018; Moeuf et al., 2018; Mittal et al., 2018; Müller et al., 2018a, 2020; Müller et al., 2018b).

Extant literature has identified some of the conditions (or drivers/opportunities/challenges) that determine the transition of SMEs towards Industry 4.0. Table 1 summarizes the conditions considered in the empirical analysis.

Concerning the definition of servitization, it has been described as a change in the business model from a product system to a product-service system (Kowalkowski et al., 2017; Neely, 2008; Vandermerwe & Rada, 1988), which represents a huge challenge for manufacturing firms (Cusumano et al., 2015; Frank et al., 2019). One major reason for developing this business strategy stems from having to cope with the competition in manufacturing costs of less developed economies (Gomes et al., 2019). Among the potential benefits of servitization are building closeness with customers and increasing their loyalty (Müller et al., 2018; Vandermerwe & Rada, 1988), expanding the sources of income (Neely, 2008; Kamp et al., 2017; Baines et al., 2017; Rabetino et al., 2018) and boosting business competitiveness (Ayala et al., 2018). However, there are also challenges to be dealt with: the risk of failure due to lack of financial and human capabilities or having to foster external collaboration (Benesova & Tupa, 2017; Birkel et al., 2019; Neely, 2008), among others. The type of services an SME provides will differ depending on the characteristics of its products and economic activity as well as on the industry's life cycle and environment (Cusumano et al., 2015; Frank et al., 2019; Visnjic et al., 2019). So, the attitudes towards servitization have implications for firms' sustainability as well as for territorial welfare (Lafuente et al., 2017).

Coreynen et al. (2020) noted that digitalization and servitization trends have a major impact on the prospects of manufacturing companies. These authors review different perspectives on the link between digitalization and servitization, one of which refers to digitalization as an "integral part" of firms' operations, although not

Table 1 Conditions for Industry 4.0 implementation

Condition	Description of the indicator	References
Aligned strategic management	Assesses whether the "Industry 4.0 plan" is aligned with the firm's strategic thinking, which requires full involvement from top management and adopting a holistic approach	Moeuf et al., (2018, 2020), Sahi et al. (2020)
Organizational model and resilience	Assesses whether the managerial and organizational models can be adapted to the requirements of Industry 4.0	Moeuf et al., (2018, 2020), Sahi et al. (2020)
Acceptance of Industry 4.0 by the market	Assesses to what extent the SME's sector is one in which there is pressure or possibilities to advance towards Industry 4.0	Müller et al. (2018, 2020), Moeuf et al., (2018, 2020), Veile et al. (2019)
Analysis of competitors' behaviour and the value chain	Identifies the SME's position in the value chain and how its relationship with other firms (often bigger and clients but also competitors) in the chain can affect the transition to Industry 4.0	Bär et al., (2018), Birkel et al. (2019), Veile et al. (2019)
Financial resources	Evaluates the SME's potential to allocate resources to Industry 4.0 related investments	Müller et al. (2018b, 2020)
Qualified staff	Assesses the qualification level of staff or the possibility of further training to be able to face Industry 4.0 related challenges	Matt et al. (2018), Moeuf et al., (2018, 2020)
Alliances and cooperation in the innovation system	Assesses the extent to which the SME is pursuing Industry 4.0 oriented cooperation with other SMEs, with customers and suppliers in the value chain or through alliances with actors from the innovation system	Bär et al. (2018), Müller et al. (2018b, 2020); Veile et al. (2019)

necessarily leading to servitization. Another view states that "digitalization is an enabler for servitization". Also, Frank et al. (2019) developed an analytic approach, stating that a demand-pull, as well as a technology-push towards servitization, exists which depends on the type of smoothing, adapting or substituting service the manufacturing company provides. According to this, servitization will be dependent on the level of digitalization and Industry 4.0 implementation. Thus, two hypotheses are developed, one related to "strategic" aspects of the implementation of Industry 4.0 and the other related to the level of use of digital technologies.

First, as mentioned before, the implementation of Industry 4.0 also requires a "strategic" adaptation, related to business models, competition, availability of resources, and so on (Schumacher et al., 2016; Müller, 2019; Navarro & Sabalza, 2016), which in turn enhances and improves their possibilities of offering higher quality services (Barret et al., 2015; Coreynen et al., 2017, 2020; Müller et al., 2020). Therefore, the following hypothesis is proposed:

H1. The more developed the conditions are for an Industry 4.0 transition, the more favourable the SME's attitude is towards servitization.
Second, a major feature of Industry 4.0 is the broad spectrum of technologies being used, including cyber-physical systems, cloud computing and the Internet of Things, and advanced manufacturing technologies (Kagermann et al., 2013; Liao et al., 2017). This variety of possibilities illustrates the complexity and diversity of options that can be applied, depending on the firm's activity, products or position in the value chain, among other aspects. With regard to this, Frank et al. (2019) also indicate that, depending on these factors, the technology push can be divided into three levels: low, moderate and high. As no typology of this matter exists, they suggest a segmentation based on the "purpose for the service offering of product firms". The low level of digitalization intensity (i.e., manual services) consists of digital tools which help to "create customer databases, to manage customers with CRM (Customer Relationship Management) software, and so on, but they do not provide the service itself". The moderate level (i.e., digital services) "comprises the use of digital tools enabling manufacturers to deliver distinct service offerings to the customer", which add value to the service provided (i.e., apps, cloud computing and embedded software). And lastly, the high level (i.e., Industry 4.0 related services) incorporates the proper integration of advanced Industry 4.0 technologies providing "value for both customers and the companies' internal processes" (Frank et al., 2019). Hence, the level of digitalization, according to the technologies applied, provides a different perspective on the Industry 4.0 conditions and their expected outcomes (e.g., servitization). Müller et al. (2018) offer similar empirical findings. Therefore, the following hypothesis is suggested:

H2: The higher the level of digitalization, the more positive the attitude towards servitization in manufacturing SMEs.
This chapter explores the links between the drivers (or conditions) for Industry 4.0 implementation, the digitalization level, and the firms' attitude towards servitization, as defined in Fig. 1.

Fig. 1 Research framework

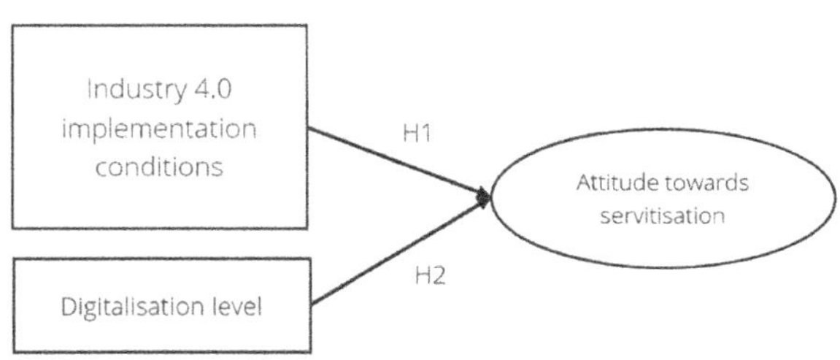

3 Methodology

3.1 Sample and Variables

Two significant features distinguish the case studied: (i) the Basque Country is one of the most industrialized regions in Europe, the weight of industry being even higher in the Gipuzkoa province, and (ii) due to its tradition in industrial policy-making, the Basque Country is considered an interesting case to analyse industrial transitions (Navarro & Sabalza, 2016).

The data analysed in the chapter was collected by the staff at Gipuzkoa's county development agencies from December 2017 to May 2018 for a research project whose aim was to foster Industry 4.0 transition within manufacturing SMEs and which involved the authors. The database contains 174 firms with between 20 and 99 employees. In Gipuzkoa, the subgroup of manufacturing SMEs with between 20 and 99 employees alone represents 23.7% of all the manufacturing firms.

As a matter of the conditions for Industry 4.0, from a managerial perspective, the collected database includes data on ten dimensions. Apart from the conditions for an Industry 4.0 transition described in Table 1, two other outcome indicators are considered: expected efficiency and profitability of Industry 4.0 investments, and servitization. Thus, servitization is used as the dependent variable, and the rest (except efficiency and profitability) are the independent variables. It should be noted that all the variables related to the Industry 4.0 conditions specified in the survey were collected using a four-point Likert scale (i.e., strongly disagree, disagree, agree and strongly agree). The main reason for choosing a four-point Likert scale is its advantage in terms of consistency in the responses since the absence of a midpoint forces the surveyed to express their agreement or disagreement.

Table 2 shows the significant degree of correlation among the variables that condition the transition to Industry 4.0. A factor analysis was carried out to divide them into different dimensions.

The iterated principal factor (IPF) method is applied to determine whether all the indicators had some commonalities. Two of the dimensions (factors) accounted for 77.58% of the total variance. Both factors were rotated using the Varimax technique (Table 3). The first one is called *internal factor* because the variables with higher loadings are those which represent the firm's assets and internal capabilities. Meanwhile, the second factor was called *external factor* due to the higher loadings in the variables which characterize the market where the firm competes. The two factors were later used in the regression analysis.

In Table 4, technologies are assigned a level of digitalization according to the classification proposed by Frank et al. (2019) and the four-point Likert scale used when collecting the data (1: no usage, 2: low usage, 3: usage and 4: high usage). If the answer was 1 or 2, it was assigned a 0; and 1 otherwise. Accordingly, three exclusive variables, each representing a digitalization level, were created, where 1 meant *applying only low-tech solutions*; 2, moderate and low-tech; and 3, that the firm used *at least one high-tech solution*.

Table 2 Correlation matrix

	Spearman's Rho	1	2	3	4	5	6	7
1	Market	1						
2	Competitors	0.465^{**}	1					
3	Strategy	0.406^{**}	0.291^{**}	1				
4	Qualified staff	0.324^{**}	0.176^{*}	0.557^{**}	1			
5	Finance	0.303^{**}	0.197^{**}	0.379^{**}	0.376^{**}	1		
6	Alliances	0.330^{**}	0.300^{**}	0.359^{**}	0.442^{**}	0.280^{**}	1	
7	Organization	0.322^{**}	0.249^{**}	0.323^{**}	0.433^{**}	0.312^{**}	0.385^{**}	1

Table 3 Rotated factor loadings and uniqueness (Varimax method)

	Factor 1 (internal)	Factor 2 (external)	Uniqueness
Market		0.6153	0.5186
Competitors		0.6555	0.5510
Strategy	0.6124		0.5334
Qualified staff	0.8722		0.2342
Finance	0.4647		0.7073
Alliances	0.5102		0.6426
Organization	0.5056		0.6673

Note Blanks represent abs (loading) < 0.4

Table 4 Technologies and level of digitalization

Technology	Digitalization level
Simulation	High
Advanced manufacturing	
Integration of vertical and horizontal systems	
Cybersecurity	
Augmented reality	
Artificial vision	
Advanced 3D inspection and metrology	
Advanced robots	
Cloud computing	Moderate
Internet of industrial things	
Embedded sensors and systems	
Remote maintenance	
Big data and analysis	
Social media technologies	Low
Mobility and geolocation	
Computer software	
Workflow	
Computer numerical control	

Source Authors' compilation based on Frank et al. (2019)

Moreover, three other control variables were taken into account in the analysis: (i) *size*, as the lastest sales reported (2017 or 2016) expressed in logarithms; (ii) *age*, calculated taking the year of company's creation from the SABI-Informa database (in logarithmic form); and the (iii) *tech level of the manufacturing activity* in consonance with the classification shown in Table 5.

Table 5 Technological level of manufacturing activities

Two-digit NACE industry	Tech level
Food products, beverages, wood products, paper, printing, furniture and other manufacturing	Low
Rubber and plastic products, other non-metallic mineral products, basic metals, fabricated metals, repair and installation of machinery	Medium–low
Chemical products, electrical equipment, machinery and motor vehicles	Medium–high
Pharmaceutical products, computer, electronic and optical products	High

Source Authors' calculations

3.2 Methods

The empirical analysis was performed using a mixed-method research approach (Creswell, 2003). First, an ordered logit model is employed to test the hypotheses since the dependent variables belong to four categories whose order has a meaning (IDRE, 2021). Accordingly, the following equation was obtained:

$$\begin{aligned} Y_i = \beta_0 + \beta_1 \text{External}_i + \beta_2 \text{Internal}_i + \beta_3 \text{External} \\ * \text{Digitalization level}_i + \beta_4 \text{Size}_i + \beta_5 \text{Age}_i + \beta_6 \text{Industry Tech intensity}_i + e_i \end{aligned}$$

The second step was a qualitative analysis based on the data collected since open questions had been included in the questionnaires given to policymakers from the county development agencies. This allowed us to gain greater insight into the drivers of servitization.

4 Results

4.1 Quantitative Results

Table 6 presents the results of the regression analysis using *attitude towards servitization* as the dependent variable. In Model 1, it is only employed control variables (size, age, technological level of industrial activity) as independent variables. As may be observed, statistical significance is only observed in firms displaying a higher level of technological development and not in those with a lower technological level. In the following models, the variables of interest were introduced one by one and then all together. In models 2 and 3, the positive and statistically significant impact of external and internal conditions is shown. Both conditions are statistically significant, but the external conditions—the competitors' behaviour along with the market and the industrial conditions—are even more so. In Model 4, when these two variables are both included, they are still relevant. Meanwhile, Model 5, in which it is introduced the *digitalization level*, shows that a higher level accounts for a more favourable attitude towards servitization. Finally,

Table 6 Regression results—dependent variable: *servitization*

	Model 1		Model 2		Model 3		Model 4		Model 5		Model 6	
External			1.060	***			1.018	***			0.918	***
			0.224				*0.226*				*0.230*	
Internal					0.670	***	0.618	***			0.598	***
					0.180		*0.185*				*0.187*	
Digitalization level												
Moderate									0.854	†	0.627	
									0.513		*0.532*	
High									1.259	***	0.894	*
									0.354		*0.373*	
Size (sales)	−0.644		−0.124		−0.119		−0.172		−0.005		−0.121	
	0.161		*0.168*		*0.165*		*0.168*		*0.166*		*0.173*	
Age	−0.046		0.086		−0.054		0.101		−0.034		0.077	
	0.222		*0.232*		*0.230*		*0.230*		*0.224*		*0.233*	
Tech level												
Medium–low	0.929	*	0.584		1.034	*	0.702		0.995	*	0.764	
	0.463		*0.494*		*0.477*		*0.500*		*0.479*		*0.507*	
Medium–high	1.695	***	1.320	**	1.672	***	1.344	**	1.735	***	1.399	**
	0.502		*0.527*		*0.511*		*0.531*		*0.515*		*0.537*	
High	2.021	*	1.127		2.131	*	1.281		1.677	†	1.104	
	0.972		*0.991*		*0.972*		*0.990*		*0.992*		*1.005*	
/cut1	−0.142		−0.516		−0.625		−0.516		1.213		0.112	
/cut2	1.542		1.385		1.168		1.385		3.029		2.193	

(continued)

Table 6 (continued)

	Model 1		Model 2		Model 3		Model 4		Model 5		Model 6	
/cut3	2.713		2.622		2.394		2.622		4.241		3.499	
No. of observations	162		162		162		162		162		162	
Likelihood ratio test	14.440		39.300		29.140		51.030		27.760		56.950	
	0.013		0.000		0.000		0.000		0.000		0.000	
McFadden's pseudo R^2	0.036		0.098		0.073		0.127		0.069		0.142	
Log likelihood	−193.330		−180.900		−185.980		−175.040		−186.670		−172.070	

in Model 6, all variables are taken into account, and the general effects can be observed.

4.2 Qualitative Results

The analysis of qualitative data allowed us to complement it with the quantitative results. The response rate of the sample was 59.5%.

Two main factors were found to hinder servitization: lack of knowledge and the remoteness of the concept (which accounted for 25.4% of the responses, although, surprisingly, 10.4% of them were using high-tech digital solutions), and the lack of strategic fit (13.3% of the responses). Comments such as "It is not one of the firm's priorities", "It is not in the strategic plan of our firm", "We don't feel the need to turn to servitization", "It is not a useful approach" or "It is not one of our strategies" are examples of this attitude.

Furthermore, among the firms already involved in servitization processes, it is worth highlighting that these processes appear to progress over different stages. Table 7 shows the different stages that make up a servitization process.

5 Discussion and Conclusion

This work has focused on the interrelationship between Industry 4.0 digitalization and servitization to be able to discern what drives servitization in manufacturing SMEs. The major findings are the following:

Table 7 Stages of the servitization process

Code	Theme	Examples
1	The remoteness of the concept or lack of strategic fit	"It is not one of the firm's priorities'"/"It is not in the strategic plan of our firm"/"We don't feel the need for servitization"/"It is not a useful approach"/"It is not one of our strategies"
2	Planning	"It is one of our objectives"/"We are analysing the change process related to a possible servitization process"
3	First steps	"They are doing something towards servitization"/ "Gradually we are implementing a new business model"/"We have started with a pilot project"/ "Selectively with some clients and/or some line of business"
4	Advanced	"We have opted for servitization"/"It has been incorporated in our strategy"

Servitization remains an unknown concept for most manufacturing SMEs. Only 23% of the firms surveyed showed some degree of advancement towards servitization. The empirical results suggest that such a low perception of this strategy is basically due to their lack of knowledge about the concept and it not being a strategic option for the firm. It should be underlined, however, that any servitization effort requires the firm to go through different stages until its business model has been transformed.

The conditions for a transition to Industry 4.0 are highly linked with servitization. In fact, the Industry 4.0 transition acts as a *facilitator* of servitization, which is determined by (mainly) external drivers—the behaviour of competitors and market conditions—and internal drivers—organizational model or qualified staff. Another determinant is the level of digitalization of the firm. It should also be highlighted that firms reaching medium to high-tech intensity levels adopt a more proactive stance towards servitization.

The implications of this analysis are:

For firms: by knowing which conditions, both external and internal, are necessary to be able to advance within the servitization process, SMEs will be able to think "one step ahead". Servitization *is* also an option for SMEs, and developing capabilities for the Industry 4.0 transition as well as digital competences can make a difference.

For policymakers: in territories such as Gipuzkoa, characterized by a dense network of manufacturing SMEs, policies that foster the transition to Industry 4.0 or servitization need to be adapted to the reality of SMEs. This means taking into account the different implementation stages and their respective drivers.

These limitations point, nonetheless, to other ideas for future research, some of which are: comparing the analysis with other territorial realities; exploring larger firms and other economic activities; or the need to continuously revise the interrelationship between the variables and the specificities of the different stages of servitization.

References

Ayala, N. F., Gerstlberger, W., & Frank, A. G. (2018). Managing servitization in product companies: The moderating role of service suppliers. *International Journal of Operations & Production Management, 39*(1), 43–74.

Baines, T., Ziaee Bigdeli, A., Bustinza, O. F., Shi, V. G., Baldwin, J., & Ridgway, K. (2017). Servitization: Revisiting the state-of-the-art and research priorities. *International Journal of Operations & Production Management, 37*(2), 256–278.

Bär, K., Herbert-Hansen, Z. N. L., & Khalid, W. (2018). Considering Industry 4.0 aspects in the supply chain for an SME. *Production Engineering. Research and Development, 12*, 747–758.

Barrett, M., Davidson, E., Prabhu, J., & Vargo, S. L. (2015). Service innovation in the digital age: Key contributions and future directions. *MIS Quarterly, 39*(1), 135–154.

Benesova, A., & Tupa, J. (2017). Requirements for education and qualification of people in Industry 4.0. *Procedia Manufacturing, 11*, 2195–2202.

Birkel, H., Veile, J., Müller, J., Hartmann, E., & Voigt, K.-I. (2019). Development of a risk framework for Industry 4.0 in the context of sustainability for established manufacturers. *Sustainability, 11*(2), 384.

Bowen, D. E., Siehl, C., & Schneider, B. (1989). A framework for analyzing customer service orientations in manufacturing. *The Academy of Management Review, 14*(1), 75–95.

Cohen, M. A., & Whang, S. (1997). Competing in product and service: A product life-cycle model. *Management Science, 43*(4), 535–545.

Coreynen, W., Matthyssens, P., & van Bockhaven, W. (2017). Boosting servitization through digitalization: Pathways and dynamic resource configurations for manufacturers. *Industrial Marketing Management, 60*, 42–53.

Coreynen, W., Matthyssens, P., Vanderstraeten, J., & van Witteloostuijn, A. (2020). Unravelling the internal and external drivers of digital servitization: A dynamic capabilities and contingency perspective on firm strategy. *Industrial Marketing Management, 89*, 265–277.

Creswell, J. (2003). *Research design: Qualitative, quantitative, and mixed method approaches* (2nd ed.). Sage.

Crozet, M., & Milet, E. (2017). Should everybody be in services? The effect of servitization on manufacturing firm performance. *Journal of Economics & Management Strategy, 26*(4), 820–841.

Cusumano, M. A., Kahl, S. J., & Suarez, F. F. (2015). Services, industry evolution, and the competitive strategies of product firms. *Strategic Management Journal, 36*(4), 559–575.

Frank, A. G., Mendes, G. H. S., Ayala, N. F., & Ghezzi, A. (2019). Servitization and Industry 4.0 convergence in the digital transformation of product firms: A business model innovation perspective. *Technological Forecasting and Social Change, 141*, 341–351.

Ghobakhloo, M. (2018). The future of manufacturing industry: a strategic roadmap toward Industry 4.0. *Journal of Manufacturing Technology Management, 29*(6), 910–936.

Gomes, E., Bustinza, O. F., Tarba, S., Khan, Z., & Ahammad, M. (2019). Antecedents and implications of territorial servitization. *Regional Studies, 53*(3), 410–423.

IDRE (2021). *Ordered logistic regression. Stat data analysis examples. UCLA: Statistical Consulting Group.* Retrieved from https://stats.idre.ucla.edu/stata/dae/ordered-logistic-regression/.

Kagermann, H., Wahlster, W., & Helbig, J. (2013). *Recommendations for implementing the strategic initiative Industrie 4.0. Securing the future of German manufacturing industry.* Final report of the Industrie 4.0 Working Group, Munich: Acatech-National Academy of Science and Engineering and Forschungsunion.

Kamp, B., Ochoa, A., & Diaz, J. (2017). Smart servitization within the context of industrial user–supplier relationships: Contingencies according to a machine tool manufacturer. *International Journal on Interactive Design and Manufacturing, 11*(3), 651–663.

Kowalkowski, C., Gebauer, H., Kamp, B., & Parry, G. (2017). Servitization and deservitization: Overview, concepts, and definitions. *Industrial Marketing Management, 60*, 4–10.

Lafuente, E., Vaillant, Y., & Vendrell-Herrero, F. (2017). Territorial servitization: Exploring the virtuous circle connecting knowledge-intensive services and new manufacturing businesses. *International Journal of Production Economics, 192*, 19–28.

Liao, Y., Deschamps, F., Roucha Loures, E., & Pierin Ramos, L. F. (2017). Past, present and future of Industry 4.0 - a systematic literature review and research agenda proposal. *International Journal of Production Research, 55*(12), 3609–3629.

Matt, D. T., Rauch, E., & Riedl, M. (2018). Knowledge transfer and introduction of Industry 4.0 in SMEs: A five-step methodology to introduce Industry 4.0. In: R. Brunet-Thornton & F. Martinez (Eds.), *Analyzing the Impacts of Industry 4.0 in Modern Business Environments* (pp. 256–282). Hershey, IGI Global.

Mittal, S., Khan, M. A., Romero, D., & Wuest, T. (2018). A critical review of smart manufacturing & Industry 4.0 maturity models: Implications for small and medium-sized enterprises (SMEs). *Journal of Manufacturing Systems, 49*, 194–214.

Moeuf, A., Pellerin, R., Lamouri, S., Tamayo-Giraldo, S., & Barbaray, R. (2018). The industrial management of SMEs in the era of Industry 4.0. *International Journal of Production Research, 56*(3), 1118–1136.

Müller, J. M. (2019). Business model innovation in small-and medium-sized enterprises: Strategies for industry 4.0 providers and users. *Journal of Manufacturing Technology Management, 30* (8), 1127–1142.

Müller, J. M., Buliga, O., & Voigt, K.-I. (2018a). Fortune favors the prepared: How SMEs approach business model innovations in Industry 4.0. *Technological Forecasting and Social Change, 132*, 2–17.

Müller, J. M., Kiel, D., & Voigt, K.-I. (2018b). What drives the implementation of Industry 4.0? The role of opportunities and challenges in the context of sustainability. *Sustainability, 10*(1), 247.

Müller, J. M., Buliga, O., & Voigt, K.-I. (2020). The role of absorptive capacity and innovation strategy in the design of industry 4.0 business Models - A comparison between SMEs and large enterprises. *European Management Journal* (in press).

Navarro-Arancegui, M., & Sabalza-Laskurain, X. (2016). Reflexiones sobre la Industria 4.0 desde el caso vasco, *Ekonomiaz, 89*(1), 143–173.

Neely, A. (2008). Exploring the financial consequences of the servitization of manufacturing. *Operations Management Research, 1*, 103–118.

Rabetino, R., Harmsen, W., Kohtamäki, M., & Sihvonen, J. (2018). Structuring servitization-related research. *International Journal of Operations & Production Management, 38*(2), 350–371.

Raddats, C., Baines, T., Burton, J., Story, V. M., & Zolkiewski, J. (2016). Motivations for servitization: The impact of product complexity. *International Journal of Operations & Production Management, 36*(5), 572–591.

Raddats, C., Kowalkowski, C., Benedettini, O., Burton, J., & Gebauer, H. (2019). Servitization: A contemporary thematic review of four major research streams. *Industrial Marketing Management, 83*, 207–223.

Sahi, G. K, Gupta, M. C., & Cheng, T. (2020). The effects of strategic orientation on operational ambidexterity: A study of Indian SMEs in the Industry 4.0 era. *International Journal of Production Economics, 220*, 107395.

Schumacher, A., Erol, S., & Sihn, W. (2016). A maturity model for assessing Industry 4.0 readiness and maturity of manufacturing enterprises. *Procedia CIRP, 52*, 161–166.

Vandermerwe, S., & Rada, J. (1988). Servitization of business: Adding value by adding services. *European Management Journal, 6*(4), 314–324.

Veile, J., Kiel, D., Müller, J., & Voigt, K.-I. (2019). Lessons learned from Industry 4.0 implementation in the German manufacturing industry. *Journal of Manufacturing Technology Management, 31*(5), 977–997.

Vendrell-Herrero, F., Bustinza, O. F., Parry, G., & Georgantzis, N. (2017). Servitization, digitalization and supply chain interdependency. *Industrial Marketing Management, 60*, 69–81.

Visnjic, I., Neely, A., & Jovanovic, M. (2018). The path to outcome delivery: Interplay of service market strategy and open business models. *Technovation, 72–73*, 46–59.

Visnjic, I., Ringov, D., & Arts, S. (2019). Which service? How industry conditions shape firms' service type choices. *Journal of Product Innovation Management, 36*(3), 381–407.

Beyond Excellence in the Automotive Industry in Industry 4.0? Lessons Learned from the creative Business Sector

Jerzy Rosiński

Abstract

In the realities of Industry 4.0, we can find the main two ways of building business models: developing existing models toward Digital Maturity and building completely new models, different from previous solutions. In the automotive industry, it seems that the search for development toward Digital Maturity, which currently ensures the development of the industry, may have its limitations. The text proposes to consider a business model taken from outside the automotive industry as a development proposal beyond Digital Maturity.

1 Transformations of the Fourth Industrial Revolution

Digitisation and automation related to Industry 4.0 (also referred to as the Industrial Internet of Things [IIoT]), together with macroeconomic factors, generates numerous opportunities, chances and challenges not only in the manufacturing industry but also in other industries (Müller & Buliga, 2019). Changes will be required in, among others, business models, models of employment, expected skills, and new challenges in terms of results. Not only business models will change, but so will social relationships (Kagermann et al., 2013). A new work environment encompassing integrated robot and cobot activities will put employees in new roles where current experience and expertise will turn out to be obsolete (Rozkwitalska & Slavik, 2017). This means that the changes associated with the fourth industrial revolution go beyond any single industry and new material technologies, and they impact not only areas related to robotics, automation of pro-

J. Rosiński (✉)
Jagiellonian University, Gołębia 24, 31-007 Kraków, Poland
e-mail: jerzy.rosinski@uj.edu.pl

K.-I. Voigt and J. M. Müller (eds.), *Digital Business Models in Industrial Ecosystems*, Future of Business and Finance, https://doi.org/10.1007/978-3-030-82003-9_14

duction, or information technology. It seems therefore that the transformations in these areas have impact in other sectors of the economy as well as the style of living of workers and consumers.

However, as regards changes within organisations themselves, there is an interesting phenomenon of the varying dynamics of technological change and organisational change described by Martec's law (Kupilas et al., 2019), which states that technology is changing faster than organisations.

The discrepancy between the speed of changes in technology and the speed of organisational change makes it necessary at some point (once the discrepancy is significant) to redefine the way the organisation operates. This re-definition can apply to, among others, business models.

2 Business Models: Types and Levels of Detail

A business model is a combination of two concepts (Kasprzak et al., 2020):

- model—a design or scheme that describes the operation and construction of a specific phenomenon or object, together with its characteristic features; a simplified representation of reality (Sławińska, 2010).
- business—an economic activity of a commercial nature, carried out in a continuous and organised manner, determined by the needs of the purchasers.

By combining the above elements, we arrive at the concept of a business model —understood as a set of elements and their relationships that allows to carry out the business logic of an enterprise (Kasprzak et al., 2020).

The existing multitude of definitions for understanding business models appears to be due to two or more reasons—the components of the concept itself. There is a level of detail associated with the formulation of the model (general/universal versus detailed/specialist). In turn, the business part means placing emphasis on various components of carrying out a business activity (e.g., delivering value, customers, process, and efficiency).

The first of these dimensions (general/universal vs. detailed/specialist) involves definitions in which a given business model describes the underlying business logic. At this level (depending on the emphasised element), the narrative is either resource-oriented or focused on the action structure or on the chain of creating value for customers. The resource-oriented model refers to key components, such as different types of company resources and relationships between them (inside and outside the company) and cause-effect relationships. Typically, resources are linked to sets of assumptions and standards describing relationships/cause-and-effect relations that help implement the company's strategy. The construction-oriented model is a way of thinking about running a business similar to architecture: it is concerned with the configuration of internal components, about their construction later on, moving to a useful function. The value chain-oriented model focuses on individual customer segments and the values offered to/co-created with them. It also informs us about segment revenue and the effectiveness of partner relationships (Kasprzak et al., 2020; Osterwalder et al., 2005).

The second of these dimensions (emphasis on individual elements) places narration around four areas: what is offered to customers, who is the target customer, how the value proposition is created, and how the business model generates profits (Jabłoński et al., 2020). These four areas can also be described in the form of the following categories: total value proposition (what?); market segments to which this proposal is addressed (who?), value collection (capture) mechanisms (how are profits gained?/how many?), the value chain structure necessary to generate and distribute the offer, complementary resources needed to support the position of the company in the chain and processes, together with the internal structure of the company supporting other elements of the business model (how is value created?/how?). Thus a business model can be defined as a system created by interdependent activities that allow an enterprise to address the questions of: "what?", "who?", "how?", and "how many" (Kasprzak et al., 2020).

It can therefore be concluded that a business model—understood as a set of elements and their relationships which allows to carry out the business logic of the company (Kasprzak et al., 2020)—encompasses two areas: a description of the organisation's basic logic of creating value and a set of elements and relationships between them explaining who the organisation's customers are, what is of value to them, and how the organisation can make a profit by delivering that value.

The description of these two areas (logic and components) can be kept on a very general (or universal) level, indicating, for example, that a business model is the rationale behind the way in which the organisation creates value and ensures and profits from that generated value. The same areas can also be defined in a more and more detailed way by describing the different elements and relationships between them and/or by giving one of the elements a leading role.

3 How Business Models Change Under Industry 4.0

Industry 4.0 may bring about fundamental changes in how business has been conducted (the logic of a business model and its components). In terms of business models, there are essentially two solutions:

1. modifying existing models and adapting them to the changing organisational environment
2. building completely new models resulting from the reality of the fourth industrial revolution.

The former solution can also be referred to as the search in Industry 4.0 for a "new way" to solve "old dilemmas" in the realm of economics and management.

In this approach, the most important area still remains the search for maximisation of company profits (“old dilemmas”). Thus, as noted by Niemczyk and Trzaska (2020), we are dealing with a management model adopted in classical and neo-classical economics, and from the point of view of management sciences a company is understood as a collection of resources undergoing optimisation processes (the so-called resource approach). The consequence of it is understanding the technologies of Industry 4.0 as an opportunity to optimise existing processes and/or expand the set of tangible and intangible assets (“new ways”). As a result, a company is able to, among other things: reduce costs, shorten time to market new products, and maintain its market position vis-à-vis competitors.

Business models that reflect this approach describe how an organisation functions in terms of the current state of the organisation, final expected state (e.g., state of Digital Maturity), and subsequent stages of approaching the desired state, along with their attributes. In some cases, the necessary priority actions are also indicated for the transitions between particular stages (Kupilas et al., 2019).What allows to classify this approach as a way of solving “old dilemmas” is the fact that the idea of achieving Digital Maturity is not specific to the current economic revolution and goes back to the third industrial revolution, as evidenced in works by R. L. Nolan about four and six stages of organisation maturity in relation to IT processes (Nolan, 1973, 1979) and publications by Paulk et al. (1995) naming five stages of process maturity. In today’s models describing adapting business models to the requirements of Industry 4.0, one can often see a reflection of what is described by Paulk et al. (1995) as the five stages of process maturity, from low maturity described as an unpredictable, poorly controlled and reactive process, to intermediate stages referring to: a project-specific and often reactive process; an organisation-specific and proactive process; a measurable and controllable process, to a mature process described as focused on continuous improvement.

A broad overview of the proposals to modify business models in the reality of Industry 4.0 is provided in the work of Kupilas et al. (2019). The overview refers to eight business models and focuses on the mechanical industry [mechanical engineering segment]. The analysed models for achieving Digital Maturity in the reality of Industry 4.0 are IMPULS Industry 4.0 Readiness; Industry 4.0/Digital Operations Self-Assessment; SIMMI 4.0; Acatech Industrie 4.0 Maturity Index; DREAMY (Digital Readiness Assessment MaturitY model); A maturity model for assessing Industry 4.0 readiness and maturity of manufacturing enterprises; 360 Digital Maturity Assessment; HADA (Spanish Government assessment).

Each of these models features between four and six degrees of reaching Digital Maturity. Comparisons between these range models can be drawn in the areas of: phases of reaching maturity, the areas described and the understanding of Digital Maturity (the last stage of development).

In terms of stages of reaching maturity, in all eight models, three phases of achieving digital maturity can be distinguished (after Cieśliński, 2020):

- Birth—processes focus on data acquisition, they are cost-generating and often unstructured,
- Growth—processes focus on processing data into the form of information, they support value creation and are organised,
- Improvement—processes provide knowledge, create value, and are self-improving.

For the areas described, the eight models mentioned relate to at least two out of three areas of operation:

- Organisation (e.g., strategy, employees, culture);
- Internal Operations (e.g., IT architecture, technology, infrastructure);
- External Operations (e.g., product and services, customers, market & customer access).

The descriptions refer mainly to the areas of Organisation and Internal Operations—these areas are present in all eight models of achieving Digital Maturity. We can therefore put forward the tentative conclusion that models for achieving Digital Maturity concentrate in areas related to the functioning of the organisation itself.

In the development stages of companies striving for Digital Maturity, the descriptions concentrate on two stages of functioning: Organisation and Internal Operations. Therefore achieving the last stage of development in a given model is the consequence of focusing on two out of three areas (Organisation and Internal Operations). Focus on the internal aspects of the organisation's functioning (Organisation oraz Internal Operations) means that also Digital Maturity in most models focuses on technological (self-)excellence, while to a small extent taking into account consumer empowerment, treating them more like a data source for one of the system's inputs. Table 1 summarises the descriptions of the highest stage of development for the eight models of Digital Maturity in relation to the consumer.

One may therefore conclude that in most of the adjustment models we focus on the organisation itself and its internal processes, marginalising environmental factors beyond the technological requirements of the market (as reflected by actions undertaken as part of Internal Operations).

As mentioned earlier, when it comes to business models in relation to the fourth industrial revolution, there are essentially two solutions. The first one (modification and adaptation of existing models) was discussed above. The other one, consisting in building completely new models resulting from the reality of the fourth industrial revolution, will be presented below.

This solution can also be referred to as the search in Industry 4.0 for a "new way" to solve "new dilemmas" in the realm of economics and management. The search is being conducted in several, increasingly advanced ways, receptive to Industry 4.0 (Niemczyk & Trzaska, 2020):

Table 1 Summary of the descriptions of the highest stage of development for the eight models of Digital Maturity in relation to the consumer (own work based on Kupilas et al., 2019)

Model of digital excellence	Name of the highest stage of development	Description of the highest stage of development in relation to the consumer
IMPULS Industry 4.0	Top performer	The producer is integrated with the customer [but most of the description at this level focuses on the technical excellence of internal processes]
Digital operations self-assessment	The digital champion	His focus is now on developing new disruptive (and often data-driven) business models and an innovative product and service portfolio to serve the individual customer requests. Collaboration is a key value driver
SIMMI 4.0	Optimised full digitisation	The company is a showcase for Industry 4.0 activities. It collaborates strongly with its business partners and therefore optimises its value networks
Acatech industrie 4.0 maturity index	Adaptability	Continuous adaptation allows a company to delegate certain decisions to IT systems so that it can adapt to a changing business environment as quickly as possible. [No person/customer]
DREAMY	Digital-oriented	Phrases like: "Digital-orientated: the process is digitally orientated and is based on a solid technology infrastructure and on a high potential growth organisation, which supports speed, robustness, and security in information exchange, in collaboration amongst the company functions and in the decision making" [No person/customer]
A maturity model for assessing Industry 4.0 readiness and maturity of manufacturing enterprises	Level 5 (the state-of-the-art of required attributes)	One of the dimensions that describe Digital Maturity applies to customers: "Customers: utilisation of customer data, digitalisation of sales/services, customer's digital media competence" [Customer treated as a "data source"]

(continued)

Table 1 (continued)

Model of digital excellence	Name of the highest stage of development	Description of the highest stage of development in relation to the consumer
360 Digital Maturity Assessment	Autonomous	Decision making is performed autonomously based on automatically synchronised data from the organisation and its direct customers and suppliers (e.g. logistics scheduling is automatically performed based on production state, customer orders and location, traffic condition, etc.) and digital development is a well-established company practice at all hierarchical levels [Customer treated as a "data source"]
HADA (Spanish Government assessment)	Leader (estimated between 800 and 1000 points)	In order to reach the highest level, it must take into account to a large extent each of the 5 scored areas, including the area: Organisation and people identify the capabilities of the organisation and its model of relationship with other stakeholders

1. seeing a company not as a set of resources, but as a set of contracts with stakeholders (in accordance with the logic of the agency theory)—we arrive at a different subject for optimisation actions than before, thus we face "new dilemmas."
2. in addition to the previous step (above), we have abandoned the concept of hierarchical enterprise structure and, thanks to Industry 4.0, adopted effective management based on one-off contacts between staff, thus we build a new organisation in terms of quality.
3. seeing human activity as embedded in Industry 4.0 technologies may lead us to a radical change in the logic of building an organisation, based on the theory of complexity (Hecklau et al., 2016); research in this respect focuses on the theory of self-organising systems, theory of chaos, path dependence, complex adaptive systems, and modeling based on agent concepts (Rokita & Dziubińska, 2016).

In publications from 2000 to 2019, we will not find too many definitions of business models dedicated to Industry 4.0. Most definitions of the business model from research papers approach the business model from a resource perspective. The models are focused on improving the traditional value chain by improving automation, increasing operational efficiency, and optimising structures (Niemczyk & Trzaska, 2020). Therefore most business models focus on "new ways" to solve "old dilemmas": the modification of existing models and their adaptation to the changing environment of the organisation. Definitions used in the majority of the current approaches focus on creating added value from the value network. These approaches very often see the aim of management in a different way. In other words, "new dilemmas" to be solved emerge. Often, the business objective is no longer a simply defined goal in the form of an expected level of profit or expected value for shareholders. Rather than that, concepts which evade easy definition emerge: the value of the ecosystem, understood as an adaptation between the company and stakeholders (actors) of the ecosystem (Jacobides et al., 2018) as well as creating value in the ecosystem and capturing it (Moller & Halinen, 2017). "New dilemmas" appear not only in the area of objectives but also of resources (whether dematerialised or digital). Resources may be described by the language of the collaborative economy, using the concept of value cloud, and the idea of building a business around an IT and information platform or by mental diagrams from the theory of complexity. Actions are also described in a new way: business models refer to the unit of analysis that is the transaction (Niemczyk & Trzaska, 2020). When at the level of objectives, resources, and actions, there are the "new dilemmas", it turns out that the answer is not "customised" models. Instead, we need a completely "new solution": a model characteristic of Industry 4.0.

According to according to Niemczyk and Trzaska (2020), a business model to be considered as an Industry 4.0 model (i.e., a "new way" of solving "new dilemmas"), the following conditions must be met:

- combine the ways of generating value following the principle of servitisation;
- it must combine in such a way as to provide the possibility of generating different value streams;
- it must combine different ways of generating value based on a uniform communication protocol;
- must combine value streams (blending transactions) by through eliminating all transaction cost carriers;
- it must generate value throughout the entire ecosystem;
- and all these combining processes must take place with the use of Industry 4.0 technologies.

Business models that meet these criteria can be divided into four groups of models:

- data-based (creating data, selling data; gathering data, selling ads; predictive analytics; gathering data, selling; predictive analytics; adding data goodness to products; adding data goodness to existing services; creating new services enabled by data mining)
- based on intelligent product and services (product-service systems);

- product-oriented business models; utilization-oriented business models; performance-oriented business models
- based on seemingly unscaled actions; the unbundled start-up; the rebundled start-up; the aggregator model; the Holding Company Mode
- based on modern market competition strategies.

Further, business models can be separated as follow: Long tail; Multilateral Platforms; Free as a business model; and Open business model. They were discussed extensively in the separate texts of the authors who created the above classification (Niemczyk & Trzaska, 2020; Niemczyk et al., 2019).

When classifying models, the subject matter can be approached not only from the side of analysis (above) but also from the side of synthesis (below), by describing the innovation archetypes in an Industry 4.0 business model. An interesting example is the classification developed by Weking et al. (2018) describing three fundamental innovation archetypes and their sub-archetypes. These are as follows:

1. New processes
   (Crowd sourced innovation; Manufacturing as a Service; Mass Personalization)
2. Servitisation
   (Long-term partnerships; Product as a service; Result as a service)
3. Expertise as a service
   (Product-related consulting; Process-related consulting; Brokerage platforms; IoT platforms)

The description of business models which are "new solutions" for "new dilemmas" within Industry 4.0 goes beyond classifications based on analysis or synthesis, as well as thinking in terms of purpose—resources—process. The new business models also give rise to a new way of business (co)operation: coopetition, going beyond traditional co-operation, and competition dilemmas (Czakon et al., 2020).

4 The Development of Current Models—Environmental Factors

Moving business models between markets or looking for an analogy with an existing model is a process that is risky and creative at the same time. On the one hand, one can surmise that every market has its own characteristics and it is unreasonable to ignore this fact. However, on the other hand, transfers from one field to have a high potential for creativity and can provide a strong boost for development in the area to which the model is transferred. As an example, one could quote a model from the realm of psychology: the perspective theory by Tverski and Kahneman (1979), which describes decision-making processes under conditions of another uncertainty. This model was transferred from cognitive psychology to economic research, creating behavioural economy (Kahneman, 2013).

Why take this risky and at the same time creative challenge with regard to Industry 4.0 and the automotive industry? The reasons may be found in the very nature of the fourth industrial revolution, as it is expected to cause the following changes:

However, the nature of the changes is shown not only by the publications of futurists but also by marketing manuals (close to the reality of the market). While between 2010 and 2019, one could think in the categories of “moving from traditional to digital” (Kotler et al., 2016) that show the world of new technologies as forcing a change in traditional thinking, after 2020 the thinking has shifted to “Technology for humanity” (Kotler et al., 2021) that shows how to integrate technology and business models into the new consumer behaviours that have emerged over the years 2010–2019.

Even when remaining within the sphere of traditional product descriptions (Kotler et al., 2019), it can be noted that a new development area is being created for business models, especially those of the first group discussed earlier: modifying existing models and adapting them to the changing environment of the organisation (looking for a “new way” in Industry 4.0 to resolve “old dilemmas”). These models aim to achieve excellence (e.g., Digital Maturity) in manufacturing, distribution and collaboration with suppliers and customers. They therefore place development within the first, second, and third product levels (respectively: Core benefit; Generic product; Expected product). The remaining product areas fourth and fifth (Augmented product: Potential product) may be less related to real technological excellence. After all, they have to do with the consumer’s beliefs about additional features, benefits, attributes or related services that serve to differentiate the product from its competitors, and consequently to customer loyalty. Areas four and five of the product offer an opportunity to modify beyond digitisation and optimisation.

The new directions available for development include (Kozarkiewicz, 2019): an orientation on continuous customer interactions (including, among others, constant on-line availability for customers), personalisation of customer offerings (through big data and web analytics tools), adding value to the company’s offer by the user/customer (e.g., creating and supporting website content by customers, generating information by customers to the supplier of goods/services), creating social networks around the provider of goods/services (e.g., video blogs, forums, chats). However, these are still changes to individual aspects.

It may be worth considering modifications of at least levels four and five of the product, or the development of the whole business model beyond Digital Maturity, using a proposal from outside the automotive industry. Such a proposal is set out below.

5 The Development of Current Models—A Proposal for Development

The business model was developed in two stages: in 2018 and 2020. In 2018, data from 2017 to 2018 were analysed with the aim of building a business model. In 2020, data from 2019 were analysed, this time with the aim of re-verifying the business model. In addition, already in 2018, references of the model created to well-functioning free time organisations were successfully found, which can be considered as part of model verification.

Due to the characteristics of the research data, the qualitative approach was used in the data analysis. In the 2018 research, the main tool was semantic analysis—a technique for categorising and processing data of a qualitative nature as well as short statements and descriptions (Liu et al., 2018; Sezgen et al., 2019; Xiong et al., 2019). Importantly for the subject of the study, this method was used for data of a similar nature from the leisure industry, as it appears to be irrespective of the specific characteristics of the local market described and the affiliation of the researchers themselves (Gorgadze et al., 2019; Homburg et al., 2019; Liu et al., 2019). Semantic analysis was used to build a model relating to entrepreneurship and new forms of business activity, which had already been practiced before (Erpf, 2019). In the 2020 research, content analysis was used. This choice had to do with a smaller number of research material. However, of key importance for the choice of the inference method were additional analyses carried out with regard to the sender of the message and the assumptions made by the sender about the recipient, which are non-material variables specific to content analysis (Klimkiewicz, 2013).

The analyses carried out in 2018 on material from 2017 to 2018 showed as a result the possibility for a 4-factor model describing conducting business in the leisure industry in the reality of the fourth industrial revolution. The result was arrived at in the following three steps:

1. Summarising the kinds of business activities in the leisure industry.
2. Putting the companies' description of their activities through semantic analysis and obtaining 4 descriptive categories as a result.
3. Verifying the overlap of the four descriptive categories with the activities of the analysed entities.

The analyses conducted in 2018, based on the 2017–2018 material, found their final form by describing how modern leisure industry organisations operate through the following categories:

- Customisation (extreme)
- Hand-made (not by a robot)
- Real time feedback (and action)
- Creativity (unordered)

Since the Start-up Challenge was also run in the next year, the next step in the analysis was to verify whether the 4-factor model, derived from 2017–2018 material, was also available to obtain based on the 2019 material. To this end, the same steps as those taken on the 2017–2018 material were repeated on the 2019 material. With the new material (from 2019), it was possible to ask new questions for the 4-factor model that had been previously created. The main dilemmas were whether there had been any changes in the structure of the companies in the described industry and whether the 4-factor model was still relevant to describe the activities carried out. In the material from 2019, as in the classification of the way in which 18 entities from 2018 operated, three categories are equally filled: Customisation (extreme), Real time feedback (and action); Creativity (unordered). As in 2017 and 2018, the material from 2019 was relatively represented in the category: Hand-made (not by a robot). This may be due to the proportion of leisure industry business initiatives that are linked to online purchases. Such services are usually intangible or are provided by software that has the nature of artificial intelligence, hence the representation for the category: Hand-made (not by a robot) is less significant.

The next step was to review the 4-factor model created based on the 2017–2018 data in relation to a non-start-up organisation. This analysis step attempted to map the obtained model with its 4 descriptive categories to a leisure time organisation which has existed for many years on the market and has been functioning in the reality of a smart city. The Norwegian Fisheries Museum in Bergen (Norges Fiskerimuseum) was selected as an adequate facility to build references in a case study, as it has been operating in Bergen, which is a smart city. Designed for modern operation in terms of the idea of its functioning, it is now considered one of the most interesting places in Bergen and Norway in general. A description of the functioning of the Norwegian museum was "imposed" on the 4-factor model obtained by analysing the functioning of start-ups (see Table 2).

As a result of the qualitative analysis (Table 2), the obtained model was confirmed with regard to an efficient organisation from the leisure industry, which is not a start-up but has been active for many years (although reformed in recent years) as a museum. Detailed analyses of the material in Table 2 are provided in a separate publication (Rosinski, 2019).

A case study of an organisation that is not a start-up also showed that the category Hand-made (not by a robot) is the second most saturated category when it comes to the descriptions of operation. Therefore, early poor saturation may be due to the specificities of the organisations being analysed (start-ups using online shopping apps in 50% cases), rather than to the characteristics of the leisure industry.

The case study analyses for the museum have also pointed to another aspect of the organisation's operation. It appears that a separate added value emerges here, resulting from the synergy between the four areas, such as, for example, solutions created with one's own hands foster creativity and facilitate considering the service as customised to one's personal needs, while all of it happens in real time. Therefore areas presented in Table 2, although they are separate, when applied in

Table 2 Description of conducting business activity by the Norwegian Fisheries Museum in Bergen as an organisation representing the leisure industry—allocation in four categories (own work)

Customisation (extreme)	Hand-made (not by a robot)
1. ways of reaching the museum building 2. switchable visiting paths (at any time) 3. elements of spatial arrangement "invite" to take breaks freely and find one's own pace 4. wide range of rest areas diverse in terms of quality 5. staff approving of the adaptation of the space for one's personal needs (picnic spots, places to have a snack)	1. manual turning, moving, pushing necessary to get content of the exhibition 2. making discoveries independently (microscopes + ability to place different objects for viewing) 3. varied "sensory experiences" for children and adult visitors 4. fishing independently on a micro scale (for children) 5. wooden jigsaw puzzles (maps, marine organisms) 6. manual skills tasks related to the sea (fishing with magnetic rods) 7. path "A world under water" allows to have a personal experience of individual "ocean floors", is composed of elements which allow a "personal experience"
Real time feedback (and action) 1. interactive exhibition screens 2. thematic computer games [and similarly as for category Hand-made (not by a robot)] 3. manual turning, moving, pushing necessary to get content of the exhibition 4. making discoveries one one's own/by oneself (microscopes + ability to place different objects for viewing) 5. varied "sensory experiences" for children and adult visitors 6. fishing with one's own hands on a micro scale (for children) 7. wooden jigsaw puzzles (maps, marine organisms) 8. manual skills tasks related to the sea (fishing with magnetic rods) 9. path "A world under water" allows to have a personal experience of individual "ocean floors", is composed of elements which allow a "personal experience"	Creativity (unordered) 1. creating one's own visit and one's own space to rest 2. interactive avatars created from photos of visitors within the space of the town (on screens) 3. wooden and electronic jigsaw puzzles 4. unexpected activities along the way (huge crab statue, fishing, entering a metal diving suit) 5. availability of objects inviting to use according to one's imagination, taking photos

individual ideas for activity may remain in interaction, increasing the added value for the user (Fig. 1).

It seems, therefore, that we can see a stability in the trend in subsequent years as regards the two ranges:

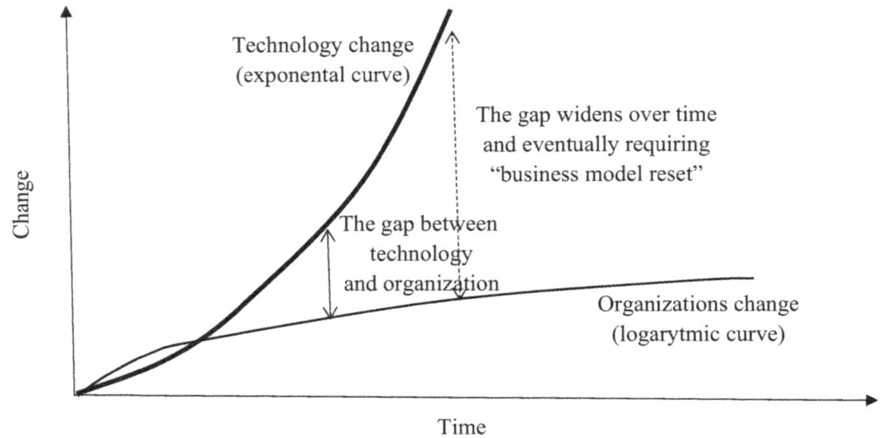

Fig. 1 Martec's law. *Source* own elaboration on base: Kupilas et al. (2019)

- the ability to describe economic initiatives within the leisure industry using the four proposed categories
- the tendency to assign entities more strongly to one of the categories, and a relatively less presence of entities described in the next of the categories, which can be linked with market trends (growth in initiatives and web services related to the leisure industry)

The proposed 4-factor business development model is shown in Fig. 2.

The proposed model does not imply the need for SMEs from the leisure industry to take up four of the 4 factors proposed. Rather, it shows the areas of opportunity and the more opportunities are met, the more beneficial it is for the company. The data based on which the model was constructed indicated that the organisations active on the market carried out three out of four or four out of the four factors of the model.

By far the most justified from the point of view of the literature (Brzeziński & Stefańczyk, 2013; Cohen et al., 2019; Tohanean & Weiss, 2019) is the element defined as creativity. At the same time, it is a very broad category (and therefore non-specific), hence the clarifying Creativity (unordered) in order to show the specificity of the category of creativity in the context of the described business entities, and therefore the specificity of the leisure industry in the realities of the fourth industrial revolution.

Already present in the economy after the third industrial revolution, Customisation (extreme), or tailoring to the needs of the customer is a well-known descriptive element. In this case, it is not so much a new descriptive element as a growth in an already existing trend.

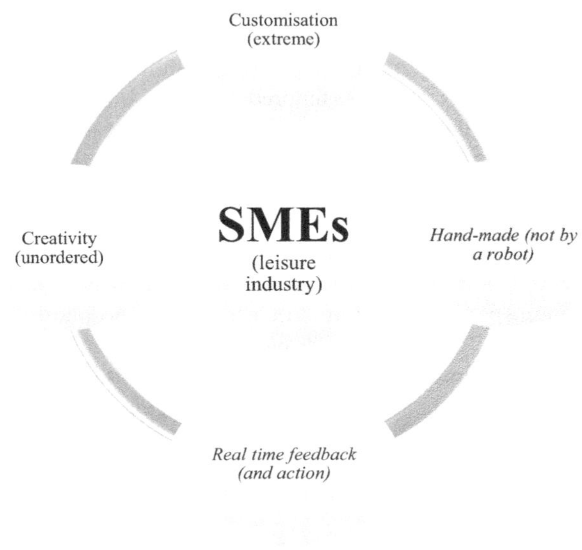

Fig. 2 Proposed 4-factor business model for SMEs operating in the leisure industry

Previously nearly absent in literature, the two remaining categories are relatively new elements in the business model:

- Hand-made (not by a robot)
- Real time feedback (and action).

What is described as real time feedback (and action) is already present in the relationship between software and user (especially in games and entertainment programs), thus in this case leisure industry organizations fit into an already existing trend.

The factor of customisation was certainly present in the earlier industrial revolution (3.0.), for example, by producing short series of products, the ability to choose additional features or supplement the product with minor differentiators (which increased the number of combinations), but in combination with the other factors (hand-made; real time feedback; creativity), it provides a new expression. These days, it is not so much the producer adjusting to the needs of his or her customers (read their needs and respond), but we witness a change in which the customer personally, on their own and by means of their activity (hand-made) creates a solution, freely combining elements in unexpected new wholes (creativity) and immediately achieves an effect (real time feedback). Such a way of thinking is already present in the leisure industry (creating a character in games such as *The Sims 4* or *World of Warcraft*). It is transferred out of the games from the virtual world to the real one (although this division seems to get increasingly fuzzy) and is transferred to new areas, outside games.

What is a non-standard element is the expectation that the product or service are not only surprising in its novelty, tailored to one's expectations and delivered quickly, but also that they are not generated automatically by robots: thus the category Hand-made (not by a robot). It seems that it is the last of these categories of descriptive categories that has the greatest potential for development for the leisure industry. It is a potential associated with redefining past activity and functioning according to new rules so as to perform new functions. Libraries have undergone such redefining. From places in which one checks out books they have become a common space to spend time in a friendly atmosphere, as well as places which "create culture" through events and permanent features carried out in the space of the library. A similar thing happened to museums, which used to be spaces for: collecting, describing, conserving, and presenting, become interactive spaces of experience, integrating groups of visitors (families, school groups).

6 Final Conclusions

The limited scope when it comes to the industry may be a constraint on the proposed model, but if it is taken as inspiration for the development of modifications to the 4th and 5th levels of the product or development of the whole business model beyond the final stage of Digital Maturity, it may be that those describing and predicting the development of Industry 4.0 will see it as (again) an increasingly oriented toward the relationship with the customer.

References

Cieśliński, W. (2020). Cyfrowa dojrzałość organizacji – założenia poznawczo-metodologiczne. In S. Gregorczyk & G. Urbanek (Eds.), *Zarządzanie strategiczne w dobie cyfrowej gospodarki sieciowej* (pp. 315–337). Wydawnictwo Uniwersytetu Łódzkiego.

Czakon, W., Manish, K., Srivastava, M. K., Le Roy, F. & Gnyawali, D. (2020). Coopetition strategies: Critical issues and research directions, *Long Range Planning, 53*(1), 101948

Erpf, P., Ripper, M. J., & Castignetti, M. (2019). Understanding Social Entrepreneurship Based on Self-Evaluations of Organizational Leaders – Insights from an International Survey. *Journal of Social Entrepreneurship, 10*(3), 288–306.

Gorgadze, A., Gordin, V., & Belyakova, N. (2019). Semantic analysis of the imperial topic: Case of St. *Petersburg, e-Review of Tourism Research, 16*(2–3), 3–13.

Gerd, L. (2016). *Technology vs. Humanity: The coming clash between man and machine*. Zurich, The Futures Agency.

Hecklau, F., Galeitzke, M., Flachs, S. & Kohl, H. (2016). Holistic approach for human resource management in Industry 4.0, *Procedia CIRP, 2016*(54), 1-6.

Homburg, T., & Boochs, F. (2019). Situation-dependent data quality analysis for geospatial data using semantic technologies. *Business Information Processing, 339*, 566–578.

Jabłoński, M., Jabłoński, A., & Szpitter, A. (2020). Dynamika modeli biznesu przedsiębiorstw w gospodarce cyfrowej – perspektywa monetyzacji. In S. Gregorczyk & G. Urbanek (Eds.), *Zarządzanie strategiczne w dobie cyfrowej gospodarki sieciowej* (pp. 295–314). Wydawnictwo Uniwersytetu Łódzkiego.

Jacobides, M. G., Cennamo, C., & Gawer, A. (2018). Towards a theory of ecosystems. *Strategic Management Journal, 39*(8), 2255–2276.

Kagermann, H., Wahlster, W. & Helbig, J. (2013). *Recommendations for implementing the strategic initiative Industrie 4.0. Securing the future of German manufacturing industry*. Final report of the Industrie 4.0 Working Group, Munich: Acatech-National Academy of Science and Engineering and Forschungsunion.

Kahneman, D., & Tversky, A. (1979). Prospect Theory: An Analysis of Decision Under Risk. *Econometrica, 47*(2), 263–292.

Kahneman, D. (2013). *Thinking, Fast and Slow*. London, Penguin.

Kasprzak, R., Tomaszewski, A., & Ziółkowska, M. (2020). Operacjonalizacja modelu biznesu w przemysłach kreatywnych – wstępne wyniki badań. In S. Gregorczyk & G. Urbanek (Eds.), *Zarządzanie strategiczne w dobie cyfrowej gospodarki sieciowej* (pp. 351–366). Wydawnictwo Uniwersytetu Łódzkiego.

Klimkiewicz, K. (2013). W poszukiwaniu paradygmatów, metodologii i strategii. Wizerunek przedsiębiorstwa społecznie odpowiedzialnego – analiza treści komunikatów. *Prace naukowe Uniwersytetu Ekonomicznego we Wrocławiu, Społeczna odpowiedzialność organizacji, 288*, Wrocław, 57-69.

Kotler, P., Armstrong, G., Harris, L. C., & He, H. (2019). *Principles of Marketing* (8th ed.). Pearson Education.

Kotler, P., Kartajaya, H. & Setiawan, I. (2021). *Marketing 5.0: Technology for Humanity, Moving from Traditional to Digital*. Hoboken, NJ: John Wiley & Sons.

Kotler, P., Kartajaya, H. & Setiawan, I., (2016). *Marketing 4.0: Moving from Traditional to Digital*. Hoboken: John Wiley & Sons.

Kozarkiewicz, A. (2019). Modele e-biznesu. In S. Kopera, M. Najda-Janoszka, & M. Bednarczyk (Eds.), *E-przedsiębiorczość Zasady i praktyka* (pp. 85–112). WUJ.

Kupilas, K. J., Rodríguez-Montequín, V., Villanueva-Balsera, J. & Álvarez-Pérez, C., (2019). Industry 4.0 and Digital Maturitys. In: M. Zaher-Pérez (Ed.) *Industria 4.0 y la Dirección e Ingeniería de Proyectos* (pp. 66-103), Universidad de Cádiz.

Liu, Y., Huang, K., Bao, J., & Chen, K. (2019). Listen to the voices from home: An analysis of Chinese tourists' sentiments regarding Australian destinations. *Tourism Management, 71*, 337–347.

Liu, W., Lai, C., & Xu, W. (2018). Tweeting about emergency: A semantic network analysis of government organizations' social media messaging during Hurricane Harvey. *Public Relations Review, 44*(5), 807–819.

Moller, K., & Halinen, A. (2017). Managing business and innovation networks – From strategic nets to business fields and ecosystems. *Industrial Marketing Management, 67*, 5–22.

Müller, J. M. & Buliga, O. (2019). Archetypes for Data-driven business models in Industry 4.0. *International Conference on Information Systems (ICIS)*, Munich.

Niemczyk, J. & Trzaska, R. (2020). Klasyfikacja modeli biznesowych w Industry 4.0. In: S. Gregorczyk & G. Urbanek (Eds.). Zarządzanie strategiczne w dobie cyfrowej gospodarki sieciowej (pp. 267-296), Wydawnictwo Uniwersytetu Łódzkiego, Łódź.

Niemczyk, J., Trzaska, R. & Trzaska, M., (2019). Scalability 4.0 as the main rent in Industry 4.0: the case study of Amazon. *Informatyka Ekonomiczna, 2019*(2), 69-84.

Nolan, R. L. (1973). Managing the computer resource: a stage hypothesis. *Communications of the ACM, 16*(7), 399–405.

Nolan, R. L. (1979). Managing Crises of Data Processing. *Harvard Business Review, 3*(4).

Osterwalder, A., Pigneur, Y., & Tucci, C. L. (2005). Clarifying business models: Origins, present, and future of the concept. *Communications of the Association for Information Systems, 16*, 1–25.

Paulk, M. C., Weber, C. V., Curtis, B., & Chrissis, M. B. (1995). *The capability maturity model: Guidelines for improving the software process*. Addison-Wesley.

Rosiński, J. (2019). Predictive factors of innovation in leisure industry organizations as an opportunity in the age of industrial revolution 4.0: a case study of the Norwegian Fisheries Museum (Bergen). In: A. Ujwary-Gil & N. R. Potoczek (Eds.), *Network, innovation, and competence-based economy* (pp. 181-203). Institute of Economics, Polish Academy of Sciences, Warsaw.

Rozkwitalska, M. & Slavik, J. (2017). Around Learning and Industry 4.0 in Management Theory. *International Journal of Contemporary Management, 16*(4), 185-206.

Sezgen, E., Mason, K. J., & Mayer, R. (2019). Voice of airline passenger: A text mining approach to understand customer satisfaction. *Journal of Air Transport Management, 77*, 65–74.

Sławińska, M. (2010). *Modele biznesu w handlu detalicznym*. Wydawnictwo Uniwersytetu Ekonomicznego w Poznaniu, Poznań.

Xiong, Y., Cho, M., & Boatwright, B. (2019). Hashtag activism and message frames among social movement organizations: Semantic network analysis and thematic analysis of Twitter during the #MeToo movement. *Public Relations Review, 45*(1), 10–23.

Geographical Factors for the Implementation of Industry 4.0 in Central Eastern Europe

Roland Z. Szabó and Lilla Hortoványi

Abstract

Studying the geographical factors for Industry 4.0 implementations is a novel research line. Only a few studies tried to define the term Geography 4.0, and we are lack empirical evidence of potential regional differences. Besides, the use of digital technologies is a key element and a triggering factor in the business model innovation nowadays. Therefore, we conducted empirical research among 302 Industry 4.0 aware business to business companies in various regions of four Central Eastern European countries to reveal the associations between the use of digital technologies and geographical factors. We found that business model innovation towards Industry 4.0 triggered by the use of digital technologies is more advanced in central and knowledge-intensive regions in the case of high-value activities, which may cause further divergence and not a convergence of regions.

1 Introduction

Despite this growing interest in research and industrial policy-making for Industry 4.0, little is known about—and mainly based on case-study findings—what the European industry and research system is doing in this context, whether there are country or region-specific differences, and whether there are few key regional hot

R. Z. Szabó (✉)
University in Győr, Egyetem tér 1., Győr 9026, Hungary
e-mail: szabozsoltroland@yahoo.com

L. Hortoványi
Corvinus University of Budapest, Fővám tér 8, Budapest 1093, Hungary
e-mail: lilla.hortovanyi@gmail.com

K.-I. Voigt and J. M. Müller (eds.), *Digital Business Models in Industrial Ecosystems*, Future of Business and Finance, https://doi.org/10.1007/978-3-030-82003-9_15

spots (Ciffolilli & Muscio, 2018). Diodato and Morrison (2019) highlights that the geographical distribution of innovative activities is an emerging subject, but still poorly understood; and relatively little attention has been devoted to investigating jointly the sectoral and the geographical dimensions behind these processes, in particular from a long-term perspective.

Since business are aware of the challenges imposed by the fourth industrial revolution and many of them already started to transform their operations, however, there is little understanding of which regions have the potential to diversify into and develop the new technologies of Industry 4.0 (Balland & Boschma, 2021). In addition, there is still limited evidence on the geography of Industry 4.0 and the factors defining the readiness of a region to transform successfully its business (De Propris & Bailey, 2020).

The stake is high. If European companies are unable to keep up with their production, new competitors will rise (Bloching et al., 2015). Consequently, the objective of the present study is to improve our understanding regarding regional differences in business model innovation towards Industry 4.0 by the analysis of the use of digital technologies in several key activities of the firms' value chain. Although, our research is based on a sample of various Central and East European regions understanding the differences is critical for providing better and more effective support to all European regions.

The next section outlines the main literature about the geography of the fourth industrial revolution where we point out the regional differences caused by the fourth industrial revolution and the importance of knowledge-intensive regions on firms' business model innovation towards Industry 4.0. Besides, we identified that the use of digital/Industry 4.0 technologies in the key activities of the firms' value chain is a good indicator for the level of the digital transformation. The theoretical chapters are followed by a brief discussion on data collection and the choice of methodology. We conducted our research in various Central Eastern European regions based on the analysis of 302 Industry 4.0 aware B2B (business to business) firms. Discussion of the results and concluding remarks will sum up the contribution of the research highlighting the importance of regional dynamics and the need for actions.

2 Geography of Industry 4.0

Over the twentieth century, improvements in transportation and communication systems allowed increasing geographical fragmentation of production and increasing global trade in intermediate inputs, which will be likely reversed by the Internet (Leamer & Storper, 2001). The growing number of studies confirmed the importance of geographic location on knowledge flow and regional innovativeness (Bell & Zaheer, 2007) which depends on the expertise and talent available in the proximity of the firm (Cantwell & Salmon, 2018).

The distribution of human capital is found to be a driving force for the growth and development of cities and regions; hence, it is considered to be an important factor in economic geography (Florida, 2002). Becattini (2015) argues that the inhabitants of a place are always engaged in the local production (aware or not) by influencing and determining the territory's knowledge base. Previous studies affirmed, in particular, that technological disruption can lead to an uneven distribution of new technologies at the regional level, benefit mainly the regions that have previously accumulated more technology-specific knowledge in their existing knowledge base. Throughout history, industrial sectors whose knowledge base and capabilities are linked to new, emerging radical innovations have been able to develop dynamically (Castellacci, 2008). Those regions are the winners of technological development that can make extensive use of new opportunities due to their previously accumulated technical-logical capabilities.

Industry 4.0 therefore will have a more dramatic effect on economic geography than previous rounds of industrial revolutions. First, Industry 4.0 will bring fundamental changes in the management of geographically dispersed value chains (Strange & Zucchella, 2017). Second, it will possibly concentrate on the economic growth in big cities and away from deindustrialised suburbs and smaller cities (Bellandi et al., 2020). Consequently, Industry 4.0 technologies are likely to be prevalent in advanced manufacturing regions with greater availability of technological capabilities (Corradini et al., 2021).

Evangelista and co-authors (2018) concluded that there is a large amount of evidence, both at national and regional levels and that competencies and capabilities are not evenly distributed, but relatively concentrated in specific areas. Analysing 294 NUTS2 regions, Ciffolilli and Muscio (2018) concluded that Industry 4.0 activities are strongly concentrated, in terms of obtained resources, in core Europe at the sub-national level, thus there are regional disparities. Moreover, Muscio and Ciffolilli (2020) concluded that the geography of Industry 4.0 is highly uneven in Europe. EU is falling behind technologically, in terms of the share of value-added in ICT goods and services in total manufacturing exports compared to the US, Japan, Korea and China, which potentially can damage the European welfare (Bachtler, 2019). This is a critical problem—continues Bachtler (2019)—especially because the EU is lack young and leading innovators in knowledge-intensive sectors that can grow to become large, thus the long-term competitiveness of European manufacturing is at stake. Indeed, in the ICT field, there is only one European company (#19 Deutsche Telekom) among the global top 20 digital companies (Forbes, 2020).

2.1 Regional Divergence Caused by the Fourth Industrial Revolution

The fourth industrial revolution is expected to have effects on the geography of knowledge production and innovation in Europe (Balland & Boschma, 2021). Although Industry 4.0 is yet unfolding, because the widespread deployment of its constituent technologies is still some years away, it has the potential to transform productive labour as we know it (Reischauer, 2018). An increasing number of tasks traditionally performed by humans will be conducted by robots (Cowen, 2013) disrupting and fundamentally changing many occupations (Brynjolfsson & McAfee, 2014; Szalavetz, 2018). It is evident, however, that the changing nature of work results in challenges for organisations' human resource needs (Barley et al., 2017).

The disruption of new technologies is costly to society (De Propris & Bailey, 2020). For example, the new skill requirements in the economy can cause a skills gap and skills obsolescence increasing unemployment and polarising the labour markets. Autor et al. (2013) found that technological change induces unemployment in routine and task-intensive production and clerical occupations both in the manufacturing and non-manufacturing sectors. Although the new technologies will also create new and complementary jobs, however, these jobs require significant and wide-ranging upskilling (Bachtler, 2019).

The creation of new skills and jobs and the loss of older ones may not be a consequence but a precondition for the transformation of local production systems (Bellandi et al., 2018). Empirical studies found evidence that workers are more productive when they locate around others with high levels of human capital, while other studies confirmed that human capital is strongly associated with urban and regional growth (Florida, 2002). The fourth industrial revolution builds on diversity and promotes urbanization (Götz & Jankowska, 2017). Socio-pessimists fear that digitisation will amplify existing inequalities because technology adds an extra hurdle to full participation, further marginalising historically disadvantaged people and countries (Helsper, 2021).

2.2 The Importance of Knowledge-Intensive Regions on Firms' Business Model Innovation Towards Industry 4.0

Due to the increasingly complex nature of technology, the boundaries of the firm cannot fully encompass any longer the challenge to generate new knowledge and innovate in isolation (Cantwell & Santangelo, 2002). It is just enormously challenging for a single organization to follow all the trends and innovations needed for staying ahead of the competition. (Diodato & Morrison, 2019) conceptualises innovation as a systemic process, which is the outcome of interactions and feedbacks between a variety of actors, public, and private.

Many other scholars share this view and argue that for companies to survive, and they need to establish research collaborations along with the development of their technological readiness (Nick et al., 2019). Because of the unprecedented speed of technological and societal change, which translates into highly uncertain environments, triple or quadruple helix partnerships are vital (Wostner, 2017). Rather, ecosystems of open, interconnected networks of stakeholders—companies, knowledge institutions, the government and NGOs—must learn to cooperate to a much greater extent through strategic partnerships (Bachtler, 2019).

Reischauer (2018) argues that Industry 4.0 is a discourse between business, academia, and politics, and all of them aims to influence and shape the course of Industry 4.0 by communicative means. These actors can innovate in ways that fit best their interests and capabilities in order to accomplish this shared vision. In summary, firms must seek access and cooperation with universities and knowledge institutions in order to succeed in the business model innovation towards Industry 4.0. Therefore, a firm located in a region where the number of higher educational institutions and scientific research and development institutes and the number of people with tertiary education is higher is more likely to use digital/Industry 4.0 technologies in various key activities of its value chain.

2.3 Digital/Industry 4.0 Technologies in the Firms' Value Chain

The use of digital/Industry 4.0 technologies is a key element and a triggering factor in the business model innovation nowadays. Several digital/Industry 4.0 technologies can be used in different activities of the firm, and some examples are shown in Fig. 1.

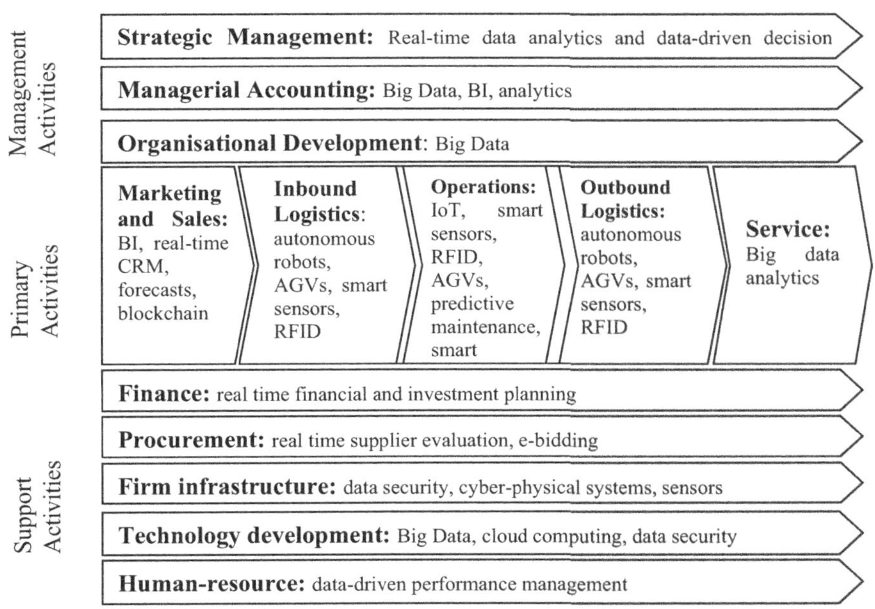

Fig. 1 Digital/Industry 4.0 technologies in the firms' value chain. *Source based on* Szabó and Hortoványi (2021)

Firms' activities and resources that used to be physical are now digital. For example, internal processes in companies were once heavily dependent on paper document flow, but now digital technologies allow remote interaction. Organizational resources can be viewed as bundles of tangible and intangible assets including a firm's management skills, organizational processes and routines, and the information and knowledge it controls (Barney et al., 2001). The value of resources, however, can be enhanced or decreased by changes in technology (Pavlou & El Sawy, 2006). Digital resources and capabilities are not simply formed as a result of technological investment (Fry & Talja, 2007), only when an ICT resource becomes firm-specific, embedded within the organizational processes, then it constitutes a digital resource and capability (Boothby et al., 2010; Wu et al., 2006).

Moreover, digital/Industry 4.0 technologies are becoming more and more 'key enabling technologies' (KETs) (Goldfarb et al., 2019; Martinelli et al., 2019; Simon, 2019). The adoption of system-wide KETs has been presented as a major source of economic benefits by the European Commission (2011) and also by many scholars (Evangelista et al., 2018; Muscio & Ciffolilli, 2020). Yet, a key consideration is that not all enabling technologies share the same transformative potential (Teece, 2018).

The above discussion on previous researches suggests region-specific factors and the use of digital/Industry 4.0 technologies in the key activities of the firms' values chain should be jointly considered to explain the ability of regions to succeed in digital transformation (Diodato & Morrison, 2019).

3 Methodology

Central and Eastern European countries due to their strong interdependencies with other European economies have an impact on Europe's competitiveness. West European societies such as Germany and France have shifted their industrial activities to locations in Central and Eastern Europe (Faust et al., 2004). Their current growth model is mostly based on assembly (Backé et al., 2019). From these countries, data were gathered in various regions in Slovakia, Hungary, Romania, and Serbia.

3.1 Sampling

The population of the sample is the Industry 4.0 aware B2B companies. The initial list of B2B firms was obtained from the local entities that help the transformation of the national manufacturing industry. For example, in Hungary, the members of the Industry 4.0 National Technology Platform Association were contacted. Altogether, in 2019, there were less than 200 companies in each participating country (Hungary, Romania, Serbia and Slovakia) that was Industry 4.0 aware.

Altogether we collected 302 full responses: 78 from Hungary, 29 from Romania, 118 from Serbia, and 77 from Slovakia. These numbers are high, considering the small population of Industry 4.0 aware B2B firms. Besides, the sample purposely comprised homogenous companies to reduce the variability of the data.

3.2 Measures of Geographical Factors

The type of settlement was divided into three categories: capital, city, smaller settlements. We measured the number of higher educational institutions and scientific research and development institutes on a settlement level in 2019.

We made socio-economic analyses of the regions at the NUTS 2 level, which are basic regions for the application of regional policies and NUTS 3 level, which are small regions for specific diagnoses (Eurostat, 2021). We used the data from Eurostat and SORS for 2019 at NUTS 2 level for the proportion of upper secondary and post-secondary non-tertiary education (levels 3 and 4) and tertiary education (levels 5–8). The classification is based on the International Standard Classification of Education (ISCED) 2011 levels (UNESCO Institute for Statistics, 2011). We used the data from Eurostat and SORS for 2017 at NUTS 2 level for the proportion of R&D personnel and researchers and NUTS 3 level for the proportion of employed persons in (manufacturing) industry.

3.3 Measures of the Use of Digital Technologies

We measured the use of digital technologies on a five point Likert-scale (from (1) strongly disagree to (5) strongly agree) using thirty items in the following six areas: (1) technology, (2) strategy and organisation, (3) marketing and sales, (4) production, (5) logistics, and (6) procurement.

4 Results

4.1 The Use of Digital Technologies

Out of the thirty items measuring the use of digital technologies, technology-related items were the most used (four out of the TOP5). They refer to that the intensive use of digitisation and automation gives a competitive advantage to the firm. Besides, the support of the top management to implement digital strategies ranked third (Fig. 2).

We reduced the thirty items to six meaningful factors using principal components analysis with varimax rotation: (1) technology, (2) strategy and organisation, (3) marketing and sales, (4) production, (5) logistics, and (6) procurement. The Kaiser–Meyer–Olkin (KMO) coefficient, a measure of sampling adequacy, was

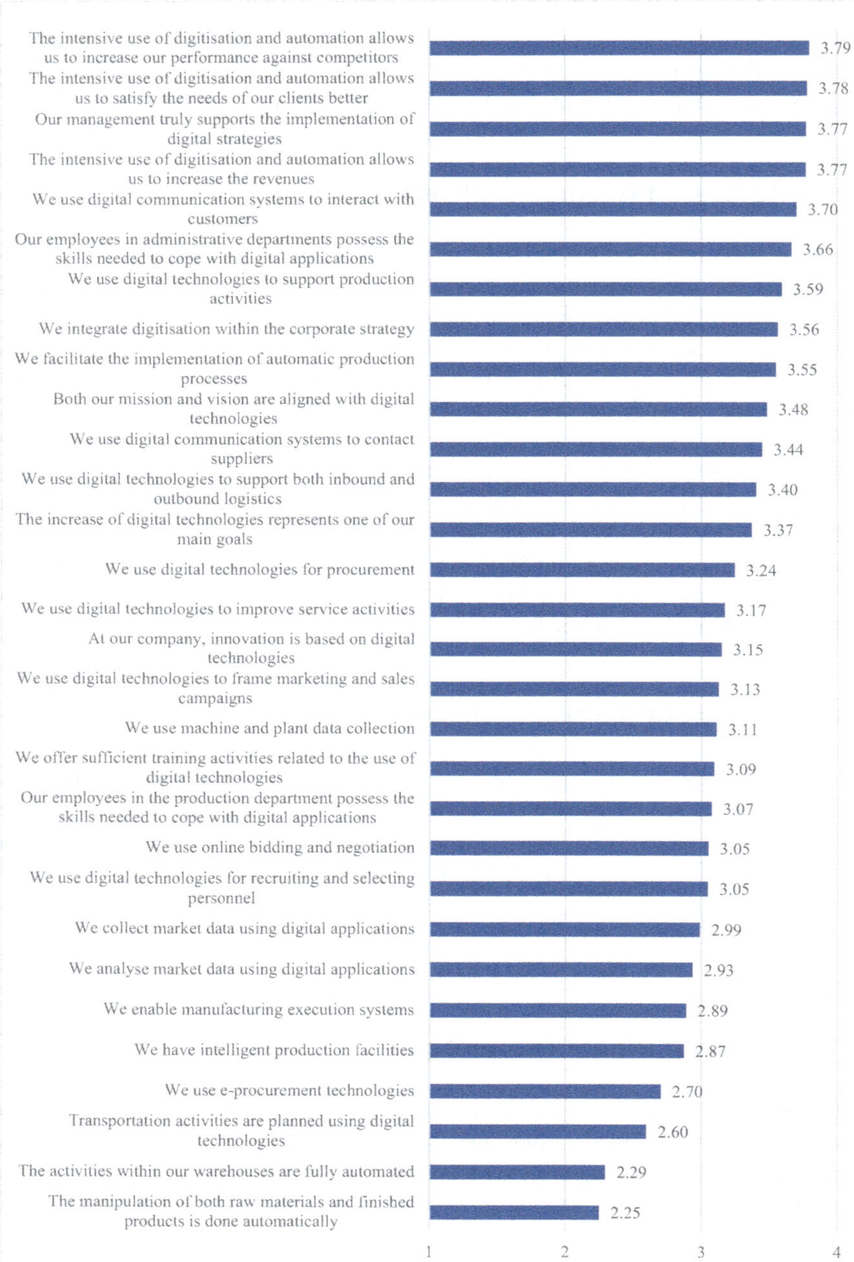

Fig. 2 The use of digital technologies

0.918, and Bartlett's test of sphericity was significant ($p < 0.001$). This solution explained 64.63% of the total variance and was characterised by strong individual loadings on each factor (Table 1). We saved the factor scores using a regression method for further analysis.

We defined these factors as digital technology use scales and tested the reliability of each scale. For each, the value of Cronbach's alpha is greater than 0.7 meaning that the items are measuring the same phenomenon (Table 1).

4.2 The Use of Digital Technologies and Geographical Factors

Marketing and sales-related digital technologies are used significantly more in firms located in capitals compared to cities or smaller settlements. Besides, the use of digital technologies in production are used significantly more in firms in smaller settlements than in capitals (Table 2).

Geographical factors influence the use of digital technologies in the areas of technology, strategy and organisation, sales and marketing and production. Technology, strategy and organisation, and marketing and sales move together, they are affected in the same direction by geographical factors, while production moves in exactly the opposite direction (Table 3).

5 Discussion and Conclusions

This paper contributes to nascent literature by analysing the diverse geographical distribution of Industry 4.0 technologies and the drivers behind their diffusion across European regions (Corradini et al., 2021). This helps us to understand to what extent the knowledge base of regions impacts their likelihood to become leaders in knowledge production and implementation in digital/Industry 4.0 technologies.

The use of digital technologies in different areas of the firms' value chain is significantly different in the studied regions, except in the field of logistics and procurement. Logistics and procurement are less developed and less digitised areas. This might be because the technology is not ready yet or these areas are not catching the top management team's attention. Another possible explanation could be that logistics are outsourced in many cases. Moreover, procurement activities are less frequent and have more individual characteristics; therefore, they are less suitable for digitisation and automation.

Central and knowledge-intensive regions with more higher education institutions and scientific research and development institutes have a clear advantage over less knowledge-intensive regions in the areas of strategy and organisation and

Table 1 The use of digital technologies: scale development and reliability

Scale	Item description	Standardised loading
Technology	The increase of digital technologies represents one of our main goals	0.713
Eigenvalue: 4.123	The intensive use of digitisation and automation allows us to increase our performance against competitors	0.830
% of variance explained: 13.74	The intensive use of digitisation and automation allows us to satisfy the needs of our clients better	0.835
Cronbach's alpha: 0.89	The intensive use of digitisation and automation allows us to increase the revenues	0.847
Strategy and organisation	Our employees in administrative departments possess the skills needed to cope with digital applications	0.527
Eigenvalue: 3.656	Our employees in the production department possess the skills needed to cope with digital applications	0.583
% of variance explained: 12.19	We offer sufficient training activities related to the use of digital technologies	0.604
Cronbach's alpha: 0.88	At our company, innovation is based on digital technologies	0.500
	We use digital communication systems to interact with customers	0.513
	Our management truly supports the implementation of digital strategies	0.582
	We integrate digitisation within the corporate strategy	0.579
	Both our mission and vision are aligned with digital technologies	0.513
Marketing and sales	We use digital technologies to frame marketing and sales campaigns	0.778
Eigenvalue: 3.607	We collect market data using digital applications	0.836
% of variance explained: 12.02	We analyse market data using digital applications	0.772
	We use digital technologies to improve service activities	0.595
Cronbach's alpha: 0.85	We use digital technologies for recruiting and selecting personnel	0.546
Production	We use digital technologies to support production activities	0.638
Eigenvalue: 3.220	We facilitate the implementation of automatic production processes	0.653
% of variance explained: 10.73	We have intelligent production facilities	0.761
	We enable manufacturing execution systems	0.642
Cronbach's alpha: 0.82	We use machine and plant data collection	0.658
Logistics	We use digital technologies to support both inbound and outbound logistics	0.555
		0.823

(continued)

Table 1 (continued)

Scale	Item description	Standardised loading
Eigenvalue: 2.580	The activities within our warehouses are fully automated	
% of variance explained: 8.60	Transportation activities are planned using digital technologies	0.692
Cronbach's alpha: 0.79	The manipulation of both raw materials and finished products is done automatically	0.696
Procurement	We use digital technologies for procurement	0.520
Eigenvalue: 2.208	We use digital communication systems to contact suppliers	0.630
% of variance explained: 7.34	We use online bidding and negotiation	0.706
Cronbach's alpha: 0.73	We use e-procurement technologies	0.543

[a]Principal component analysis with varimax rotation and Kaiser normalisation converged in nine iterations

Table 2 Differences in the use of digital technologies in settlement types

	Settlement type				
	Group means[a]				
Scale dimensions	Smaller settlement (n = 27)	City (n = 63)	Capital (n = 72)	Univariate F-value	Scheffe multiple comparison[b]
Technology	−0.057	−0.041	0.107	0.642	
Strategy and organisation	−0.118	−0.055	0.240	2.757	
Marketing and sales	−0.295	−0.085	0.391	9.025**	Ca > Ci, Ca > Ss
Production	0.197	0.047	−0.252	3.613*	Ss > Ca
Logistics	0.070	0.011	−0.100	0.489	
Procurement	0.191	−0.048	−0.016	1.201	

[a]Standardised values (Mean = 0, STD = 1), below 0 means below average, above 0 means above average

[b]Post-hoc analysis of differences ($p \leq 0.05$) demonstrating the extent to which settlement types differ in the extent to which they use digital technologies where: Ca = "Capital"; Ci = "City" and Ss = "Smaller settlement"

**F-value is significant $p \leq 0.01$

*F-value is significant $p \leq 0.05$

marketing and sales. Marketing and sales-related digital technologies are used in capitals more than in cities and smaller settlements. Management activities and marketing and sales-related activities are high added value activities, thus supporting them with digital technologies are rewarding.

Table 3 Geographical factors and the use of digital technologies correlations

	Geographical factors					
Scale dimensions	HEI	RDI	RDP	TE	USE	EPI
Technology	0,079	0,046	0,130*	0,125*	–0,182**	–0,077
Strategy and organisation	0,118*	0,122*	0,167**	0,168**	–0,176**	–0,139*
Marketing and sales	0,255**	0,165**	0,196**	0,206**	–0,176**	–0,174**
Production	–0,200**	–0,126*	–0,075	–0,082	0,199**	0,122*
Logistics	–0,075	–0,002	0,017	0,007	0,035	0,000
Procurement	–0,045	–0,039	–0,049	–0,021	0,090	–0,041

HEI: the number of higher educational institutions, RDI: the number of scientific research and development institutes, RDP: the proportion of R&D personnel and researchers, TE: the proportion of tertiary education, USE: the proportion of upper secondary and post-secondary non-tertiary education, EPI: the proportion of employed persons in (manufacturing) industry

**Pearson correlation is significant $p \leq 0.01$

*Pearson correlation is significant $p \leq 0.05$

The business model change in the fields of technology, strategy and organisation and marketing and sales, is harder and slower in less knowledge-intensive regions where the proportion of R&D personnel and researchers and people with tertiary education is lower and the proportion of people with upper secondary and post-secondary non-tertiary education is higher. Moreover, the use of strategy and organisation and marketing and sales-related digital technologies are lower in regions where the proportion of employed people in the (manufacturing) industry is higher. Digital technologies in production are used significantly more in firms located in smaller settlements than in capitals. A possible explanation for this is that production is a low added value activity, and mass production is displaced from the capital to rural areas. Using digital technologies in production does not require the presence of a high number of higher educational institutions or scientific development and research institutes but specialized entities are enough.

The Industry 4.0 implementation initiatives in production are targeting the replacement of low skilled workers, especially in those regions, where the proportion of employees with upper secondary and post-secondary non-tertiary education and the proportion of employed people in (manufacturing) industry are currently higher. This could lead to massive structural unemployment there in the forthcoming years or it could mean a potential for further industrialization. Time will tell.

To summarize the above-mentioned, it means that digitalisation/Industry 4.0 causes further divergence and not a convergence of the regions. The policy implication derives from the above is that investing in higher education institutions and scientific research and development institutes is essential in the Industry 4.0 competitiveness of a region. The high proportion of low skilled workers and a high proportion of employed people in the (manufacturing) industry might be drivers for further digitisation and automation of production; however, this leads to further divergence and leads to a permanent middle or low-income trap of the region. Regional aspects should be noted in the digital transformation towards Industry 4.0. Policymakers should act accordingly.

The managerial implication is that location matters more than we might think. The chances are significantly higher for digital transformation in high added-value activities in the capital and knowledge-intensive regions. Further digitisation and automation is a must for production which is low added value activity. Production facilities may be pushed out into peripheral regions/settlements forever.

References

Autor, D. H., Dorn, D. & Hanson, G. H. (2013). Untangling Trade and Technology: Evidence from Local Labor Markets. *NBER Working Paper Series, 18938*, Article 18938.

Bachtler, J. (2019). The Challenge of Economic Change for Europe. *Regional Studies Policy Impact Books, 1*(1), 9–16.

Backé, P., Korhonen, I., Ritzberger-Grünwald, D., & Solanko, L. (2019). A tribute to 30 years of transition in CESEE. *Focus on European Economic Integration, Q3*, 11–28.

Balland, P. A. & Boschma, R. (2021). Mapping the potentials of regions in Europe to contribute to new knowledge production in Industry 4.0 technologies. *Regional Studies*, 1–15.

Barley, S. R., Bechky, B. A., & Milliken, F. J. (2017). The changing nature of work: Careers, identities, and work lives in the 21st century. *Academy of Management Discoveries, 3*(2), 111–115.

Barney, J., Wright, M., & Ketchen, D. J. (2001). The resource-based view of the firm: Ten years after 1991. *Journal of Management, 27*(6), 625–641.

Becattini, G. (2015). Beyond geo-sectoriality: The productive chorality of places. *Journal of Regional Research, 32*, 31–41.

Bell, G. G., & Zaheer, A. (2007). Geography, Networks, and Knowledge Flow. *Organization Science, 18*(6), 955–972.

Bellandi, M., De Propris, L. & Santini, E. (2020). A Place-Based View on Industry 4.0 in Local Productive Systems. *L'industria, 41*(1), 51–69.

Bellandi, M., Santini, E., & Vecciolini, C. (2018). Learning, unlearning and forgetting processes in industrial districts. *Cambridge Journal of Economics, 42*, 1671–1685.

Bloching, B., Leutiger, P., Oltmanns, T., Rossbach, C., Schlick, T., Remane, G., Quick, P. & Shafranyuk, O. (2015). The Digital Transformation of Industry. *Roland Berger Strategy Consultants GmbH & BDI.*

Boothby, D., Dufour, A., & Tang, J. (2010). Technology adoption, training and productivity performance. *Research Policy, 39*(5), 650–661.

Brynjolfsson, E. & McAfee, A. (2014). *The second machine age: work, progress, and prosperity in a time of brilliant technologies*. New York, W. W. Norton & Company.

Cantwell, J., & Salmon, J. (2018). The effects of global connectivity on knowledge complexity in the information age. *Progress in International Business Research, 13*, 123–137.

Cantwell, J., & Santangelo, G. D. (2002). The new geography of corporate research in Information and Communications Technology (ICT). *Journal of Evolutionary Economics, 12*, 163–197.

Castellacci, F. (2008). Technological paradigms, regimes and trajectories: Manufacturing and service industries in a new taxonomy of sectoral patterns of innovation. *Research Policy, 37*(6–7), 978–994.

Ciffolilli, A. & Muscio, A. (2018). Industry 4.0: national and regional comparative advantages in key enabling technologies. *European Planning Studies, 26*(12), 2323–2343.

Corradini, C., Santini, E. & Vecciolini, C. (2021). The geography of Industry 4.0 technologies across European regions. *Regional Studies*, 1–14.

Cowen, T. (2013). *Average is over: Powering America beyond the age of the great stagnation*. Dutton.

De Propris, L. & Bailey, D. (2020). *Industry 4.0 and regional transformations*. London, Taylor & Francis.

Diodato, D. & Morrison, A. (2019). Technological regimes and the geography of innovation: a long-run perspective on US inventions. *Papers in Evolutionary Economic Geography, 1924*.

Eurostat (2021). *Background - NUTS - Nomenclature of territorial units for statistics*. Retrieved from https://ec.europa.eu/eurostat/web/nuts/background.

Evangelista, R., Meliciani, V., & Vezzani, A. (2018). Specialisation in key enabling technologies and regional growth in Europe. *Economics of Innovation and New Technology, 27*(3), 273–289.

Faust, M., Voskamp, U. & Wittke, V. (2004). *European Industrial Restructuring in a Global Economy: Fragmentation and Relocation of Value Chains*. Göttingen, Soziologisches Forschungsinstitut.

Florida, R. (2002). The economic geography of talent. *Annals of the Association of American Geographers, 92*(4), 743–755.

Forbes. (2020). Top 100 digitalcompanies list (2019 Ranking). Retrived from https://www.forbes.com/top-digital-companies/list/#tab:rank.

Fry, J., & Talja, S. (2007). The intellectual and social organization of academic fields and the shaping of digital resources. *Journal of Information Science, 33*(2), 115–133.

Götz, M. & Jankowska, B. (2017). Clusters and Industry 4.0–do they fit together? *European Planning Studies, 25*(9), 1633–1653.

Helsper, E. J. (2021). *The Digital Disconnect: The Social Causes and Consequences of Digital Inequalities*. Sage.

Leamer, E. E. & Storper, M. (2001). The economic geography of the internet age, *NBER Working Paper Series, 8450*.

Muscio, A. & Ciffolilli, A. (2020). What drives the capacity to integrate Industry 4.0 technologies? Evidence from European R&D projects. *Economics of Innovation and New Technology, 29*(2), 169–183.

Pavlou, P. A., & El Sawy, O. A. (2006). From IT leveraging competence to competitive advantage in turbulent environments: The case of new product development. *Information Systems Research, 17*(3), 198–227.

Reischauer, G. (2018). Industry 4.0 as policy-driven discourse to institutionalize innovation systems in manufacturing. *Technological Forecasting and Social Change, 132*, 26–33.

Sambamurthy, V., Bharadwaj, A. S., & Grover, V. (2003). Shaping agility through digital options: Reconceptualizing the role of IT in contemporary organizations. *MIS Quarterly Executive, 27* (2), 237–263.

Strange, R. & Zucchella, A. (2017). Industry 4.0, global value chains and international business. *Multinational Business Review, 25*(3), 174–184.

Szabó, Z. R. & Hortoványi, L. (2021). Digitális transzformáció és Ipar 4.0: magyar, szerb, szlovák és román tapasztalatok [Digital transformation and industry 4.0: Experiences from Hungary, Serbia, Slovakia and Romania]. *Külgazdaság, 65*(5–6), 56–76.

Szalavetz, A. (2018). Ipari fejlődés és munka a tudásalapú társadalomban [Industrial development and work in knowledge-based societies]. *Magyar Tudomány/Hungarian Science, 179*(1), 55–60.

UNESCO Institute for Statistics. (2011). *International Standard Classification of Education*. Retrieved from http://www.uis.unesco.org.

Wostner, P. (2017). From projects to transformations: Why do only some countries and regions advance? The case of the Slovenian S4. *European Structural and Investment Funds Journal, 5* (1), 84–96.

Wu, F., Yeniyurt, S., Kim, D., & Cavusgil, S. T. (2006). The impact of information technology on supply chain capabilities and firm performance: A resource-based view. *Industrial Marketing Management, 35*(4), 493–504.

The manufacturer's authorised representative in the EU is Springer Nature Customer Service Centre GmbH, Europaplatz 3, 69115 Heidelberg, Germany. If you have any concerns regarding our products, please contact ProductSafety@springernature.com

Printed and bound by CPI Group (UK) Ltd, Croydon, CR0 4YY
28/09/2026
02224086-0005